A YEAR OF ADVENTURES

A GUIDE TO THE WORLD'S MOST EXCITING EXPERIENCES

lonely planet

MELBOURNE | LONDON | OAKLAND

⊿ CONTENTS:

↗ **PACK YOUR SENSE OF**

ADVENTURE!

It's time to put some excitement into your next journey. *A Year of Adventures* takes you to over 250 amazing destinations, where you'll experience wild places and adrenaline-fuelled activities – at the time when they're at their best. Choosing the right time of the year can turn a good trip into an incredible one. Scheduled events, rainy seasons, peak tourist times, migration patterns...they're all critical factors when planning your trip. We've organised experiences by month and week of the year, so you're ensured the best chance of glimpsing tigers in India, ski touring the Haute Route, or catching the perfect wave in Indonesia.

The diversity of activities covered in this book caters to all passions and ability levels. You'll find inspiration for all times of the year, all around the world, whether it's an ultramarathon requiring almost superhuman endurance in Greece, or the more sedentary but just as heart-pounding pursuit of whale watching in Mexico. The last page of each week lists some additional events that occur around that time of year, with links for more information.

At intervals through the book we've also delved a bit deeper into four of humankind's favourite physical activities – cycling, jumping, paddling and walking. Whichever your passion, these sections will help you find the best place and time to ride, bungee jump, kayak and hike.

While the word 'adventure' might conjure up images of scaling mountains, sailing the globe solo or surviving on a desert island, it doesn't have to mean extreme. Visiting an exotic part of the world, taking in the view from a hot air balloon or shooting wild animals (with your camera) are all about experiencing something new and out of the everyday. So make some time for adventure – any time of the year. They'll be the experiences you'll never forget.

⌐ JANUARY
WEEK.01

GO: QUEENSTOWN, NEW ZEALAND

(ABOVE) ↗
Pinch yourself to
check it's not a dream
as you take in the
sweeping vista over
Lake Wakatipu out to
the Remarkables.

(RIGHT) ↗
Feel the need
for speed? Try
bobsledding at Lake
Placid to rocket your
body into the 4th
dimension.

WHY NOW? GET STARTED ON AN ADVENTURE BEFORE THE SUN'S EVEN RISEN ON THE REST OF THE WORLD

One of New Zealand's proud claims is that it's among the first lands on earth to see the sun rise on the New Year. Get an early adventuring start, then, by beginning the year in the South Island town of Queenstown, where the adrenaline flows as fast as the water in its churning rivers. This self-appointed 'adventure capital of the world' has one of the finest settings ever handed a town, hugging the shores of Lake Wakatipu and looking across to the aptly named Remarkables mountain range. Yet it was neither water nor peaks that spawned Queenstown's reputation for thrills; it was an elastic band.

In 1988 the world's first commercial bungee jump began operating from the Kawarau Suspension Bridge, 23km from Queenstown. For those who fancied it – and there were queues of them – this was the opportunity to plunge 43m towards the Kawarau River without worrying about a landing.

↗ DO: **BOBSLED AT LAKE PLACID**

COUNTRY USA **TYPE OF ACTIVITY** Bobsledding **FITNESS/EXPERTISE LEVEL** Not required. **WHY NOW?** The season usually opens in late December; be certain of a run by visiting in January. **DESCRIPTION** Become a momentary Olympian as you step aboard a bobsled on Mt Van Hoevenberg at Lake Placid, the venue for the 1932 and 1980 Olympic Winter Games, host to the 2009 World Bobsled Championships, and the United States' only dedicated bobsled track. Pressed between a professional driver and brakeman, you'll spend little more than 30 seconds covering the 800m public run, whooshing through the self-explanatory Zig Zag turns and up the finishing curve at such speed you'll think you're on the launch pad at Cape Canaveral rather than in the Adirondacks. If you prefer to be your own pilot, take a seat on the Luge Rocket and scurry through its 17 bends. www.orda.org

Years on, bungee remains Queenstown's signature activity but there are more highs in this town than there are peaks in the Southern Alps. For bungee basics, the Kawarau Suspension Bridge continues its stock in trade, but if 43m sounds pedestrian, try a jump from the Nevis Highwire, a cable car suspended 134m above the Nevis River, or combine sightseeing with bungee jumping by leaping from the Ledge, 400m above Queenstown.

Even after you've completed the inevitable bungee jump, your adventuring dance card for the week remains full. If you still fancy aeronautics, you can paraglide, skydive, hang glide or parafly on the lake. You can jet boat or raft the foaming Shotover or Kawarau Rivers, or get even more intimate with the river by clinging to a glorified boogie board as you discover white-water sledging. Ride the 800m-long luge, go canyoning, mountain biking, heli-skiing or heli-biking, or skip town to revel in the awesome beauty of nearby Fiordland and Mt Aspiring National Parks. Here, you'll find some of the world's great walking tracks – the Milford, Routeburn, Kepler, Hollyford and Dusky Tracks – and fiords and lakes that scream to be paddled.

www.queenstownadventure.com

[ABOVE] ↗
Share a magic moment
with one of the last
mountain gorillas
in the world.

[TOP RIGHT] ↗
Coast around Cuba for
an exhilarating escape.

[BOTTOM RIGHT] ↗
It's a long way down
from the slopes of the
world's highest ski field.

DO: GORILLA TRACKING AT BWINDI

COUNTRY Uganda **TYPE OF ACTIVITY** Wildlife watching
FITNESS/EXPERTISE LEVEL Good fitness a benefit.
WHY NOW? It's the middle of the dry season in Uganda's rainforested southwest.

DESCRIPTION It's estimated that there are only about 600 mountain gorillas remaining in the world, and half of these live in Uganda's Bwindi Impenetrable National Park. Seeing them is one of Africa's magic moments.

There are four groups of gorillas habituated to the presence of humans in the so-called Impenetrable Forest, and they move daily. They may be only 15 minutes' walk from the park entrance, or they may be hours of hard walking away, up hillsides and along slippery paths (wear gloves for grasping branches and nettles).

Only 24 tracking permits are issued per day, with each permitted group limited to six people. Most of the permits are snapped up by the big safari companies, so plan ahead. If you're determined to snaffle your own permit, all bookings must be made through the office of the Uganda Wildlife Authority in Kampala (www.uwa.or.ug) – the authority recommends booking two years in advance! Children under 15 years of age are not permitted, and anyone with a cold or other illness is likewise excluded, because such sicknesses could endanger these rare creatures' lives.

Once you finally join a trekking group, the chances of finding the gorillas are excellent, though the time you actually spend with the gorillas is limited to exactly one hour.

An adult male mountain gorilla – a silverback – can grow to more than 160kg, but despite his size he's usually placid and gentle unless he feels threatened. His reaction to danger – and sometimes strangers – is to scream and charge at the intruder. It's important not to lose your nerve. Stay still and look away from him. He may come close but there's little chance he'll actually hurt you.

↗ DO: CYCLE CUBA

COUNTRY Cuba **TYPE OF ACTIVITY** Cycle touring
FITNESS/EXPERTISE LEVEL Moderate fitness required.
WHY NOW? It's Cuba's coolest, driest time of the year.
DESCRIPTION See the land behind the politics as you pedal across the
Caribbean's largest island. Fly into the capital, Havana, and stretch out your
legs with a ride along the waterfront Malecón (complete with bike lane),
where you'll have waves on one side and colonial grandeur on the other.
Continue east out of Havana to find the tropical treats of the Varadero
beaches. Cross to the island's eastern tip to pit yourself against the 300km-
long Sierra Maestra, Cuba's highest range, or to attempt the country's most
notorious climb, ascending 1200m over 12km to the enormous La Gran
Piedra rock. There's always the descent to look forward to.

↗ DO: SKI AT JADE DRAGON

COUNTRY China **TYPE OF ACTIVITY** Skiing
FITNESS/EXPERTISE LEVEL Beginner to intermediate runs; the greater
difficulty is the altitude.
WHY NOW? Chinese winter means Chinese snow.
DESCRIPTION Once second to Bolivia's Chacaltaya glacier for the claim
as the world's highest ski field, Yunnan province's Jade Dragon Snow
Mountain Ski Resort was elevated into the top post in 2009 when the
South American glacier melted away to nothing. The gondola at Jade
Dragon (Yùlóng Xuěshān) reaches to 4516m above sea level, and surface
tows have also created a small ski area above the gondola station. Such
is the scarcity of oxygen at this height that the ski resort sells altitude
sickness pills and oxygen bags. Conversely, owing to its southern location,
Jade Dragon is also China's warmest ski field so you can come here to
bask in more than altitude records.

↗ DO: CLIMB ADAM'S PEAK

COUNTRY Sri Lanka **TYPE OF ACTIVITY** Hiking
FITNESS/EXPERTISE LEVEL Moderate fitness required.
WHY NOW? Blend into the pilgrims.
DESCRIPTION Adam's Peak (2243m) has fired imaginations for centuries.
Sri Lanka's holiest peak has a huge 'footprint' on its summit, which is
variously claimed to be the place where Adam first set foot on earth, a
sacred footprint left by Buddha as he ascended to paradise, or the indent
of St Thomas or Shiva. Little wonder it's become a haunt for pilgrims. The
pilgrimage season begins in December and runs until May, during which
time a steady stream of people make the climb up the countless steps
from the small settlement of Dalhousie. The route is illuminated in season
by a string of lights, making it possible to come for the peak's other great
attraction, the dawn view across the hill country to the east and the land
sloping away to the ocean to the west. The Sri Lankan capital, Colombo,
65km away, is easily visible on a clear day.

↗ **Ice Marathon**
www.adventure-network.com
Run a marathon, half-marathon or 100km race
in Antarctica at 80° south

↗ **Siberian Ice Half-Marathon**
http://runsim.ru
Drag your feet through 21km
of Siberian snow.

↗ **Lorne Pier to Pub**
www.lornesurfclub.com.au
A 1.2km open-water swim off the Great Ocean
Road, Victoria, Australia.

↗ **Turquoise Lake 20 Mile
Snowshoe Run**
www.salidarec.com/ccrc
Plough through 32km of powder in snowshoes
around Colorado's Turquoise Lake.

GO: ANDAMAN COAST, THAILAND

[ABOVE] ↗
Discover a world of hidden beauty as you kayak through the ancient *hong* (caves) of Ao Phang-Nga Marine National Park.

[RIGHT] ↗
Push pedal power to the limit in the Desafio de los Volcanes.

WHY NOW? VISIT THE ANDAMAN COAST NOW, WHEN YOU'LL FIND AN ENTICING MIX OF GOOD WEATHER AND CLEAR WATER

Soaring peaks of jagged limestone provide a heady backdrop to the emerald-green waters and white-sand beaches of Thailand's Andaman Coast. The region is a feast for the eyes, serving overflowing portions of some of Southeast Asia's most striking scenery, though it's unlikely that you'll be content to just look at it.

Pinched between Malaysia and Myanmar (Burma), the Andaman Coast is not long but there's something for every adventuring appetite. For divers, the coast is a watery wonderland, with around 210 hard corals and 108 reef fish recorded here.

Glam, glitzy Phuket is indisputably the hub of diving in Thailand and is one of the world's top dive destinations. It's also a good place to arrange live-aboard boats to the Surin and Similan Islands to the north. The nine

↗ DO: **RACE IN THE DESAFIO DE LOS VOLCANES**

COUNTRY Argentina/Chile
TYPE OF ACTIVITY Adventure Race
FITNESS/EXPERTISE LEVEL Superior fitness and navigation skills required.
WHY NOW? To race others across the Andes.
DESCRIPTION The Andes is the longest mountain chain in the world and this week it's also the setting for one of the longest and most challenging multisport races. For seven days and seven nights, competitors race in teams of four west across the mountains, covering 560km by mountain biking, trekking, kayaking and climbing, guided only by map and compass. The race begins in San Martin de los Andes in Argentina and finishes in Pucón in Chile, passing through dramatic volcanic landscapes, fording rivers and treading precariously over partially frozen lakes. Navigation skills are crucial to success, and competitors come from around the world hoping for lava-hot performances in this land of volcanoes.
http://eldesafiodelosvolcanes.com

Similan Islands are world-renowned, with their huge and smooth granite formations plunging into the Andaman Sea and forming seamounts, rock reefs and dive-throughs. At the Surin Islands, you'll find granite islands and coral reefs, and whale sharks and manta rays with which to share the water.

What's good below the water is equally delightful on top. With a sea kayak you have the opportunity to go where other vessels cannot, namely into the semi-submerged *hong* (caves), that characterise kayaking on the Andaman Coast. A good place to explore *hong* is in Ao Phang-Nga Marine National Park.

For landlubbers, central Krabi is synonymous with rock climbing. Blessed with some amazing scenic karst formations along its coast (and even in the middle of Krabi River) there are endless climbing opportunities, though the industry and most climbers' attentions are on the serrated peninsula of Railay, west of Krabi city. The cliff-backed isthmus is one of the world's leading climbing destinations, providing high-quality limestone with steep, pocketed walls, overhangs and the occasional hanging stalactite. About 700 sport routes have been bolted. Novices usually begin with Muay Thai, a 50m wall with around 20 climbs.

[ABOVE] ↗
Find your own
Lost World dreamscape
high on the
Venezuelan mesas.

[RIGHT] ↗
White-water sledging.
It's kind of like this, but
by yourself and without
a raft. Are you crazy?!

DO: **TREK TO RORAIMA**

COUNTRY Venezuela **TYPE OF ACTIVITY** Trekking
FITNESS/EXPERTISE LEVEL Moderate fitness required.
WHY NOW? Be thankful it's the dry season (December to March); at other times of the year it
really rains.

DESCRIPTION Sir Arthur Conan Doyle's *Lost World* was a place frozen in time, a plateau so removed from
the world that dinosaurs continued to roam atop it. The inspiration for Sir Arthur's tale were the sandstone
tepuis (mesas) of the South American jungles, and particularly the tales of exploration then emanating from
the *tepui* Roraima.

Stretching 34 sq km across the borders of Venezuela, Guyana and Brazil, Roraima is the highest of the
tepuis – its plateau is at about 2700m and its tallest peak at 2810m – but it is also the easiest to ascend. A trek
to this massive table mountain provides some of the most memorable experiences a trip to Venezuela can
offer. The hike up the steep walls is fascinating, and the top of the plateau is nothing short of otherworldly.

It will take a minimum of five days to do the round trip, and you'll need camping equipment and food. Be
prepared for a strenuous trek and some discomfort, including plenty of rain, cold and *jejenes* (a biting gnat).

Gather up guides and porters (independent trekking is not allowed) in the village of Paraitepui and walk
for two days to the plateau, where the scenery is a dreamscape evocative of a science-fiction movie:
impressive blackened rocks in myriad shapes, gorges, creeks and pink beaches. Few living organisms have
adapted to the inhospitable conditions of the barren, rocky plateau. Those that have include curious endemic
species such as a little, black frog that crawls instead of jumps, and the *heliamphora*, a carnivorous plant
that traps unwary insects in beautiful, bucket-shaped, red flowers filled with rainwater. Plan on staying at
least two days on the summit to allow time for exploration.

↗ DO: **WHITE-WATER SLEDGE IN ROTORUA**

COUNTRY New Zealand **TYPE OF ACTIVITY** River surfing
FITNESS/EXPERTISE LEVEL Moderate fitness required.
WHY NOW? If you're going to expose yourself to glacial-melt rivers, do it when New Zealand is at its warmest.
DESCRIPTION Essentially rafting for one, white-water sledging is a personal fight-or-flow with the rapids of a river, aided only by flippers and the sledge you push ahead of you. One moment you might have proudly backed your sledge into a standing wave, surfing it like a master; the next, you'll be yanked underwater into a damp black hole, wondering where – and if – you'll get your next breath. The activity isn't unique to Rotorua - Wanaka and Queenstown also offer sledging trips - but here you can helicopter up to the Okere River and fight your way back through grade-five rapids.
www.kaitiaki.co.nz

↗ DO: **KAYAK BASS STRAIT**

COUNTRY Australia **TYPE OF ACTIVITY** Kayaking
FITNESS/EXPERTISE LEVEL High degree of expertise required.
WHY NOW? Paddle in summer in hope of the smoothest crossing.
DESCRIPTION Around 15,000 years ago, Australia's island state of Tasmania was joined to the mainland by a land bridge across the eastern end of what is now stormy, shipwreck-sprinkled Bass Strait. Today, the remains of that bridge form a chain of islands that serve as stepping stones for a small number of sea kayakers willing to brave the strait's notorious currents and swells. Most kayakers leave from Wilsons Promontory National Park, the southernmost point of the Australian mainland, and paddle through the Hogan Group to two of the country's most striking islands: Deal and Flinders. After a final tussle with the tidal races of Banks Strait, the 300km journey ends in Tasmania's Musselroe Bay. A trip for the experienced paddler only.

The 24 Hours of Telemark
www.the24hoursoftelemark.com
Cross-country ski for a full day at the Telemark Resort in Wisconsin.

- -

Dolomitenlauf
www.dolomitensport-lienz.com
A 60km ski marathon through the Austrian Dolomites.

- -

Fulda Challenge
http://fulda-challenge.com
Deep-winter, 2500km Arctic Circle race involving such means as skidoo, bike, dog-sledding and ice climbing.

↗ DO: **SKI THE ALBORZ MOUNTAINS**

COUNTRY Iran **TYPE OF ACTIVITY** Skiing
FITNESS/EXPERTISE LEVEL Beginners to powder hounds.
WHY NOW? For mid-winter's best skiing conditions.
DESCRIPTION Iran has several ski resorts in the Alborz Mountains, a range higher than the European Alps, including four within day-trip distance of the capital, Tehran. Dizin is the largest of Iran's ski fields, and thanks to its altitude – its highest run begins at around 3500m, making it one of the world's highest ski fields – it gets about a six-month season (and converts to a grass-skiing venue in summer). Another ski field worth a look is Shemshak, nearer to Tehran and offering the chance for night skiing on floodlit slopes. Expect easy to moderate runs at Dizin, while Shemshak is noted for its moguls and more difficult runs. Just be aware that if you come to ski in the Alborz it's purely about the snow, not the parties.

GO: PAYS DOGON, MALI

[ABOVE] ↗
Drop into a sun-baked version of Middle Earth as you trek along the Bandiagara Escarpment.

[RIGHT] ↗
Frozen waterfalls? Check. Easy access? Check. Is this the best ice climbing in the USA?

WHY NOW? NOW IS THE COOLEST TIME OF THE YEAR, THOUGH TEMPERATURES MAY STILL BE ABOVE 30°C

Mali's Dogon Country – the land of the Dogon people – resembles Hobbiton, with villages like scattered rocks, granaries with witch-hat straw roofs, shocked-looking baobab trees and perfect, small fields spread across unlikely, inhospitable terrain. What sets it apart from Middle Earth, and into an adventuring world of its own, is the 150km-long, copper-red, cracked and wrinkled Bandiagara Escarpment that towers through the scene.

The best way to see the Pays Dogon is to trek along this escarpment for anything between two days and three weeks, walking from village to village along ancient tracks, sometimes above the escarpment, sometimes below it, and sometimes zigzagging along it.

Food and accommodation are available in the villages, and guides can be hired in the gateway towns of Bandiagara, Bankass and Sanga. While

↗ DO: ICE CLIMB VALDEZ

COUNTRY USA **TYPE OF ACTIVITY** Ice climbing **FITNESS/EXPERTISE LEVEL** High level of expertise required. **WHY NOW?** Get the best of the winter ice. **DESCRIPTION** Alaska's Prince William Sound and the town of Valdez might be remembered most for the *Exxon Valdez* oil spill, but ask anyone with an ice-axe and this is climbing central. Drive about 20km out of town to the Keystone Canyon, where you'll find arguably the best ice climbing in the United States. The waterfalls through this 5km-long canyon freeze into glorious multipitch routes such as Bridalveil Falls and, just a few metres away, Keystone Greensteps, which is ascended in four 60m pitches. Dozens of climbs, including Bridalveil Falls, begin right beside the main road, so you won't have to hump all your equipment to climbs. Stick around a while for Valdez's annual Ice Climbing Festival in early March. www.valdezalaska.org

guides aren't essential, they will help you get the most out of the Pays Dogon. They'll show you the route, help with translation, find accommodation and food, stop you stumbling over sacred sites, and take you to the abandoned cliff dwellings that pockmark the 600m-high cliff face. Built as homes by the Tellem people, who were forced away by the Dogon, these caves are now used for Dogon burials.

The trekking options along the escarpment are numerous. The central area between Dourou and Banani is the most spectacular, but also receives the most visitors. The area north of Banani sees far fewer visitors, but the landscape is less striking. The southern section from Dorou to Djiguibombo is also very beautiful, and again popular. The far south of

the Dogon, between Kani-Kombolé and Nombori, is more tranquil but less dramatic.

Distances between villages are short, allowing you time to appreciate the people and the landscape, while escaping the midday heat.

The unusual Dogon calendar has five days per week (although villages on the plateau tend to keep a seven-day week), with once-weekly markets. These are lively and colourful, and an opportunity for beer drinking. Try to catch one during your trek.

[ABOVE] ↗
Your *Finding Nemo*
moment will be
painless, as the sting
of these harmless
jellies is either
nonexistent or mild.

[TOP RIGHT] ↗
Say hello to whale
mums who've made a
10,000km journey to
give birth

[BOTTOM RIGHT] ↗
Launch yourself down
the steepest slopes of
Whistler-Blackcomb
and watch the white
powdery world whizz by.

DO: SNORKEL IN JELLYFISH LAKE

COUNTRY Palau **TYPE OF ACTIVITY** Diving/snorkelling

FITNESS/EXPERTISE LEVEL Snorkelling has no requirements; diving covers all abilities.

WHY NOW? Palau's diving is good year-round, but come in January and you'll have seen off the wet season.

DESCRIPTION Palau is one of the world's truly spectacular dive spots, with coral reefs, blue holes, WWII wrecks, hidden caves and more than 60 vertical drop-offs. The epicentre is the Rock Islands, where 200-plus rounded knobs of limestone, covered with jungle, dot the waters for a 32km stretch southwest of Koror.

The waters surrounding the Rock Islands are teeming with more than 1500 varieties of reef and pelagic fish. There are four times the number of coral species in Palau than in the Caribbean. Divers can see manta rays, sea turtles, moray eels, giant tridacna clams, grey reef sharks and sometimes sea snakes, dugongs and chambered nautiluses. But the real fish-of-the-day is jellyfish. Among the Rock Islands' 80 marine salt lakes – former sinkholes – is Jellyfish Lake. Here, millions of harmless, transparent jellyfish swim en masse following the path of the sun. Diving is not allowed but snorkelling in this pulsating mass is an unearthly sensation.

For a more traditional dive experience, head for the Ngemelis Wall, widely considered to be the world's best wall dive. From knee-deep water, the wall drops about 300m. Divers can float past a brilliant rainbow of sponges and soft corals, their intense blues, reds and whites forming a backdrop for quivering 3m orange and yellow sea fans and giant black coral trees.

Blue Corner, Palau's most popular dive, is noted for its abundance of marine life. Expect to be totally bedazzled by the variety of fish, including barracudas and schooling sharks, as well as hard and soft corals. Strong tidal currents make this a dive for the more experienced. Novice divers will prefer the German Channel and Turtle Cove; manta rays are frequently spotted in the former.

↗ DO: **WHALE WATCH AT BAJA CALIFORNIA**

COUNTRY Mexico **TYPE OF ACTIVITY** Wildlife watching
FITNESS/EXPERTISE LEVEL Not required.
WHY NOW? To enjoy the company of California grey whales.
DESCRIPTION Even if you don't like the super-development of Los Cabos at the height of the tourist season, the whales do, so pack everything but your prejudices. From January to March, California grey whales have their own winter vacation from the cold Siberian and Alaskan waters, travelling almost 10,000km to give birth in the warmth of the Sea of Cortez. You'll easily spot whales from the shores of Los Cabos, or you can journey north to the shallow lagoons of San Ignacio, Ojo de Liebre and Bahía Magdalena, mating and breeding grounds for the grey whale, where hundreds of whales might be seen. You'll find boats for Ojo de Liebre in the town of Guerrero Negro.

↗ DO: **SKI RUBY BOWL**

COUNTRY Canada **TYPE OF ACTIVITY** Skiing
FITNESS/EXPERTISE LEVEL Black diamonds (ie experts) only.
WHY NOW? Both Whistler and Blackcomb are at their snowy best right now.
DESCRIPTION Consistently voted North America's best ski resort, and considered by many people to be the best in the world, Whistler-Blackcomb – the principal venue for the 2010 Olympic Winter Games – contains almost 200 longer-than-average marked trails and the highest vertical drop (1609m) of any North American ski field. Wander round the back of Blackcomb to Ruby Bowl and it gets even sexier. Ruby Bowl is one of 12 alpine bowls on Whistler-Blackcomb and is reached by a climb up Spanky's Ladder from the top of the Glacier Express chairlift. It has Whistler-Blackcomb's best powder, falling in continuous steeps for more than 600m.

↗ DO: **RIDE THE CRESTA RUN**

COUNTRY Switzerland **TYPE OF ACTIVITY** Skeleton tobogganing
FITNESS/EXPERTISE LEVEL Not required.
WHY NOW? The Cresta Run opens a few days before Christmas and operates until the end of February. **DESCRIPTION** In 1885 the Cresta Run was first built on the slopes of the Swiss resort of St Moritz, and continues to be reconstructed each winter season. This most famous of skeleton (head-first tobogganing) runs is used for both competition and play, though visitors can only park their own skeletons on the club's skeleton toboggans on non-race days (and women cannot ride at all). The best in the game can reach speeds of up to 130km/h on the Cresta Run, but beginners have trouble enough just mastering braking, for which you use only the rakes on your boots. Fail in this and you'll almost certainly come a cropper at the run's most famous corner, the Shuttlecock. This at least grants you entry into the Shuttlecock Club and the right to wear the special Shuttlecock tie. www.cresta-run.com

↗ **Inferno Race**
www.inferno-muerren.ch
The world's oldest ski race, covering 15.8km, in the Swiss resort of Mürren.

↗ **Dusi Marathon**
www.dusi.org.za
Paddle 120km through the Valley of 1000 Hills to Durban; watch for crocodiles.

↗ **The Coastal Challenge**
www.thecoastalchallenge.com
Run 250km across seven stages through the jungles, beaches and mountains of Costa Rica.

↗ **Jizerská 50**
http://bezky.jiz50.cz
A 50km ski marathon at the Czech resort Bedrichov.

JANURY

↗ **JANUARY**

WEEK.04

GO: PATAGONIA, ARGENTINA/CHILE

[ABOVE] ↗
The 'end of the earth'
is the beginning of
an adventure of fire
and ice.

[RIGHT] ↗
A mere six-hour flight
and you can be making
the world's most
southerly snowman...

WHY NOW? COME TO PATAGONIA NOW WHEN IT'S AT ITS APPROACHABLE BEST, SNOW-TOPPED NOT SNOWBOUND

Patagonia is the literal end-of-the-earth, a raw and rugged place where South America tapers away to a chilly nothing. The star feature of this great southern land is the tail end of the Andes, the longest mountain chain on earth. Assaulted by wind, snow and ice for millennia, the Patagonian Andes are not especially high – they average 2000m – but they've been blasted into an array of peculiar mountain shapes, from the Torres del Paine, which look like a hand of broken fingers, to the 1.2km-high domed summit rock of Monte FitzRoy that so intoxicates climbers. Hidden beneath FitzRoy is the South Patagonian Icecap, the world's third-largest icecap (behind Antarctica and Greenland). From it springs a host of glaciers like tributaries, including the pin-up of world ice, 60m-high Moreno Glacier. Stand in awe for a while as it noisily calves seracs into the milky waters of Lago Argentino.

↗ DO: FLY TO THE SOUTH POLE

REGION Antarctica **TYPE OF ACTIVITY** Adventure travel **FITNESS/EXPERTISE LEVEL** Not required. **WHY NOW?** It's a short summer at 90° south. **DESCRIPTION** Once upon a time you had to be prepared to eat your dogs and bury your companions to set foot on the South Pole. Today you need only endure a bumpy six-hour flight, and you can be making the world's most southerly snowman. Air journeys to the South Pole begin with a preliminary flight from the Chilean town of Punta Arenas to your Antarctic base camp at Patriot Hills (at 80° south). Over the coming week you can explore your icy surrounds as you await conditions that permit flights into the Pole. You'll refuel halfway before landing beside the Amundsen-Scott Research Station at the Pole, where you will pay another price beyond the US$38,000 you have already shelled out – you will probably have a headache from the altitude as you stand atop the 3000m-thick ice. The temperature is also likely to be around -30°C.
www.adventure-network.com

The Andes separate two vastly different landscapes. To their rain-shadowed east is the arid Argentine steppe, which extends to the wildlife wonderland of Península Valdés, populated by Magellanic penguins, sea lions, elephant seals and rheas. To the range's west is the fiord-slashed Chilean coast, where rivers such as Río Serrano provide kayakers with access to iceberg-choked lakes beneath the Torres del Paine. For a more turbulent experience, consider a rafting trip on Chile's Río Futaleufú, one of the world's wildest white-water experiences.

The full stop to this land is Tierra del Fuego, the paradoxically named 'Land of Fire', perched just above the Antarctic Circle. Split between Chile and Argentina, the Chilean side is a practically untamed expanse of massive sheep farms and mountains, sprinkled with remote lakes. The Argentine half boasts the energetic regional capital of Ushuaia and the impressive Darwin Range, which is technically the death throe of the Andes. Ushuaia is also the departure point for most Antarctica-bound ships.

(ABOVE) ↗
Connect with the African
land and people as you
cross the continent on
two wheels during the
Tour d'Afrique.

(TOP RIGHT) ↗
Stormy weather: take a
front-row seat for some
spectacular tempests in
North America.

(BOTTOM RIGHT) ↗
The world's longest
waves are close to
perfect at Superbank on
Australia's
Gold Coast.

DO: RIDE THE TOUR D'AFRIQUE

COUNTRIES Various **TYPE OF ACTIVITY** Cycling
FITNESS/EXPERTISE LEVEL High level of fitness and endurance required.
WHY NOW? To ride in one of the world's epic cycling events.

DESCRIPTION The Tour d'Afrique is an 11,900km bike race starting at the pyramids of Giza, outside Cairo, and finishing in Cape Town, South Africa. For four months cyclists average around 120km a day, pedalling through Egypt, Sudan, Ethiopia, Kenya, Tanzania, Malawi, Zambia, Botswana, Namibia and South Africa. It travels through both hemispheres and past some of Africa's greatest sights – Luxor, the Blue Nile Gorge, mountains Kenya and Kilimanjaro, Lake Malawi, Victoria Falls – and as much wildlife as a colonialist could poke a blunderbuss at.

The Tour d'Afrique is foremost a race and the pace is cracking – in 2003 nine riders were listed by Guinness World Records as completing the fastest human-powered crossing of Africa – but you can also cycle as a so-called 'expedition rider', trundling along at more of a touring speed.

For many riders, the commitment in time and energy to ride for four months is beyond them, but it is possible to ride individual sections, of which there are eight in total, ranging in distance between 1000km and 2000km. There are particularly brutal sections, such as that between Khartoum (Sudan) and Addis Ababa (Ethiopia) where the altitude of the highlands will be as much a drag as the roads; and there are more open sections such as the all-sealed route from Iringa (Tanzania) to Lilongwe (Malawi) along the shores of Lake Malawi. Entry fees for individual sections range from around €850 to €2150, or you can 'treat' yourself to the whole shebang for a little more than €8000. www.tourdafrique.com

↗ DO: STORM WATCH ON VANCOUVER ISLAND

COUNTRY Canada **TYPE OF ACTIVITY** Natural phenomena
FITNESS/EXPERTISE LEVEL Not required.
WHY NOW? It's the depths of the Canadian winter, with regular storms rolling in.
DESCRIPTION Each winter, Vancouver Island's west coast becomes a front-row seat to the most spectacular storms on the North American west coast. With nothing but the Pacific Ocean between the island and Japan, these well-travelled storms – driven here by a persistent low-pressure system in the Gulf of Alaska – roar ashore, bringing high winds and waves that hit harder than a boxer. Wander the beaches to experience the storms' full fury, follow the aptly named Wild Pacific Trail for a cliff-top view, take a storm-watching tour from the town of Tofino or simply watch the action from the windows of your hotel room.
www.tofino-bc.com; www.my-tofino.com

↗ DO: SURF THE SUPERBANK

COUNTRY Australia **TYPE OF ACTIVITY** Surfing
FITNESS/EXPERTISE LEVEL Beginners and pros alike.
WHY NOW? Cyclone swells will be lighting up the Superbank.
DESCRIPTION Until a few years ago, there was no such place as Superbank, the great white sandbar off Queensland's Gold Coast that's now home to the world's longest waves and barrels. In 1999 a 'sand bypass' project aimed to move northerly flowing sand past the mouth of the Tweed River and on to the Gold Coast. Instead it resulted in the creation of Superbank – all praise to failed bureaucracy – which stretches in a ruler-straight line from Snapper Rocks to Kirra, with summer cyclone swells creating tubes as long as an oil pipeline. So good is it at this time of year that you'll even find a handful of surfers still riding their fortune at night. The waters are always packed, but there are waves enough here for everyone.

↗ DO: TWITCH AT PARC NATIONAL DU BANC D'ARGUIN

COUNTRY Mauritania **TYPE OF ACTIVITY** Birdwatching
FITNESS/EXPERTISE LEVEL Not required.
WHY NOW? Midwinter sees the highest concentration of birds.
DESCRIPTION Pinched between the Atlantic Ocean and the ocean of sand that is the Sahara, Mauritania's Parc National du Banc d'Arguin is one of the world's great birdwatching destinations. Stretching 200km north from Cape Timiris, it's the wintering site for around 2 million wading birds – around 30% of the waders that use the Atlantic flyway – the largest concentration of such birds in the world. Among the 108 recorded species, expect to see broad-billed sandpipers, pink flamingos, white and grey pelicans, black terns and spoonbills. The park's islands – largely formed by wind-blown sand from the Sahara – are the prime birding sites, and the only way to see them is by small boat. You'll find boats for hire in the fishing village of Twik. Bush taxis between Nouakchott and Nouâdhibou will generally stop at Ten Alloul, 14km from Twik.

↗ **Tring to Town**
www.tring2town.com
Two-day, 130km run in and out of London along the Grand Union Canal

↗ **Raid de la Savane**
http://maiarmor.free.fr/BF-accueil.php (in French)
Five-stage, 120km run through the African nation of Burkina Faso.

↗ **Alpine Classic**
www.audax.org.au
Cycle 200km between three of the highest points in the Australian state of Victoria, ascending more than 3000m.

↗ **Regata del Rio Negro**
www.regatadelrionegro.com.ar
Eight-day paddle in Argentina; said to be the longest kayak race in the world.

FEBRUARY

WEEK.01

GO: YEMEN

(ABOVE) ↗
Immerse yourself in tranquil waters on Suqutra, known as the Galápagos of the Indian Ocean.

(RIGHT) ↗
The Zanskar River is your chance to walk on water among Himalayan peaks and fantastic ice formations.

WHY NOW? THE BEST TIME TO VISIT TIHAMA – THE RED SEA COASTAL STRIP – IS BETWEEN NOVEMBER AND FEBRUARY

There's extraordinary history and legend in Yemen. Dragons were reputed to have lived on its largest island, Noah's sons knew it as the land of milk and honey, wise men gathered frankincense and myrrh from its mountains, and Gilgamesh came here to search for the secret of eternal life.

A land virtually untouched by modernity – one local legend tells of God's pride in Yemen because it hasn't changed since the day he made it – any journey here has the whiff of adventure.

Yemen's sheer-sided Haraz Mountains, rising abruptly off the steamy Red Sea coastal plains, are prime trekking country with their tapestry of terraced fields and fortified villages, all huddled together on the most unlikely crags. For those with a little self-sufficiency, it's possible to spend

↗ DO: ICE TREK ON THE ZANSKAR RIVER

COUNTRY India **TYPE OF ACTIVITY** Winter trekking **FITNESS/EXPERTISE LEVEL** Good fitness required – cold blood an asset. **WHY NOW?** Trek while the Zanskar River has a skin of ice. **DESCRIPTION** The extremes of cold in the Himalayan region of Ladakh mean that it's little visited in winter. The mountain passes close and the only way in and out is by air. For those hardy souls who not only take the challenge to visit in winter but want to do something even more outlandish, there's the chance to trek along the frozen Zanskar River from Chilling to Padum, sleeping in rock shelters. For Zanskaris this is a traditional route, the only way in and out when the high passes are snowed in, but for trekkers it usually means about eight days of walking, including through a canyon that's inaccessible at any other time of year. Expect severe cold (winter in Leh can reach -20˚C) but be cheered by the news that Ladakh receives 300 days of sun a year, making for crisp, clear trekking days on the river.

days, or even weeks, weaving along the mule trails that link up the different villages.

Yemen's natural jewel lies about 510km off the mainland, with the remote Suqutra island having been described as an Arabian Garden of Eden and the Galápagos of the Indian Ocean. The unique and otherworldly island is known for its high level of endemic plants and animals: there are around 850 plant species, of which approximately 250 species are endemic. Rumoured to have once been a refuge for dragons, it today offers a nascent tourism industry (the island airport was only built in 2002) erring towards activity. There is great hiking potential in the green hills and granite outcrops of the 1500m Haggeher Mountains. The diving is world-class,

with the attraction being fish rather than corals. The island is also thought to boast one of the world's largest cave systems (though they remain almost entirely unexplored to date). Surfers will also find some excellent breaks hidden in the more remote reaches of the island, and the windsurfing potential is enormous.
www.yementourism.com

[ABOVE] ↗
Aconcagua,
the 'stone sentinel', was
first summited in 1897.
Now it's your turn.

[RIGHT] ↗
Elevator full? Power your
way up 1576 steps to
the 86th floor to win the
Empire State Run-Up.

DO: CLIMB CERRO ACONCAGUA

COUNTRY Argentina **TYPE OF ACTIVITY** Trekking/mountaineering
FITNESS/EXPERTISE LEVEL Good fitness (and acclimatisation) required.
WHY NOW? The climbing season is November to March; come late to avoid deep snow.
DESCRIPTION At 6960m, Cerro Aconcagua is the highest mountain outside of the Himalayas, but it yields to determined trekkers. Known as the 'roof of the Americas', the Andean peak rises above the Argentine city of Mendoza, and reaching its summit requires at least 13 to 15 days, including time to acclimatise to the altitude.

The traditional ascent on Aconcagua is the Northwest Route, approached on a 40km trail from the park entrance at Laguna los Horcones. The Polish Glacier Route is longer (76km) but more scenic and less crowded. It's also more technical, requiring the use of ropes, ice screws and ice axes. A third route, the South Face, is a demanding technical climb.

Only highly experienced climbers should consider tackling Aconcagua without the relative safety of an organised tour; even skilled climbers often hire guides who know the mountain's Jekyll-and-Hyde weather. Nonclimbers can also have a taste of Aconcagua, albeit a diluted one, by trekking to camps and refuges beneath the permanent snow line. Tour operators and climbing guides set up seasonal tents at the best camp sites, so independent trekkers and climbers usually get only the leftover spots.

From December to March, permits are obligatory for both trekking and climbing in Parque Provincial Aconcagua. They are available only in Mendoza.

Buses from Mendoza will stop at Puente del Inca, just a couple of kilometres from Laguna los Horcones, allowing easy access to the Northwest Route. Tread carefully; Aconcagua claims several lives each year. www.aconcagua.mendoza.gov.ar (in Spanish)

⏶ DO: RUN UP THE EMPIRE STATE BUILDING

COUNTRY USA **TYPE OF ACTIVITY** Stair climbing/running
FITNESS/EXPERTISE LEVEL High level of fitness required.
WHY NOW? To compete in the Empire State Building Run-Up
DESCRIPTION First held in 1978, the Empire State Building Run-Up challenges competitors to sprint up 1576 steps to the 86th-floor observation deck in New York's Empire State Building. This stairwell run is part of a growing worldwide circuit of organised runs up the staircases of buildings and Australian Paul Crake (a five-time winner of the race) holds the record time of nine minutes and 33 seconds, set in 2003; the fastest woman is Austrian Andrea Mayr, who dashed up in 11 minutes and 23 seconds in 2006. Competitors are chosen according to their running history and ability, with applications accepted through the New York Road Runners (www.nyrr.org). If you thought shoving your way into a New York elevator was tough, wait until you experience this race's mass start. www.esbnyc.com

⏶ DO: DIVE GLOVER'S REEF

COUNTRY Belize **TYPE OF ACTIVITY** Diving
FITNESS/EXPERTISE LEVEL Beginners to pros.
WHY NOW? It's the middle of Belize's dry season. **DESCRIPTION**
Named after 18th-century English pirate John Glover, Glover's Reef is the southernmost of Belize's three atolls. Six small cayes of white sand and palm trees are dotted along the atoll's southeastern rim, supporting a handful of low-key resorts and diving bases. The reef sits atop a submerged mountain ridge on the edge of the continental shelf, surrounded by enormous drop-offs with world-class dive sites. On the east side, where visibility is usually more than 30m, the ocean floor plummets away to 800m. Divers regularly see spotted eagle rays, southern stingrays, turtles, moray eels, dolphins, several shark species, large groupers, barracudas and many tropical reef fish. In the shallow central lagoon 700 coral patches brim with marine life – brilliant for snorkellers. In a week here you could probably manage about 17 dives, including some at other atolls. www.gloversreef.org

⏶ DO: VISIT THE EMPTY QUARTER

COUNTRY Saudi Arabia **TYPE OF ACTIVITY** Adventure travel
FITNESS/EXPERTISE LEVEL Not required.
WHY NOW? Come while desert conditions are bearable. **DESCRIPTION**
The Empty Quarter (Rub al-Khali), aka the Abode of Silence, is the largest area covered by sand on the planet, encompassing 655,000 sq km (an area larger than France). For early European adventurers, it conjured up all that was romantic and forbidden about Arabia, and it has lost little of this allure. The remarkable, sculpted dunes for which it's famous can rise more than 300m and form vast chains of longitudinal dune ridges stretching over hundreds of kilometres. Pushed by the wind, the dunes can move at a rate of up to 30m per year. Exploring the Empty Quarter requires more preparation than any other destination in Saudi Arabia. Permission is free and rarely denied, but must be obtained from the National Commission for Wildlife Conservation and Development in Riyadh. Most Empty Quarter expeditions start and end at either Sharurah or Sulayyil.

⏶ Cole Classic
www.coleclassic.com
Rough-water swim off Sydney beaches: roll your arms over for 1km, 2km or 10km.

⏶ Cradle Mountain Run
www.cradlemtnrun.asn.au
Run 82km along Australia's finest bushwalking trail, the Overland Track.

⏶ Bonk Hard Chill
www.bonkhardchill.com
A 12-hour winter adventure race in Missouri, involving mountain biking, trekking, running and paddling.

⏶ Temple to Temple
www.templetotemple.com
Seven-day, 750km bike race between major temples in Belize.

↗ **FEBRUARY**

WEEK.02

GO: TASMANIA, AUSTRALIA

[ABOVE] ↗
Revel in that middle-of-nowhere feeling. Around 40% of Tasmania is a World Heritage Area or a reserve.

[RIGHT] ↗
Grade-two rapids mean relatively easy paddling – a good breather after 36km of running and 140km of cycling.

WHY NOW? VISIT AT THE END OF SUMMER FOR THE MOST RELIABLY WARM CONDITIONS

Tasmania is Australia's smallest state, yet it packs more opportunity into its outdoors than the other states and territories combined. Furnished with mountains shaped as peculiarly as the country's native fauna, 20% of Tasmania is made up of national parks, with most listed as World Heritage. Both the air and water in parts of the state are claimed to be the purest on the planet.

Suck in this air and drink the water as you discover Tassie's wealth of bushwalking trails. The Overland Track, between Cradle Mountain and Lake St Clair, is Australia's premier bushwalk, attracting summer crowds like outback flies. For an encore, you can select from a roll call of fantastic walks, such as the South Coast Track, Freycinet Peninsula, Western Arthurs, Federation Peak, Frenchmans Cap, Walls of Jerusalem and Bay of Fires.

↗ DO: COMPETE IN THE COAST TO COAST

COUNTRY New Zealand **TYPE OF ACTIVITY** Adventure race **FITNESS/EXPERTISE LEVEL** Superior fitness required. **WHY NOW?** To compete in one of adventure racing's marquee events. **DESCRIPTION** The Coast to Coast is the event that gave birth to the rise and rise of adventure racing. First contested in 1980, this multisport race traverses New Zealand's South Island, beginning in Kumara Beach on the wild west coast and ending in the coastal suburbs of Christchurch. Competitors run 36km, cycle 140km and kayak 67km through the grade-two rapids of the Waimakariri Canyon. You can choose to compete individually or in teams of two, in a single day or extended across two days with an overnight rest/collapse in Arthurs Pass. Heavy rain – not uncommon on the South Island even in February – can add all sorts of surprises to the challenge. Entries to the event are accepted from 1 June of the previous year, and close on 30 June. www.coasttocoast.co.nz

Footsore? Tasmania still has plenty to offer. Rack up a selection of activities and the island state can knock them down.

Cycling? Tasmania is about the only place in Australia that can be comfortably circuited by bike, so each summer it becomes the scene of a wheeled migration worthy of wildebeests. Mountain bikers are not forgotten, with the Tasmanian Trail running 480km from Tassie's top to tip on back roads and trails.

Climbing? Set on the Tasman Peninsula next to Australia's highest cliffs, and rising 65m out of the Tasman Sea, is a famous and spectacular dolerite stack called the Totem Pole – your first pitch begins from your boat.

Caving? Niggly Cave near Maydena is Australia's longest explored cave at 375m, and contains the longest single pitch in the country: 191m.

Even the things that mar the Tasmanian landscape have been turned into an adventure, with the Gordon Dam, a concrete abscess in the World Heritage-listed Southwest, doubling as the site for the world's highest commercial abseil – 140m to valley floor.

All things considered, Tasmania is the kind of place you want to live, not just visit, but if you must only visit, do so at the end of summer for the most reliably warm conditions – you're nearing the Antarctic when you hit Tasmania. www.discovertasmania.com.au

[ABOVE] ↗
Hit the ice and explore Mälaren as the lake freezes around Stockholm.

[TOP RIGHT] ↗
The Vallée Blanche offers the longest ski run in Europe.

[BOTTOM RIGHT] ↗
The price of perfect conditions is company on the waves.

DO: **TOUR SKATE ON MÄLAREN**

COUNTRY Sweden **TYPE OF ACTIVITY** Nordic skating

FITNESS/EXPERTISE LEVEL Some skating experience.

WHY NOW? The skating season usually lasts from December to March; come now to coincide with the likely running of Vikingarännet.

DESCRIPTION One look at the name 'Nordic skating' and it's apparent that Sweden is a heartland for the pursuit of touring on ice skates. Whenever the ice is thick enough, Stockholm's lake and canal system is exploited by skating enthusiasts seeking the longest possible 'run'.

Stretching west from Stockholm, Mälaren is Sweden's third-largest lake (1140 sq km) and one of the country's prime Nordic skating venues. A short ride on public transport and you can be skating across the freshwater lake, covering up to 100km a day and stopping at towns, villages and cultural landmarks as you go. Among the stops you can make is the World Heritage–listed Viking trading centre of Birka on the island of Björkö, containing the largest Viking Age cemetery in Scandinavia, with around 3000 graves.

Each year – or at least those years the ice will support it – Mälaren hosts the skating race Vikingarännet. Started in 1999, this marathon event sees thousands of skaters cross the lake from Uppsala to Stockholm, a distance of around 80km – the record winning time is two hours 35 minutes. Vikingarännet is held when the lake ice is thick enough to support great numbers of skaters. The most probable date is during February.

Stockholm offers an extra skating thrill when the Baltic Sea freezes, though this occurs only once or twice every 10 years. When it does, fantastic tours of the archipelago are possible, but never skate alone.

Sharpen your blades and your Nordic skating interest at the Stockholm Ice Skate Sailing Association website (www.sssk.se). www.vikingarannet.com

↗ DO: SKI VALLÉE BLANCHE

COUNTRY France **TYPE OF ACTIVITY** Skiing
FITNESS/EXPERTISE LEVEL Good fitness and endurance required.
WHY NOW? You need a lot of snow to ski 22km, so come in deep winter.
DESCRIPTION From the evergreen Alpine resort town of Chamonix – the venue for the very first Olympic Winter Games in 1924 – ride the Aiguille du Midi cable car to its needle-tip end high above the town, climb out nervously on an arête and strap on your skis for the longest run in Europe. The Vallée Blanche switches between glaciers, including the famous Mer de Glace (the Alps' second-longest glacier), as it descends 22km back to Chamonix, dropping every one of the 2760m the cable car has carried you. It's fairly easy skiing, though you'll be on your planks for up to five hours. At times you'll also be threading between crevasses so it's imperative you make the descent with a qualified guide – Chamonix is chock-full of them; begin your search at www.chamonix-guides.com.

↗ DO: WINDSURF AT CABARETE

COUNTRY Dominican Republic **TYPE OF ACTIVITY** Windsurfing
FITNESS/EXPERTISE LEVEL Beginner to pro.
WHY NOW? From December to March, the waves are big enough to make even the inner bay a bit choppy. **DESCRIPTION** Cabarete's bay seems custom-made for windsurfing. A small coral reef on the bay's upwind side protects it from waves and currents, leaving a huge area of shallow, flat water. With light morning winds and mellow seas, the bay is ideal for beginners. In the afternoon, thermal winds pick up, blowing east to west and reaching speeds of between 25km/h and 40km/h. About 1km out, waves break over a second coral reef, and expert windsurfers head here to practice their 360° spins and end-over-end flips. Don't come expecting a travelling secret because windsurfing has transformed Cabarete. Its single road, once a sandy track along the coast, is now crammed with hotels, resorts and shops catering to wind-sport enthusiasts. Kiteboarding is also a mainstay here. www.activecabarete.com; www.cabaretewindsurfing.com

↗ DO: SNOWSHOE AT MESA VERDE

COUNTRY USA **TYPE OF ACTIVITY** Snowshoeing
FITNESS/EXPERTISE LEVEL Basic snowshoeing skills required.
WHY NOW? Snow conditions are patchy, with mid-February among the most likely snowshoeing times. **DESCRIPTION** Even if you've never been snowshoeing, you've no doubt seen images of cold people in cold places wearing what appear to be tennis racquets on their feet. Snowshoeing allows you to walk trails in the depth of winter, when all other hikers are home keeping their toes warm for summer. And at Mesa Verde National Park, nestled into the crook of the Four Corners, it comes with a surreal edge: snowshoeing in the desert, among ancestral Puebloan sites. Winter here brings unreliable snows, opening the park to snowshoeing for only a few days a year. The Cliff Palace Loop Rd offers a 10km stroll past lookouts onto the cliff dwellings, while the Morefield Campground Loop Rds offers a variety of choices, both short and long. www.nps.gov/meve

↗ Yukon Quest
www.yukonquest.com
A 1600km dog-sled race in jet-black-winter Alaska and Canada's Yukon, across frozen rivers and through four mountain ranges.

↗ Yukon Arctic Ultra
www.4ar.info/races.php
Race 42km, 160km, 480km or 750km on skis, snowshoes or mountain bike; begins a few hours after the Yukon Quest.

↗ Patagonia Expedition Race
www.patagoniaexpeditionrace.com
Up to 10 days of mountain biking, trekking, sea kayaking, orienteering, and rope activities, covering more than 500 Patagonian kilometres.

↗ Sapporo International Ski Marathon
www.shsf.jp/ski
Ski 50km within seven hours on the Japanese island of Hokkaido.

↗ FEBRUARY

WEEK.03

GO:
SOUTH GEORGIA ISLAND

[ABOVE] ↗
Take February off
to march with the
penguins.

[RIGHT] ↗
Thanks to its height
and equatorial location,
Kilimanjaro guarantees
climbers four seasons
in one day.

WHY NOW? AT THIS END OF SUMMER IT HAS ONE OF
THE WORLD'S MOST EXTRAORDINARY COLLECTIONS OF
WILDLIFE

More than 2000km west of Tierra del Fuego, the South Atlantic island of
South Georgia has been part of the adventuring psyche ever since Ernest
Shackleton made his dramatic walk across the uncharted island after the
Endurance was crushed by the Antarctic pack ice. After sailing 1300km
from Elephant Island in a 6m lifeboat, across some of the world's roughest
seas, Shackleton and two members of his crew trekked for
36 hours across the mountainous island on frostbitten feet (with screws
from the lifeboat as makeshift crampons) to reach the whaling station at
Stromness. For fit and well-equipped adventurers the possibility of following
this amazing trek has become one of the key Antarctic challenges.

With its snowcapped peaks and glaciers plunging towards the sea,
South Georgia has been described as an alpine mountain range rising

↗ DO: CLIMB MT KILIMANJARO

COUNTRY Tanzania **TYPE OF ACTIVITY** Trekking **FITNESS/EXPERTISE LEVEL** Good fitness and acclimatisation required. **WHY NOW?** Warm temperatures and little rain, while avoiding the New Year high season when huts may be booked out. **DESCRIPTION** Mt Kilimanjaro (5896m) is Africa's highest mountain and can be climbed along six routes. The majority of trekkers take Kili's easiest path, the Marangu Route (so popular it's been dubbed the 'Coca-Cola Route'). Most trekkers on this route only go as far as Gillman's Point, on the crater rim at 5685m, with another two hours of high-altitude walking required to reach the summit at Uhuru Peak. Of the other routes, Umbwe is the most direct, and Lemosho the longest, while the Machame (with a descent on the Mweka Route) is the most scenic option. You'll go through the pain barrier on the way to the top of the mountain, but the reward is unforgettable – a sunrise view over what seems like half of Africa.

straight out of the ocean. But at this end of summer there are swathes of green and it has one of the world's most extraordinary collections of wildlife. If you want to see king penguins or fur seals, this is the place to come – there are millions of fur seals, while single colonies of king penguins can number in the tens of thousands. There are also substantial numbers of elephant seals as well as a variety of other penguin species.

South Georgia and its outlying islands are also home to a substantial proportion of the world's albatross population, including important colonies of the largest of these astonishing birds, the gigantic wandering albatross, which can have a wing span of more than 3m.

While on South Georgia, pay homage to Shackleton's grave in the cemetery at Grytviken whaling station – Sir Ernest died in January 1922 aboard his ship moored off Grytviken.

Unless you're one of the few people who come by private yacht, the only way to reach South Georgia is by cruise ship. www.sgisland.org

[ABOVE] ↗
Receive a watery smile from a *butanding* (whale shark) as you take a dip near Donsol.

[TOP RIGHT] ↗
Treading on thick ice: the 15-storey-high Moreno Glacier.

[BOTTOM RIGHT] ↗
Naked wrestling wearing loin cloths? Clear as mud.

DO: SWIM WITH SHARKS AT DONSOL

COUNTRY Philippines **TYPE OF ACTIVITY** Snorkelling/wildlife watching
FITNESS/EXPERTISE LEVEL Good swimming skills an asset.

WHY NOW? Whale sharks visit the waters off Donsol between about February and May.

DESCRIPTION Until 1998 Donsol, on the Luzon Peninsula, was an obscure, sleepy and remote village. Then a local diver shot a video of whale sharks in the area. Days after a newspaper story about the 'discovery' was published, poachers from other provinces arrived in the area. The local and central governments quickly drafted a municipal ordinance together, prohibiting the hunting of whale sharks. Since then Donsol has quickly become one of Luzon's best-known locations, with travellers and media from around the world descending on the town to see the famous *butanding* (the local word for whale shark).

Today, Donsol is one of the world's top locations to swim with the largest fish in the sea – these gentle giants can grow to 18m in length, although it's more common to see them about half that size.

It's truly an exhilarating experience swimming along with these huge blue-grey, silver-spotted creatures. Only snorkelling equipment is allowed, with scuba diving prohibited. There's a limited supply of snorkelling equipment available for rent at Donsol's visitor centre, so it's advisable to bring your own.

During the peak months of March and April, the question isn't whether you will see a shark, but how many you will see. Occasionally the sharks migrate here as early as November and stay until around late June, but you shouldn't bank on it.

Upon arrival in town, stop in at the visitor centre. It will arrange a boat, spotter and a Butanding Interaction Officer for you. You'll find a small selection of accommodation in Donsol, and this once unknown town now even has a direct bus service to the capital, Manila.

↗ DO: **GLACIER WALK ON MORENO GLACIER**

COUNTRY Argentina **TYPE OF ACTIVITY** Glacier walking
FITNESS/EXPERTISE LEVEL Not required.
WHY NOW? Stay warm atop the giant ice block.
DESCRIPTION Discover the true meaning of the term 'cold feet' as you take a boat across the glacial melt of Lago Argentino, wander through beech forest and emerge at the edge of 15-storey-high Moreno Glacier. It's one of the few glaciers in the world not in retreat, defying global trends to have shown signs of advancing. Fit your crampons and head out onto the ice, which is twisted, broken and covered in seracs like giant, blue blades of grass. Water streams across its top, disappearing into seemingly endless holes, and you walk past crevasses that yawn wider than a lion – welcome to the world of the mountaineer, without any of the requisite hardships. At the end of your walk you get a whisky with ice chipped directly from the glacier. Make base camp at the Patagonian town of El Calafate, from where buses run daily to Moreno Glacier. www.hieloyaventura.com

↗ DO: **FIGHT IN A NAKED FESTIVAL**

COUNTRY Japan **TYPE OF ACTIVITY** Adventure travel
FITNESS/EXPERTISE LEVEL A good boxing defence and wrestling technique an asset.
WHY NOW? To fight with 10,000 men over two sticks.
DESCRIPTION Naked festivals are common (if a little overstated, since participants wear loincloths) throughout Japan in the early new year but the most extraordinary is that in the Kannon-in temple outside of Okayama. Taking place in the chilly depths of winter, Saidai-ji Eyō sees thousands of near-naked men fighting for possession of two sacred *shingi* (wooden sticks), while freezing water is poured over them. Fuelled by alcohol, fights and skirmishes are common and an indicator of the seriousness of the battle is the fact that the *yakuza* – Japan's mafia – fields competitors in the event. You're free to participate, but even if you manage to grab one of the *shingi*, that's only an invitation to be savaged.

↗ DO: **RACE OF HOPE**

COUNTRY Cameroon **TYPE OF ACTIVITY** Mountain running
FITNESS/EXPERTISE LEVEL High level of fitness required.
WHY NOW? To compete in the Mt Cameroon Race.
DESCRIPTION Mt Cameroon (4095m) is the highest peak in West Africa, rising direct from the Gulf of Guinea through rainforest to an alpine summit. An active volcano, it erupted seven times last century, most recently in 2000, but that doesn't deter runners from scaling it in the marathon-length Race of Hope (Mt Cameroon Race), held around this time each year. Beginning in the sprawling town of Buea, competitors follow the most direct of the mountain's trekking trails – the so-called Guinness Route – to the summit. If you dance to a slower drum, you can always just walk up the mountain. While the quickest of the runners complete the Guinness Route in 4½ hours, allow two nights to comfortably trek it.

↗ **Susitna 100**
www.susitna100.com
Mountain bike, ski, run or snowshoe for 160km through wintry South Central Alaska.

↗ **Tartu Maraton**
www.tartumaraton.ee/tm
A 63km cross-country ski marathon in Estonia.

↗ **Kili[MAN]jaro**
http://kilimanjaro-man.com
Climb Mt Kilimanjaro in eight days, cycle around it in two, then run the Kilimanjaro Marathon.

↗ **RAW Africa**
www.runacrosstheworld.com
Five-day, 250km running race across Namibia's Sossusvlei, which are among the highest sand dunes in the world.

↗ **FEBRUARY**

WEEK.04

GO:
COSTA RICA

(ABOVE) ↗
Get lost in the tree tops
of Costa Rica, home to
more animal species
than any other country
in the world.

(RIGHT) ↗
Fly up in a chopper, fly
down on two wheels.

WHY NOW? FEBRUARY IS TRADITIONALLY THE DRIEST MONTH ACROSS COSTA RICA

Costa Rica covers less than 0.01% of the planet, yet it has almost as many birds as the USA and Canada combined, more reptiles than Europe and five times more butterflies than Australia. Measured in terms of number of species per 10,000 sq km, Costa Rica tops the list of countries at 615 species, compared to the relatively impoverished USA with its 104 species. This simple fact alone makes Costa Rica among the premier destinations for naturalists.

More than 850 animal species have been recorded in Costa Rica, but birds are the primary attraction, and they come in every imaginable colour, from the strawberry-red of scarlet macaws to the iridescent violet of sabrewings. Because many of the birds have restricted ranges, you are guaranteed to find completely different species almost everywhere you travel in the country.

↗ DO: HELI-BIKING IN NEW ZEALAND

COUNTRY New Zealand **TYPE OF ACTIVITY** Mountain biking **FITNESS/EXPERTISE LEVEL** Some technical skills required over the rugged terrain. **WHY NOW?** To hit the mountain tops when they're snow-free. **DESCRIPTION** In New Zealand, adventures are never content to stay simple. White-water rafting became black-water rafting, bungee jumping became plunging from the country's tallest building, and for mountain bikers the ante has now been upped to heli-biking, in which riders and bikes are choppered into the mountains and left to freewheel through alpine or subalpine lands back into town. The activity is available in various locations – Twizel, Coromandel Peninsula, Nelson, Rotorua, Taupo and, inevitably, the country's twin adventure capitals Wanaka and Queenstown. From Queenstown, helicopters deposit bikes on the summit of Ben Cruachan for a 1600m descent back towards town. Wanaka rides begin in the Cardrona Valley and can be tailored to suit most riding abilities. www.helibike.com

Not all that's wild in Costa Rica is wildlife. If you take your inspiration from the birds and not the sloths, you can bungy jump from the Río Colorado bridge in the capital, San José. And if you're more manatee than macaw, you'll find legendary surf at Witches Rock, with its tubular 3m curls, and Ollie's Point, situated near the old airstrip that was once used to smuggle goods to the Nicaraguan Contras in the 1980s (and named after US colonel Oliver North). White-water warriors consider the Río Pacuare to be among the 10 best river raft runs in the world.

Land mammals will appreciate the dry season for some great hiking among fumaroles and tropical dry forest in Parque Nacional Rincón de la Vieja, or in the cloud forest reserves of Santa Elena and Monteverde. Those with higher ambitions can scale Costa Rica's highest mountain, Cerro Chirripó (3820m), on a 16km trail – of the Central American countries, only Guatemala has higher peaks.

And those who want something with the lot will gravitate to Península de Osa. Largely covered by Parque Nacional Corcovado, it offers spectacular wildlife viewing at the Sirena Research Station, and the best way into Sirena is on foot. There are three trails to the station, two of which follow the coast and produce an endless pageant of birds. Scarlet macaws are guaranteed, with the tropical almond trees that line the coast a favourite macaw food. There's also the opportunity to swim with dolphins in Bahía Drake.

· (ABOVE) ↗
Explore the eerie depths
of Piccaninnie Ponds for
an out-of-this-world
dive experience.

(TOP RIGHT) ↗
Make sure you take
a guide when visiting
Ethiopia's churches
and temples.

(BOTTOM RIGHT) ↗
Scramble through
shifting desert sands
as you tackle the
Sahara Marathon.

DO: CAVE DIVE AT PICCANINNIE PONDS

COUNTRY Australia **TYPE OF ACTIVITY** Cave diving

FITNESS/EXPERTISE LEVEL High level of expertise required.

WHY NOW? Freezing waters but at least the air is warm.

DESCRIPTION The ground around the South Australian city of Mt Gambier has more holes than fishnet stockings (even balls pitched to some greens at the local golf club can produce a subterranean echo) but of all the caves that puncture the so-called Limestone Coast, the Piccaninnie Ponds demand most attention.

The standout attraction at the Ponds is the Cathedral, which has a reputation as one of the world's greatest freshwater dive features. Filled by underground springs and filtered by the limestone, visibility inside this scalloped cavern reaches to 40m, and is only then impeded by the walls of the cave. The Chasm offers greater depth, plunging more than 100m, its white walls covered in algal growth.

Controls on snorkelling and diving at Piccaninnie Ponds are strict. To dive at the Ponds you must be a member of the Cave Divers Association of Australia and certified to sinkhole level. Permits are required – obtainable from the Department for Environment and Heritage (DEH) office in Mt Gambier – and these are issued by timeslots: only four divers are allowed in the Ponds at any one time. All divers are allowed one hour.

Snorkellers also need to obtain permits from the DEH office, though you don't need any qualifications or affiliations to apply for them. Timeslot conditions are the same as for divers.

To experience a different sort of cave dive, head to nearby Ewens Ponds. These three ponds, connected by shallow channels, reach nowhere near the depths of Piccaninnie – their maximum depth is around 10m – but are inhabited by eels and freshwater crays. They are fed by a greater flow of spring water, creating a current that will almost imperceptibly carry you along. www.cavedivers.com.au; www.environment.sa.gov.au

↗ DO: SCRAMBLE TO TIGRAY'S ROCK CHURCHES

COUNTRY Ethiopia **TYPE OF ACTIVITY** Scrambling/adventure travel
FITNESS/EXPERTISE LEVEL Not required.

WHY NOW? Come at the end of the cool and dry winter. **DESCRIPTION**
Between the northern Ethiopian towns of Adigrat and Mekele lie around
120 churches carved into cliff faces or pre-existing caves. Visiting some
of these churches involves a scramble up almost sheer rock faces using
just footholds in the rock. Although daunting at first sight, the ascents
aren't difficult if taken carefully. Abuna Yemata is considered the most
challenging climb, taking about an hour, using footholds up a sheer
20-minute ascent and crossing a narrow ledge. For your effort you'll find
a church famed for its beautiful and well-preserved frescoes, and with
stunning views. Mekele makes the best base from which to explore the
churches; it can be reached by plane or bus from the capital, Addis Ababa.
Guides are available through Mekele travel agencies and are essential, not
only to locate the more remote churches, but also for tracking down the
often-elusive priests, keepers of the all-important church keys.

↗ DO: SAHARA MARATHON

REGION Western Sahara **TYPE OF ACTIVITY** Running
FITNESS/EXPERTISE LEVEL High level of fitness required.

WHY NOW? To run through the world's largest desert. **DESCRIPTION**
Imagine the least likely place in the world in which to run 42km, and
it'd probably be the Sahara. This annual event between the towns of El
Aaiun and Smara is staged in the disputed region of Western Sahara to
demonstrate solidarity with the local Saharawi people, around 200,000 of
whom live in refugee camps near Tindouf in Algeria. The good news for
runners is that most of the course isn't ankle deep in Saharan sand; the
bad news is that it's across hard and rocky terrain, with the second half of
the race also hilly with dunes. The Sahara Marathon is held in the desert's
coolest season, so forget the heat and brace yourself for dawn's chill.
www.saharamarathon.org

↗ DO: SURF PIPELINE

COUNTRY USA **TYPE OF ACTIVITY** Surfing
FITNESS/EXPERTISE LEVEL High skill level required.

WHY NOW? About your only chance to be allowed a wave here is to come
on a February or March dawn. **DESCRIPTION** Hawaii lies smack in the
path of all the major swells that race across the Pacific Ocean, with the
biggest waves rolling into the north shores of the islands from November
through February. On Oahu's north shore, the glassy tubes of Banzai
Pipeline have become the unofficial world mecca of surfing. Winter
swells can bring in towering 10m waves, creating conditions that can be
insane. The waves break onto a dangerously shallow reef, while equally
hazardous currents pull at the surfers, boogie boarders and bodysurfers
who crowd the sea. To find the Pipeline, head for Ehukai Beach Park
and, facing the ocean, walk about 100m to the left; come at dawn if you
want any space on a wave. Wait until summer and the Pipeline will have
mellowed into a swimmers' delight.

↗ **Iditarod Trail Invitational**
www.alaskaultrasport.com
Cycle, ski or walk 560km or 1770km along
Alaska's Iditarod Trail; a hell of a way to finish
winter.

↗ **Bergson Winter Challenge**
www.adventurerace.pl
Trek, ski or mountain bike 400km in five days
in Poland.

↗ **Avalanche Peak Challenge**
www.avalanchepeak.co.nz
Twenty-six kilometre mountain run across New
Zealand's spectacular Avalanche Peak.

↗ **Tai Po Mountain Marathon**
www.seyonasia.com/koth/tp.html
Run 36km through the Hong Kong mountains,
climbing around 2000m.

GO:
MONSERRAT

[ABOVE] ↗
Check out the steaming vents of Montserrat's volcano from a safe distance, then explore the superb diving opportunities that lie beneath the waves.

[RIGHT] ↗
For an extreme take on 'Fetch', take on the 1850km Iditarod..

WHY NOW? CLIMATE VARIES LITTLE ON TROPICAL MONTSERRAT, BUT THE BEGINNING OF MARCH IS ONE OF THE (MARGINALLY) COOLER TIMES, AND IS WELL REMOVED FROM THE HURRICANE SEASON

There was a time when travelling to the island of Montserrat combined two usually unrelated activities: Caribbean holiday and a death wish. You don't need a death wish to visit Montserrat anymore, just an ash mask.

After spending decades as a tight-knit community, proud of its image as an unspoiled Caribbean island with no pretensions, Montserrat was given a big how-do-you-do by the Soufrière Hills Volcano on 18 July 1995, ending 400 years of dormancy. The capital and only significant town, Plymouth, was covered in ash and subsequently abandoned. The 11,000 residents resettled around the island or emigrated, and tourists all but disappeared. In 1997 the volcano erupted again, killing 19 people. Two months later, a superheated pyroclastic flow wiped out the remainder of Plymouth.

↗ DO: IDITAROD

COUNTRY USA **TYPE OF ACTIVITY** Dog-sledding **FITNESS/EXPERTISE LEVEL** Epic endurance and sledding skills required. **WHY NOW?** To gut yourself in one of the world's toughest races. **DESCRIPTION** The greatest dog-sled event of all, and one of the blockbuster endurance events, the Iditarod is an 1850km race between Anchorage and faraway Nome on the Bering Sea. Held along the Iditarod National Historic Trail, the event has become known as the 'last great race' and has been held since 1973 to commemorate the role that dogs and sleds played in the settlement of remote Alaska. From a winning time of more than 20 days in the first couple of years, the record is now less than nine days. The start in Anchorage is ceremonial, with the true race beginning in the town of Willow the following day. www.iditarod.com

The volcano still lets off the occasional puff of steam, but life has regained some normalcy for Montserratians, with almost 5000 people living in the northern one-third of the island not affected by the eruptions. Tourism is now low-key and the real sights here are the central volcano and accompanying devastation.

The volcano itself isn't accessible, but there are several good viewing points, and you can visit the Montserrat Volcano Observatory (www.mvo.ms), set up by an international team of vulcanologists. There's an excellent film, and displays of things such as 'breadcrust bombs' that are spat out of the earth during eruptions.

Although much of the ocean surrounding the southern part of the island is still off-limits, what is left of Montserrat's diving is legendary. Best of all, it's been left in near pristine condition because the volcano virtually wiped out tourism.

In July 2005 Monserrat's new airport (replacing the one destroyed by the eruption) opened, and there are now flights from Antigua and St Maarten. You can also take the one-hour Montserrat Ferry from St John's Bay in Antigua. www.visitmontserrat.com

[ABOVE] ↗
Swap greens for 'whites'
and perhaps spot an
albatross.

[TOP RIGHT] ↗
Get caught between
a rock and a hard place
in Majlis al-Jinn.

[BOTTOM RIGHT] ↗
Cheer on newly hatched
baby loggerhead turtles
as they battle to reach
their ocean destination.

DO: **PLAY THE WEIRDEST GOLF COURSES**

COUNTRIES Greenland/Australia/South Korea **TYPE OF ACTIVITY** Golf
FITNESS/EXPERTISE LEVEL Not required.
WHY NOW? To play in the World Ice Golf Championship.

DESCRIPTION Each March on the small Greenland island of Uummannaq, a golf course is carved anew
in the ice. The course differs each year, according to what ice shapes and structure the winter season
has left behind, but by the start of March the nine-hole course is being fashioned ready for the World Ice
Golf Championship. Golfers in the 36-hole tournament – open to anyone with a handicap but limited to 20
players – play with bright-red balls in the white ice, driving, chipping and putting along fairways and 'whites'
(rather than greens) framed by icebergs.

Far away in Australia there's a very different golf experience on the Nullarbor Plain, where the world's
longest golf course opened in 2009. The 18-hole Nullarbor Links covers almost 1400km, with one hole
at each of the towns and roadhouse stops along the Eyre Highway as it crosses through the so-called
treeless plain. Golfers play a hole, drive on and play the next on a course befitting the vast landscape of the
Australian outback.

For a course where the word 'bunker' has more than one connotation, head to Camp Bonifas, abutting
the Demilitarised Zone between South and North Korea. Home to South Korean and American troops,
the camp is also the location of a golf course now all but accredited as the most dangerous on the planet.
Actually, 'course' is an exaggeration; what's here is a single par-three hole, 176m in length and ideal for the
golfer who wants to cure a hook in their swing. With an artificial green, and lined by barbed wire, it's also
positioned beside a live minefield – an erratic drive here can have explosive results. www.greenland-guide.

↗ DO: CAVING AT MAJLIS AL-JINN

COUNTRY Oman **TYPE OF ACTIVITY** Caving
FITNESS/EXPERTISE LEVEL Abseiling experience necessary.
WHY NOW? The best time to visit Oman is between November and mid-March, when daytime temperatures average 25°C. **DESCRIPTION** The so-called Meeting Place of the Spirits is one of the largest cave chambers in the world, drilled into the Selma Plateau in Oman's Ash Sharqiyah region. Discovered in 1983 but brought to world spelunking attention by *National Geographic* 20 years later, the cave features a 120m-high ceiling. Cavers must abseil more than 150m into the sun-pierced chamber and then climb back out. The cave contains three entrances, with cavers entering through Cheryl's Drop, named after one of the cave's discoverers. Putting a further spin on what was already a spin, BASE jumpers have also discovered the cave, leading to talk that entry may be banned, though the Oman government announced plans in 2008 to turn it into a show cave.

↗ DO: VIEW LOGGERHEAD TURTLES AT MON REPOS

COUNTRY Australia **TYPE OF ACTIVITY** Wildlife watching
FITNESS/EXPERTISE LEVEL Not required.
WHY NOW? To witness hatching turtles scurry for the ocean.
DESCRIPTION The lovely Queensland beach of Mon Repos, near Bundaberg, is Australia's most accessible mainland turtle rookery and one of only two nesting sites in the South Pacific for the endangered loggerhead turtle. Every year between November and February, large numbers of loggerhead and occasional green and flatback turtles drag themselves up the beach to lay their eggs. The time to be here is when they hatch – mid-January to March – to watch the young turtles emerge and begin their often ill-fated dash for the ocean. During the laying and hatching seasons, access to the beach is controlled by staff from the Mon Repos information centre, with rangers leading visitors onto the beach between 7pm and 6am. Bookings are essential. www.epa.qld.gov.au

↗ DO: TREK IN THE RWENZORI MOUNTAINS

COUNTRY Uganda **TYPE OF ACTIVITY** Trekking
FITNESS/EXPERTISE LEVEL High level of fitness required.
WHY NOW? The best trekking is in the dry season from November to March. **DESCRIPTION** Straddling the border of Uganda and the Democratic Republic of the Congo, the Rwenzori Mountains (often called the Mountains of the Moon) contain six main massifs, culminating in Margherita Peak on Mt Stanley (5109m), the third-highest point in Africa. If you want your wilderness easy this is not the place, for the paths are narrow and you must push through dense bush and bamboo forest, and wade through deep bogs. To reach the three main peaks requires technical skills and the use of ice axe, rope and crampons. The highest point normally reached by trekkers is Elena Hut (4540m), at the snout of Elena Glacier, where the technical routes up Mt Stanley begin. It's also possible for trekkers to cross two major cols, the Scott-Elliot Pass (4370m) and the Freshfield Pass (4280m). The main access town for treks is Kasese, about a 500km drive west from the capital, Kampala. www.uwa.or.ug/rwenzori.html

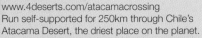

Ultimate Florida Challenge
www.watertribe.com
Circumnavigate peninsular Florida – about 1900km – by kayak, canoe or small boat, taking up to 29 days.

Everglades Challenge
www.watertribe.com
Paddle or sail 500km of Florida water between Fort Desoto and Key Largo; nine-day limit.

Atacama Crossing
www.4deserts.com/atacamacrossing
Run self-supported for 250km through Chile's Atacama Desert, the driest place on the planet.

High Peak Marathon
www.highpeakclub.union.shef.ac.uk
A 67km overnight mountain run (or 'bog trot') along the Derwent Watershed near Sheffield, England.

↗ MARCH

WEEK.02

GO: SABAH, MALAYSIA

[ABOVE] ↗
Join a school of fish weaving its way through an iridescent underwater playground.

[RIGHT] ↗
There may have been water here once, but now the Sahara is an ocean of sand.

WHY NOW? IN MARCH, YOU'LL FIND HAWKSBILLS LAYING EGGS ON PULAU GULISAN

On evocative Borneo, in the semi-autonomous Malaysian state of Sabah, rises the highest mountain between the Himalayas and New Guinea. The good news is that Mt Kinabalu (4095m) is one of the easiest climbs among the world's high peaks, and atop its summit you may even be greeted by an international view – on a clear day you can see the Philippines. Clear days are rare, however, and dawn on the summit is often an all-too-brief glimpse across Borneo before the clouds roll in along the mountainous spine.

Climbing Mt Kinabalu is typically a two-day exercise. Most people climb as far as Laban Rata or the nearby huts on the first day, then climb to the summit at dawn and return to park headquarters on the next day. A climbing permit and insurance are compulsory for any ascent, and guides are also mandatory for all summit attempts. March and April are the driest

↗ DO: 100KM DEL SAHARA

COUNTRY Tunisia **TYPE OF ACTIVITY** Endurance running **FITNESS/EXPERTISE LEVEL** Superior fitness required. **WHY NOW?** To race through the world's largest desert. **DESCRIPTION** Spend four days running more than 100km through the Sahara on a course where, if you have the energy to look up from your shuffling feet, you'll discover some of the desert's finest scenery. Beginning from the oasis of Ksar Ghilane, an amazing spot surrounded by dunes and sublime desert scenery (many of the scenes from *The English Patient* were filmed here) the race is run over four days, ending at another oasis in Duoz. Three of the days are around half-marathon length, with the third day's run being over the full marathon distance of 42km. www.100kmdelsahara.com

times on the mountain and offer the best climbing opportunities.

Beyond the mountain, Sabah is noted for other incredible natural features. There are beautiful coral reefs to explore, and birds, animals, trees and plants to seek out. Foremost among these is the amazing rafflesia, the world's largest flower, up to 1m in diameter. A parasitic plant, you will see no roots or leaves, just the blossom…if you're lucky. It only blooms infrequently and randomly, and lasts just a few days. One of the best places to try your floral luck is the Tambunan Rafflesia Reserve, south of the Sabah capital, Kota Kinabalu. Staff at the information centre can fill you in on the latest sightings.

More reliable are Sabah's critters. Marvel at how cute unruly red hair can be at the Sepilok Orang-Utan Rehabilitation Centre, one of just four orang-utan sanctuaries in the world, or head out to the three small islands that comprise Turtle Islands National Park. Although their numbers have fallen off, two species of marine turtle – green and hawksbill – come ashore here to lay their eggs at certain times of the year. In March you will find hawksbills laying eggs on Pulau Gulisan.

(ABOVE) ↗
Unearth a verdant
sanctuary as you
tramp the Milford Track.

(TOP RIGHT) ↗
Monkey business at Yala
National Park.

(BOTTOM RIGHT) ↗
Almost 20,000km of
trails await serious
snowmobilers in
Moosehead.

DO: **TRAMP THE MILFORD TRACK**

COUNTRY New Zealand **TYPE OF ACTIVITY** Hiking

FITNESS/EXPERTISE LEVEL Moderate fitness required.

WHY NOW? The holiday crowds have gone but the good conditions have not.

DESCRIPTION The famous Milford Track is a four-day, 53.5km walk described in a newspaper report a century ago as the finest in the world, a moniker it now wears like a tattoo. So popular is the track that in the tramping season (late October to April) permits are required and strict conditions are placed on all walkers: the number of walkers starting the track each day is limited to 40; accommodation is only in huts (camping isn't allowed); you must follow a set four-day itinerary; and you can only walk in the one direction (Lake Te Anau to Milford Sound). For your trouble you're treated to a wild (and invariably wet) piece of New Zealand's World Heritage–listed Fiordland National Park. The tramp funnels through the Clinton Valley, with its glacier-scratched walls closing to little more than a crack at its head. From here it climbs to the crest of wind-whipped Mackinnon Pass which, though not particularly high (1069m), bears all the hallmarks and beauty of a high alpine pass – the view of the drop down into the Arthur Valley is especially heady, as are the sharp Mt Balloon and Mt Hart peaks rising above it. The descent follows the headwaters of the Arthur River, passing by 580m-high Sutherland Falls, the highest waterfall in New Zealand (and among the highest in the world), before arriving on the shores of Milford Sound, where it's possible to kayak out for a bit of a multisport end to the tramp. www.doc.govt.nz

↗ DO: SAFARI AT YALA NATIONAL PARK

COUNTRY Sri Lanka **TYPE OF ACTIVITY** Wildlife watching
FITNESS/EXPERTISE LEVEL Not required.
WHY NOW? Best time of year to see leopards and elephants.
DESCRIPTION On Sri Lanka's southeast coast, Yala West (Ruhuna) National Park is around 1270 sq km of scrub, plains, brackish lagoons and rocky outcrops. Lurking within the park is one of the world's densest leopard populations with around 35 resident cats. The most reliable time to see the big cats is from February to about June, when water levels are low. For good measure, this is also the time you're most likely to see elephants in Yala West. Most people use a tour company or safari operator to get into Sri Lanka's largest national park, and you won't have to go far to find somebody willing to take you; the coastal town of Tissamaharama is flush with guides and drivers. There is no accommodation inside the national park and it has been plagued by security issues so check ahead that it is open to visitors.

↗ DO: SNOWMOBILE THE MOOSEHEAD TRAIL

COUNTRY USA **TYPE OF ACTIVITY** Snowmobiling
FITNESS/EXPERTISE LEVEL Basic snowmobiling skills required.
WHY NOW? To be mobile you'll need snow; the most reliable conditions are from January to mid-March. **DESCRIPTION** In the rural far north of New England, snowmobile trail systems wind throughout the woods (much on private land and usually with the owner's blessing). Most state parks are open for cruising and local clubs are sprinkled everywhere. Maine's Interconnecting Trail System alone contains almost 20,000km of trails, so it's no wonder that this state is also home to snowmobiling heaven: Moosehead Lake. There are a number of trails around Moosehead Lake (you can even snowmobile to a wrecked B-52 bomber) but the standout ride is the Moosehead Trail, a 267km track that circumnavigates the lake. If you have petrol for blood, you can tear around the trail in a day, but you can also break it with overnight stops in the towns of Greenville, Kokadjo, NE Carry, Seboomook, Pittston Farm and Rockwood.

↗ DO: RIVER-TUBE IN BELIZE

COUNTRY Belize **TYPE OF ACTIVITY** River-tubing
FITNESS/EXPERTISE LEVEL Not required.
WHY NOW? Tubing is best in the dry season (February to April).
DESCRIPTION River-tubing – sitting in an inflated inner-tube and floating or paddling along a river – is all the rage in Belize, blessed as the country is with many fairly gentle and not-too-cold watercourses working their way through gorgeous scenery. You go downstream most of the time and the only technique that needs to be learnt is to avoid getting beached, eddied or snagged on rocks while continuing to face in roughly the right direction! The Mopan River near San Ignacio is a popular tubing river, but the mother of Belizean tubing adventures is the float in and out of a sequence of caves on the Caves Branch River, inside the Nohoch Che'en Archaeological Reserve. People come on day trips from all over Belize for this.

↗ Six Foot Track Marathon
www.sixfoot.com
A 45km foot race along a popular bushwalkng trail through the Blue Mountains near Sydney.

↗ Cape Argus Cycle Tour
www.cycletour.co.za
Join around 30,000 cyclists riding 110km around Cape Town's Table Mountain.

↗ La Ruta Maya Belize River Challenge
www.larutamayabelize.com
Paddle 274km in four days between San Ignacio and Belize City.

↗ ARC Winter Adventure Race
www.adventureracingcanada.com/winter
Multisport race with an icy twist; snowshoe, ski and mountain bike for up to six hours.

WEEK.03

GO: **LA MOSQUITIA, HONDURAS**

(ABOVE) ↗
Navigate the Río Plátano on a *pipante* (wooden canoe) to get to the heart of La Mosquitia.

(RIGHT) ↗
Delve into the cathedral-like Lang Cave to behold illuminated helictites.

WHY NOW? THE BEST TIME FOR SEEING BIRDS IS NOW, WHEN MANY MIGRATORY SPECIES ARE PRESENT

La Mosquitia – the Mosquito Coast – covers the entire northeast portion of Honduras. It has few roads and inhabitants, and a pristine natural beauty that's awe-inspiring. Manatees and other wildlife live in the eastern lagoons. Monkeys visit the forested areas along the rivers in the dawn, and there is abundant birdlife, including toucans, macaws, parrots, egrets and herons. Those who go deep into the jungle may even spot a jaguar, and crocodiles can be seen in many of the waters. As the name may suggest, mosquitoes and sand flies are even more abundant.

La Mosquitia is a genuinely remote place, of the sort that exists in very few places in Latin America and the world. At its core is the Río Plátano Biosphere Reserve, one of the most magnificent nature reserves in Central America. A World Heritage site, established jointly in 1980 by

↗ DO: CAVE AT GUNUNG MULU NATIONAL PARK

COUNTRY Malaysia **TYPE OF ACTIVITY** Caving **FITNESS/EXPERTISE LEVEL** Fear of the dark is a hindrance. **WHY NOW?** It's the driest month of the year, making it only seriously damp in Sarawak. **DESCRIPTION** Gunung Mulu is the largest national park in the Borneo state of Sarawak, containing abutting mountain ranges, one composed of sandstone and the other of limestone. Beneath the limestone range is a network of underground passages, stretching around 51km. In 1981 cave explorers discovered the largest chamber in the world in Gunung Mulu (the Sarawak Chamber) reputed to be the size of 16 football fields. The park's show caves are Deer, Lang, Clearwater, Cave of the Winds and Lagang. If you want a more daring cave crawl, there's also a series of adventure caves, all graded as beginner, intermediate or advanced. Experienced spelunkers can also journey into the Sarawak Chamber if you're up for an all-day epic. www.mulupark.com

Honduras and the United Nations, it is home to abundant bird, mammal and aquatic life, including a number of exotic and endangered species in the river and surrounding jungle.

Large (5251 sq km) and mostly well preserved, Río Plátano consists of lowland tropical rainforest with remarkable natural, archaeological and cultural resources. Access to the southern zone is through Olancho by road, beyond Dulce Nombre de Culmí; access to the northern zone is by plane from La Ceiba to Palacios and then by motorised canoe to other destinations. The central zone is very remote and seeing it requires long expeditions.

The main jumping-off point for trips into the Mosquitia is Palacios, which has an airport and

several accommodation options. Visiting La Mosquitia is not cheap; prices are fixed at relatively high levels and are rarely negotiable. The best time of year to visit is from November to July.

[ABOVE] ↗
Prepare for confined
inner space in infinite
outer space as you orbit
the earth 120 times.

[TOP RIGHT] ↗
Forget the scientific
explanation and be
blown away by the
beauty of the Aurora
Borealis.

[BOTTOM RIGHT] ↗
Share a giggle with
some locals in Sapa
on your way up to the
summit of Fansipan.

DO: BLAST OFF INTO SPACE

COUNTRY Russia **TYPE OF ACTIVITY** Space tourism
FITNESS/EXPERTISE LEVEL Large wallet required.
WHY NOW? Hit space in the month named after Mars.

DESCRIPTION Ever fancied flying into space, or at twice the speed of sound? In Russia, it can be arranged at a price. In April 2001, American billionaire Dennis Tito made history as the first paying customer of the Russian Space Agency, forking out a cool US$20 million to take a shot at space travel. After several months of training at Star City, Zvezdny Gorodok (30km from Moscow), Tito joined cosmonauts on board a Russian Soyuz spacecraft for a week-long visit to the International Space Station. Tito's trip, initially opposed by NASA, was considered a success and six other cashed-up astroheads have since followed in Tito's space boots.

The same journey can still be made, orbiting the earth around 120 times, and at the same price – can't be fairer than that – but there's also now the option of a shorter space trip that'll make significantly less impact on your hulking bank account. Backed by four days of intensive training, you can be blasted 100km above the earth to the point at which space begins. The rocket engines are shut down, and for five minutes you experience the sensation of weightlessness and a view that really is out of this world. All up, you'll be off the ground for about an hour – less time than on a Moscow–St Petersburg flight.

The price for this space trip is US$102,000, but that includes an astronaut pin as a souvenir.
www.spaceadventures.com

↗ DO: **VIEW THE AURORA BOREALIS**

REGIONS Greenland, Scandinavia, Russia, USA, Canada
TYPE OF ACTIVITY Natural phenomena
FITNESS/EXPERTISE LEVEL Not required.
WHY NOW? Viewing of the Northern Lights is best around the spring equinox. **DESCRIPTION** Watch the northern sky turn into a Pollock canvas as the heavenly phenomenon of the Aurora Borealis (Northern Lights), wafts across the prolonged night sky. The lights form from solar particles thrown out by explosions on the sun; nearing earth they're drawn to the magnetic poles, colliding with atmospheric gases to emit photons (light particles) of myriad shapes and colours. Often, they can look like celestial waterfalls. Viewing of the Northern Lights is best in the so-called auroral zone, which runs close to the Arctic Circle.

↗ DO: **CLIMB FANSIPAN**

COUNTRY Vietnam **TYPE OF ACTIVITY** Hiking
FITNESS/EXPERTISE LEVEL Moderate fitness required.
WHY NOW? It's the driest month around the mountain and the wildflowers are out. **DESCRIPTION** On the infrequent occasions that it's not obscured by cloud, Vietnam's highest peak (3143m) towers above the northern hill station of Sapa. Technical skills are not required to reach Fansipan's summit, although a substantial amount of endurance, as well as proper equipment and a guide, are required. The terrain is rough and adverse weather is frequent. Despite the short distance (19km) the round-trip hike to the summit will take around three to four days. After the first morning you won't see any villages; just the forest, striking mountain vistas and perhaps some local wildlife such as monkeys, mountain goats and birds. There are no mountain huts or other facilities along the way, so you'll need to be self-sufficient.

↗ Rock & Ice Ultra
www.rockandiceultra.com
Week-long, self-supported 225km race (run, snowshoe, ski) through Arctic Canada in winter.

↗ Goldrush
www.goldrush.co.nz
A 375km multisport event along the old gold trails of New Zealand's South Island.

↗ Terra Australis
www.terraaustralismtbepic.com.au
Seven stages and 550km of singletrack through Australia's high country.

↗ DO: **MOUNTAIN BIKE ON SNOW**

COUNTRY France **TYPE OF ACTIVITY** Mountain biking
FITNESS/EXPERTISE LEVEL Decent technical skills required.
WHY NOW? To race in Razorsnowbike.
DESCRIPTION Why pack away your trusty mountain bike just because it's winter and the earth is buried in snow? In the ski resort of Chatel, in the French Alps, they are convinced that mountain biking is just as relevant on hard snow as on hard single track. Held as part of the resort's 3 Style Days, Razorsnowbike sees up to 50 amateur mountain bikers sprinting downhill on a groomed track, poised above steep drops and swivelling through tight hairpins. This is followed by a four-cross race, in which four mountain bikers race along a specially prepared track, negotiating snow jumps as they try to beat the other three mountain bikers to the finish line. Super knobbly tyres a must. www.chatel.com

GO: GALÁPAGOS ISLANDS, ECUADOR

(ABOVE) ↗
Bask and bark with
sea lions in this highly
diverse and rich
ecosystem.

(RIGHT) ↗
Jaguars are
exceptionally elusive;
only a handful of visitors
a year actually see one.

WHY NOW? IN MARCH THE SEA IS WARM, TURTLES ARE NESTING AND THERE'LL BE SEA-LION PUPS CRAWLING AROUND THE SHORES

Like perhaps no other place on earth, the Galápagos Islands guarantee close encounters of the wildlife kind – above and below the sea. This remote, barren archipelago was known to early explorers as Las Islas Encantadas (the Enchanted Isles) and none of its enchantment has been lost down the centuries. Visitors continue to fall under the islands' spell as they step over dozing sea lions to come face-to-face with abundant birdlife and lumbering giant tortoises.

The bird-species tally in the Galápagos stands at about 140, including 28 endemic species. Two seabirds stand out: the waved albatross – the world's only tropical albatross species – and the flightless cormorant, which lost the power of flight in the absence of land-based predators.

↗ DO: COCKSCOMB BASIN WILDLIFE SANCTUARY

COUNTRY Belize **TYPE OF ACTIVITY** Wildlife watching **FITNESS/EXPERTISE LEVEL** Not required. **WHY NOW?** Drying waterholes are concentrating the jaguar population into smaller areas. **DESCRIPTION** As southern Belize's waterholes dry up, you could be one of the handful of visitors each year who spot a jaguar in the world's first dedicated jaguar reserve. Cockscomb has a number of walking trails, ranging from very accessible short walks near the park headquarters to a four-day hike to Victoria Peak (1120m), Belize's second-highest point. But if it's wildlife you want, you needn't venture far from park headquarters. More than 300 bird species have been recorded here, and a thriving community of black howler monkeys lives close to the visitor centre. Nine-banded armadillos and striped hog-nosed skunks also sometimes turn up at the bins behind the office. Night holds the best, if rare, chance for a cat sighting; jaguars, ocelots and pumas often walk along the entrance road late at night. www.belizeaudubon.org

The only land mammals that occur naturally on the islands are bats and native rats. Large marine mammals, however, are common and abundant. Sea lions and fur seals thrive in the rich waters of the Humboldt Current and visitors are almost guaranteed close interactions. While cruising between islands keep an eye out for dolphins and whales.

Reptiles are the islands' pin-up inhabitants. The giant tortoise has a lower shell up to 1.5m long, can weight 270kg and plods around the islands of Santa Cruz, Isabela and San Cristóbal. The land iguana has skin as rough as a Florida retiree, but despite its fearsome appearance is a harmless vegetarian. The marine iguana is the world's only truly marine lizard and lives only in the Galápagos. It's found on every island and you'll see many at close range; early morning is the best time to see them on land.

The most feasible way to visit the islands is on a boat tour – day trips operate out of the town of Puerto Ayora, but most visitors go on longer tours and sleep aboard overnight.

The Galápagos can be inviting at any time of year, but in March you'll be at the tail end of the warmest (and wettest) season.

[ABOVE] ↗
Take the five-day hike to the top of El Capitan for rewarding panoramas over Yosemite's treetops.

[RIGHT] ↗
You're in control when you take to the sky with a paraglider, so relax and enjoy the view.

DO: CLIMB EL CAPITAN'S NOSE

COUNTRY USA **TYPE OF ACTIVITY** Rock climbing
FITNESS/EXPERTISE LEVEL Rock gods only.
WHY NOW? Spring and autumn are the best times to climb on El Cap.

DESCRIPTION The most famous route on the most famous bit of climbing rock in the world, El Capitan's Nose is where big-wall climbing was born. Guarding the entrance to the sublime Yosemite Valley, El Capitan is an imposing granite monolith rising 1000m above the Merced River. It's a rock to which most climbers can only aspire.

The first ascent of the Nose, an epochal climbing moment, was made in 1958 (one year after the first climb on nearby Half Dome) and took the combined efforts of 45 days of climbing. Most climbers now take five days to make the 31-pitch ascent, bivvying each night and hauling food up the rock with them. The elite scale it in a single day. The quickest have done it in less than three hours.

A combination of aid and free climbing, the Nose is not regarded as being technically difficult but it is long, and more exposed than Paris Hilton, and a great number of climbers who set out from the Southeast Buttress fail to complete the route. That doesn't deter those with rock dreams of conquering this route; the Nose can be so 'blocked' with climbers there's often a two-day wait at the base.

For the complete El Cap experience, base yourself at Camp 4 in the Yosemite Valley. This crowded, walk-in site is as much a part of rock folklore as El Cap itself, and is now listed on the National Register of Historic Places. There's little to it but dusty clearings and bear-proof food lockers but no self-respecting climber would be seen sleeping anywhere else in the valley. Camp 4 even comes with a built-in alarm – the sound of shotguns as rangers shoot noisemakers in attempts to chase away curious bears. www.nps.gov/yose

↗ DO: **PARAGLIDE IN WESTERN CAPE**

COUNTRY South Africa **TYPE OF ACTIVITY** Paragliding
FITNESS/EXPERTISE LEVEL From tandem tag-alongs to top guns.
WHY NOW? The strongest thermals are from November to April; March and April provide the best conditions for beginners to take a leap from Table Mountain. **DESCRIPTION** South Africa is one of the world's top paragliding destinations. For experienced pilots, airspace restrictions are minimal and the potential for long-distance, cross-country flying is tremendous. Your own transport is essential to escape the strong winds in Cape Town and reach the best sheltered sites in Porterville (a ridge site), Hermanus (a coastal site) and at Sir Lowry's Pass (a ridge site). When conditions permit, it's also possible to fly from Table Mountain, Lion's Head and Signal Hill and land on the beach at Clifton or Camps Bay. Soaring along the Twelve Apostles as the tablecloth cloud forms around you is a near-biblical experience. Mornings typically offer the best conditions for beginners. The South African Hang Gliding and Paragliding Association (www.sahpa.co.za) can provide names of operators, and plenty of schools offer courses for beginners.

↗ DO: **DOG-SLED IN GREENLAND**

COUNTRY Greenland **TYPE OF ACTIVITY** Dog-sledding
FITNESS/EXPERTISE LEVEL Not required.
WHY NOW? Sledding high season is March to May. **DESCRIPTION** During the eight or nine months of continuous snow and frozen seas in Arctic and east Greenland, dog-sled is the most common method of getting around. For visitors with money to spend, it's exciting to do a 'winter' tour. Popular dog-sledding venues include Tasiilaq, Uummannaq, Ilulissat and Sisimiut. Greenlanders aren't permitted to keep sled dogs south of the Arctic Circle, so dog-sledding isn't available in the south. Dog-sled trips range from one-day samplers to two-week expeditions, and some include accommodation in villages or hunting camps along the way. Greenlandic sled dogs bear little resemblance to the drippy-tongued, tail-wagging pooches most visitors probably associate with the breed. Most dogs seem only a generation or two removed from wolves and their reputation for snarling, howling and a generally ill-tempered demeanour should be taken seriously. Trying to pat adult dogs is courting disaster.

↗ DO: **HIKE THE ISRAEL NATIONAL TRAIL**

COUNTRY Israel **TYPE OF ACTIVITY** Hiking
FITNESS/EXPERTISE LEVEL Good fitness and endurance required.
WHY NOW? Hit the desert before summer does. **DESCRIPTION** Somebody you know has beaten you to all the great trekking routes, but surely not the Israel National Trail. Rambling for 900km through Israel's least-populated and most scenic areas, from Tel Dan in the north to Taba in the south, it's a remarkably varied and beautiful route. If you want just a taste of it, head to the Eilat Mountains at the southern end of the trail. From the waterfall at Ein Netafim, less than 1km off the main road, you can follow the trail to the spectacular Shehoret Canyon, 15km away. Near the mouth of Shehoret Canyon lie the impressive Amram Pillars, where there's an official camp site (no water). Keep walking south for a few hours, to the trail's end, and you'll pass through the spectacular Nakhal Gishron gorge to the Egyptian border.

↗ **Polaris Challenge**
www.polarischallenge.com
Two-day mountain-bike navigation event in southern England; summer and autumn events follow in the year.

↗ **Manx Mountain Marathon Challenge**
www.manxfellrunners.org
A 50km mountain running event with around 2500m of climbing; staged every Easter on the Isle of Man.

↗ **Red Rock Rendezvous**
www.mountaingear.com/RedRock
Ignore the Vegas slots and head the few kilometres to Red Rock Canyon for a weekend of climbing.

↗ **International Rolex Regatta**
www.rolexcupregatta.com
Four days of sailing competition in the US Virgin Islands.

CYCLE

The humble bicycle may well be the perfect adventuring vehicle. As at home on bitumen roads as on ribbon-thin singletrack, a bicycle can journey almost anywhere cars can travel and yet also take to you lands and terrain once accessible only to walkers.

A select few road trips around the world have become cycling favourites, prized for their scenery, lightly trafficked roads and often their challenging climbs. Pumped full of the latter is the Indian route between Manali and Leh (p126-7), stretching 475km through the Himalaya and struggling over four high passes that reach up to 5328m above sea level. To close the ride in style, you can then ride from Leh up to Khardung La which, at about 5600m, is often spruiked as the highest road in the world. Not far away, the Friendship Highway (p66) connects Kathmandu to Lhasa, also climbing above 5000m and flattening out above 4000m on the Tibetan plateau;

while the third great route in the Asian cycling trilogy is the Karakoram Highway (p159), crossing between Pakistan and China through some of the most gobstopping mountain scenery on the planet. Other extended touring classics include Britain's top-to-toe ride between Land's End and John o'Groats (p102); Canada's Icefields Parkway, which threads through the Rockies between Lake Louise and Jasper; and the wild Carretera Austral in deepest Patagonia. In France you can hit the road to test your pro prospects with gruelling climbs up the Alpe d'Huez or Mont Ventoux (p114-15), the two most famous Tour de France ascents.

Away from the roads, Europe is the undisputed standard bearer in cycle paths – you can just about ride from corner to corner on this continent without touching a road. Prime among the European cycle paths is the Danube Trail (p113), which also connects

partway along in Donauworth with the Via Claudia Augusta (p141). This ancient Roman route combines paths and roads to hit the Mediterranean in Venice. For the ultimate long-distance path, there's the emerging Trans Canada Trail (p85), which will eventually reach from coast to coast. By late 2009, around 14,500km of the eventual 21,500km trail had been completed, which will be enough to satisfy most legs anyway.

Mountain bikers have found the world opening up wide over recent years. On a mountain bike the riding options are almost unlimited: you can sample what is statistically the world's most dangerous road (p163); pedal on safari through Botswana's Mashatu Game Reserve (p87), where the presence of big cats and elephants will ensure you maintain a decent cadence; heli-bike out of New Zealand mountains (p35); or race through snow at a French ski resort (p49).

If you want to test your endurance or skills against others, there's a host of ambitious cycling events. On road, nonstop randonnées stretch out to as long as 1200km, with the matriarch of randonnées being Paris-Brest-Paris (p136). The Race Across America (p93) is even more gruelling, with riders racking up more than 500km a day; while Tour d'Afrique (p20) cyclists can pedal the length of Africa if they have the time and money.

Off road, the Australian outback offers a couple of true challenges. The Simpson Desert Cycle Challenge (p153) pits competitors against each other and about 750 sand dunes, while the Crocodile Trophy (p169) in Far North Queensland – billed as the longest and hottest mountain-bike race in the world – stirs together bulldust, corrugations, epic distances, crocodiles and 33% gradients. Whether the crocs or the gradients are scarier is open to debate.

GO:
NORTH KOREA

(ABOVE) ↗
Performances of epic
proportions take place
during Pyongyang's
Mass Games.

(RIGHT) ↗
Ancient tombs stand
sentinel along the
Lycian Way.

WHY NOW? APRIL IS A BEAUTIFUL TIME IN KOREA, WITH MILD TEMPERATURES AND FLOWERS BLOOMING EVERYWHERE

North Korea is probably the most mysterious country in the world today and one almost entirely untouched by tourism. Off the beaten path seems too slight a term for a nation that admits fewer than 2000 Westerners a year, and whose overwhelming attraction is its isolation and backwardness.

North Korea is a place frozen in the Cold War. Visitors are escorted at all times outside their hotel by guides. Only the party elite can use mobile phones in North Korea, there's no internet access to be had for tourists and there are just a handful of international flights into the capital, Pyongyang, each week. These zealous measures to keep the country isolated make North Korea a magnet for those seeking a cultural adventure, and while travel here is not easy or cheap, the rewards

↗ DO: HIKE THE LYCIAN WAY

COUNTRY Turkey **TYPE OF ACTIVITY** Hiking
FITNESS/EXPERTISE LEVEL Moderate level
of fitness and good endurance required.
WHY NOW? Summer in Lycia is hot, so beat
it to the punch. **DESCRIPTION** The Lycian
Way was Turkey's first long-distance hiking
trail, created in 1999. It's a 509km trail around
the coast and mountains of Lycia, starting
at Fethiye and finishing at Antalya. It gets
progressively more difficult as it winds around
the coast and into the mountain ranges, and
can be trekked in its entirety in about 30 days,
or can be walked in smaller, easier chunks.
Good places for starting out are Ölüdeniz, Kaş,
Adrasan or Olympos. The Lycian Way offers
great views over Turkey's Mediterranean coast
and a variety of flora, and you'll find a few
pensions and hotels along the route in which
to seek some relief from your tent.
www.lycianway.com

are many and will instantly make you the most
interesting person you know.

Once through all the North Korean red tape,
trips here usually run like clockwork. Two guides
will accompany you everywhere you go outside
the hotel, controlling what you see and the spiel
you hear while seeing it. Forward planning is a
must – almost everything you want to see needs
to be approved before your arrival, and ad hoc
arrangements make the guides very nervous and
thus less fun to be around. Being accompanied
is non-negotiable, and if you are not prepared
to be controlled throughout the duration of your
stay, North Korea is not a destination you should
consider.

To add some adventure beyond that of simply
visiting the most reclusive member of the 'axis of
evil', plan a trip to Mt Paekdu, the highest peak in
Korea (2744m) and, according to official sources, the
birthplace of Kim Jong-il – in fact, he was probably
born in Khabarovsk, Russia, where his father was in
exile at the time, but the necessity of maintaining
the Kim myth supersedes such niggling facts.

Visit the Demilitarized Zone (DMZ), rolling down
a deserted six-lane highway to Panmunjom, where
you will face off against US troops across the DMZ in
South Korea.

[ABOVE] ↗
Tokelau's outrigger canoes are known for their open-water stability and safety.

[TOP RIGHT] ↗
Just a stone's throw from San Francisco, Marin County is home to some of the USA's last stands of skyscraping coastal redwoods.

[BOTTOM RIGHT] ↗
Make like Spiderman, and get to grips with El Chorro Gorge.

DO: SAIL TO TOKELAU

COUNTRY New Zealand administration **TYPE OF ACTIVITY** Boat travel/sailing
FITNESS/EXPERTISE LEVEL Not required.
WHY NOW? The best months to travel to Tokelau are from April to October, avoiding both cyclones and full cargo ships.

DESCRIPTION The three small atolls of Tokelau lie in a rough line 480km north of their nearest neighbour, Samoa. Just getting here is a major achievement and might not be available to future generations – the low-lying islands have a maximum elevation of only 5m above sea level and it's predicted that, with global warming, they'll be uninhabitable by the end of the 21st century.

Already, Tokelau is one of the most isolated spots on earth and getting here can be difficult. It has no airstrip, and every two to three weeks a cargo ship from Apia in Samoa is the only way travellers can get to Tokelau without a yacht. In fact, because of the hazards of anchoring, yachting to Tokelau is not much easier!

The MV *Tokelau* sails from Apia fortnightly, with the trip to Fakaofo (the closest atoll to Samoa) taking about 24 hours. There is no harbour in any of the atolls. The ship waits offshore while passengers and cargo are transferred via small boats and dinghies – a hair-raising experience if seas are heavy.

For yachties, one of the first dilemmas in finding the atolls is their low elevation, which makes them difficult visual targets. There are no harbours and anchoring offshore is difficult, especially in an offshore wind. The sea floor drops off sharply outside the coral reef and the water is too deep for most anchor chains. There's one anchorage beyond the reefs at each atoll, but leave a crew member aboard in case the anchor doesn't hold. The channels blasted through the coral are shallow and are intended for dinghies only.

↗ DO: **MOUNTAIN BIKE IN MARIN**

COUNTRY USA **TYPE OF ACTIVITY** Mountain biking
FITNESS/EXPERTISE LEVEL Something for all levels.
WHY NOW? Spring provides ideal conditions.
DESCRIPTION Mountain biking is said to have had its beginnings in the
1970s in Marin County, out of San Francisco, where a group of riders
would charge off Pine Mountain in races along Repack Rd. Today, it's a
pursuit of almost global reach, even gaining admission to the Olympic
Games in 1996, but if you're a sentimentalist, or just partial to a decent bit
of riding, there's still plenty of good mountain biking in ancestral Marin.
The county has more than 300km of trails and fire roads – not all open
to cyclists – offering hair-parting descents or off-road tours. Two of the
legendary rides involve circuits of Pine Mountain (where you can pay
homage to Repack Rd) and Mt Tamalpais. www.marintrails.com/biking

↗ DO: **CLIMB EL CHORRO**

COUNTRY Spain **TYPE OF ACTIVITY** Rock climbing **FITNESS/EXPERTISE
LEVEL** A variety of grades, but more on offer for experienced climbers.
WHY NOW? Enjoy the rock before summer turns it to hot coals.
DESCRIPTION Mountainous Andalucía is full of crags, walls and slabs that
invite *escalada* (climbing), now a popular sport here. The sheer walls of El
Chorro Gorge, one of several great sites in the north of Málaga province,
are the biggest magnet, with more than 600 routes incorporating almost
every degree of difficulty. El Chorro presents a great variety of both
classical and sport climbing, from slab climbs to towering walls to bolted
multipitch routes. The walk-ins can be lengthy but you'll find the crags
more than reward the effort. There's accommodation for all budgets in the
El Chorro area, and quite a climbers' scene at Bar Isabel at El Chorro train
station.

↗ **Marathon des Sables**
www.saharamarathon.co.uk
Six-day, 243km endurance run through the
Moroccan Sahara.

↗ **Devizes to Westminster International
Canoe Marathon**
www.dwrace.org.uk
Begin paddling on Easter Saturday and stop
on Easter Sunday, 200km later.

↗ **Elk Mountains Grand Traverse**
www.elkmountaintraverse.org
A 64km backcountry ski race between Crested
Butte and Aspen, Colorado.

↗ **XTERRA Saipan Championship**
www.saipansports.com
Off-road Micronesian triathlon: ocean swim,
mountain-bike ride and a trail run.

↗ DO: **PARAGLIDE AT MEDELLÍN**

COUNTRY Colombia **TYPE OF ACTIVITY** Paragliding
FITNESS/EXPERTISE LEVEL Not required.
WHY NOW? Medellín claims perfect, unchanging weather year-round, but
elsewhere Colombia's dry season is generally December to April.
DESCRIPTION Colombia is one of South America's best places to try
paragliding, with the northern city of Medellín emerging as one of the
continent's premier destinations – it's also one of the cheapest. It's home
to some of the best national glide pilots, and gliding here is more popular
than in any other Colombian city, Bogotá included. Thanks to the rugged
topography and favourable winds, the city and the region provide good
conditions for gliding. Gliding schools in Colombia's second city offer
tandem flights with a skilled pilot, or you can settle in for a 10-day course
that'll set you on the way to becoming a pilot yourself.

GO: DARIÉN GAP,
PANAMA

[ABOVE] ↗
The waterways of the Darién Gap are sources of food for locals, but they present challenges for travellers.

[RIGHT] ↗
Depending on where the ice floats, a runner might travel right across 90°N – the geographic North Pole.

WHY NOW? VISIT NOW AND YOU'LL SNEAK IN BEFORE THE WET SEASON

Panama's far south is one of the wildest and most ravaged areas in the Americas. It's home to the country's most spectacular national park, and the point at which North America clips onto South America. Even the Pan-American Hwy, which runs from Alaska to the south of Chile, hasn't been able to fight a way through here, earning the area the name of the Darién Gap.

Most of the region falls within Parque Nacional Darién – 5760 sq km containing sandy beaches, rocky coasts, mangrove swamps, freshwater marshes and four mountain ranges covered with double- and triple-canopy jungle. The birdwatching here is among the world's finest – there are places where you can see four species of macaw fly by with outstanding frequency. The harpy eagle, the world's most powerful bird of prey, resides here, as do giant anteaters, jaguars, ocelots, monkeys, Baird's

↗ DO: NORTH POLE MARATHON

REGION The Arctic

TYPE OF ACTIVITY Ice running

FITNESS/EXPERTISE LEVEL Superior fitness (and partiality to cold) required.

WHY NOW? To run to the geographic North Pole. **DESCRIPTION** Dubbed the 'world's coolest marathon', this is almost certainly also the only marathon run on water. Competitors in this unique event fly out of Svalbard, Norway, to a temporary camp near the North Pole. The following day they run 42km across the frozen Arctic Ocean, which may be just a couple of metres beneath them – the course of the race is chosen a day ahead to avoid breaks in the ice. Soft conditions can force runners into snowshoes, while temperatures of around -20°C to -30°C can be expected. The winning time in the 2009 race was four hours and 27 minutes by Russian Evgeniy Gorkov. www.npmarathon.com

tapirs, white-lipped peccaries, caimans and American crocodiles.

It's an adventurer's dream, offering spectacular opportunities for rainforest exploration by trail or river, and a place where the primeval meets the present, with the scenery appearing much as it did a million years ago. Indians perfected the use of poison-dart guns here and still maintain many of their traditional practices.

The heart of this World Heritage Site is the former mining valley of Cana, the most isolated place in Panama. Except for a hike of several days, the only way into the valley is by chartered aircraft.

The area around Pirre Station is the most accessible section of the park, and two good hiking trails originate from here. The longest of these trails leads to Pirre Mountain ridge, which takes most hikers two days to reach – bring a tent. This walk shouldn't be attempted without a guide. It's not well marked and if you get lost out here, you're finished. Fifteen kilometres separate the station and Cana, and between the two there's nothing but virgin, inaccessible rainforest. The only way in is by hiking or a combination of hiking and boating from El Real. Visit now and you'll sneak in before the wet season. You'll also witness the end of the nesting season for the mighty harpy eagle, a powerful predator that'll please any twitcher.

[ABOVE] ↗
By the time you finish the Haute Route, you'll have dragged your ski-strapped feet over climbs equivalent to 10,000m of ascent.

[TOP RIGHT] ↗
On a windy day this tree can sway up to 1.5m. Bring a head for heights.

[BOTTOM RIGHT] ↗
Don't let the spectacular scenery take your breath away – you'll need it for your freedive.

DO: SKI TOURING THE HAUTE ROUTE

COUNTRIES France, Italy and Switzerland **TYPE OF ACTIVITY** Cross-country skiing
FITNESS/EXPERTISE LEVEL High level of fitness and experience required.
WHY NOW? April is the prime month to be on the Haute Route.

DESCRIPTION Unquestionably one of the world's great ski-touring trails, the Haute Route links the two most celebrated mountains of the European Alps, crossing from the evergreen French resort of Chamonix, at the foot of Mont Blanc, to the Swiss town of Zermatt, in the shadow of the shapely Matterhorn. Covering around 140km, the route was pioneered on foot by members of the Alpine Club and their guides in the 1860s, and while it remains a popular summer trek (on a slightly different route), it's best known as a classic and popular spring ski-mountaineering expedition. It's prized both for its challenging terrain and its parade of big-name mountains – Mont Blanc, Monte Rosa, Grand Combin and the Matterhorn will be your ever-present touring companions.

Ski tourers usually take six or seven days to complete this hut-to-hut route, which crosses more than 20 glaciers and, as the name suggests (Haute Route translates as High Route), follows a high line across the snow-plastered slopes of the Alps, rarely dipping into valleys. Pushing across a number of passes, including the spectacular Val d'Arpette, with its views down onto the fractured surface of Glacier du Trient, the route tops out on the summit of Pigne d'Arolla, at around 3800m – high enough to make your head spin from more than the exertion.

All up, you'll drag your ski-strapped feet over climbs totalling around 10,000m, enough to have summited Mt Everest from sea level with Ben Nevis as a warm-down. Skiing days on the Haute Route can be long and difficult, so limber up on less gruelling tours elsewhere before slapping on the skins at Chamonix.

↗ DO: **TREE CLIMB IN PEMBERTON**

COUNTRY Australia **TYPE OF ACTIVITY** Tree climbing
FITNESS/EXPERTISE LEVEL A head for heights welcome.
WHY NOW? April is the least windy month around Pemberton; you'll
appreciate it when you're 75m up a tree. **DESCRIPTION** Western
Australia's endemic karri tree is one of the giants of the wooden world.
Growing to 90m it's the tallest tree in the state and among the tallest in
the world. Poking above the canopy of the thick forests of the southwest,
eight karri trees were chosen in the first half of the 20th century as
fire-lookout trees, with platforms built at their tops and metal spikes
hammered into their trunks as ladders. Today, three of the trees have been
designated as 'climbing trees', allowing visitors to climb up for a windy
view over hillsides thick with forest. The most popular of the trees is the
Gloucester Tree, just 3km from the milling town of Pemberton, but nearby
Dave Evans Bicentennial Tree is the tallest of the climbing trees at 75m.
www.pembertontourist.com.au

↗ DO: **FREEDIVE IN A BLUE HOLE**

COUNTRY Bahamas **TYPE OF ACTIVITY** Freediving
FITNESS/EXPERTISE LEVEL Big lungs preferred.
WHY NOW? To experience Vertical Blue.
DESCRIPTION Holding your breath underwater in the public pool was
one thing, but freediving is another all together. In this lung-bursting
sport, competitors attempt to conquer great depths, times or distances
on a single breath without weights, fins or tanks. By 2009 somebody
had freedived to a depth of 88m; another had stayed underwater for
11½ minutes. There have also been freediving deaths. In the Bahamas,
at Dean's Blue Hole, you can take a three-day introductory course in
freediving or hone your skills with advanced classes, overseen by world-
record holder William Trubridge. Newcomers are taught breathing and
relaxation techniques on a live-aboard boat. More advanced courses focus
on technique, yoga and meditation. This week is also the date for the
Vertical Blue Invitational Freediving competition if you want to see how the
lung legends do it. www.verticalblue.net

↗ DO: **WALK THE 88 TEMPLE CIRCUIT**

COUNTRY Japan **TYPE OF ACTIVITY** Hiking/pilgrimage
FITNESS/EXPERTISE LEVEL Moderate fitness required.
WHY NOW? It's a long walk and you want to be finished before summer
fully kicks in. **DESCRIPTION** Japan's best-known pilgrimage is the 88 Temple
Circuit on the island of Shikoku. Kōbō Daishi, the most revered of Japan's
saints, is said to have personally selected the circuit route. Today, most
pilgrims travel it by tour bus, but many still walk. Set aside two months if
you want to join them over the 1500km route. Some temples are only a
few hundred metres apart, but it can be more than 100km between others.
Individually, none of the temples is exceptionally interesting; it's the whole
circuit that counts. The 88 temples represent the number of evil human
passions defined by the Buddhist doctrine, and completing the circuit is said
to rid you of these. The route begins in Tokushima and is generally walked
clockwise. About half the temples have lodging facilities for pilgrims.

Sea Otter Classic
www.seaotterclassic.com
Cycling festival in Monterey, California, with
races, recreational rides and a trade show.

Oxfam Trailwalker NZ
www.oxfamtrailwalker.org.nz
Cover 100km on foot near Taupo in less than
48 hours.

Three Peaks Race
www.threepeaks.org.au
Easter event in which you sail halfway around
Tasmania and climb Mts Wellington, Freycinet
and Strzelecki.

Dead Sea Ultramarathon
www.deadseamarathon.com
A 50km run from Amman to the
Dead Sea.

GO:
VANUATU

[ABOVE] ↗
Men from tho Small
Nambas tribe will take
part in the death-defying
land-diving ritual,
the forerunner of the
modern bungee jump.

[RIGHT] ↗
Never smile at a
crocodile. Spend 15
minutes in the Cage of
Death and live
to tell the tale.

WHY NOW? THE LAND-DIVING TOWERS SHOULD BE FINISHED OR NEARLY FINISHED AND READY FOR ACTION

One of the most remarkable customs you're ever likely to see is the *naghol* (land diving) on the Vanuatu island of Pentecost. Every year in early April, as soon as the first yam crop emerges, the islanders in the south build tall wooden towers in the villages. A full-sized tower is vertical for 16m, then leans backwards. Each tower takes several weeks to erect. The soil in front of the tower is cleared of rocks, then loosened to reduce the chance of injury.

Once completed, and until early June, men and boys dive from these rickety structures with only two springy vines to break their fall, a leap that is said to guarantee a bountiful yam harvest.

Between 20 and 60 males per village will dive. As a diver raises his hands he tells the crowd his most intimate thoughts; the people stop their singing and dancing, and stand quietly – these could be his last words.

↗ DO: SWIM WITH A CROCODILE

COUNTRY Australia **TYPE OF ACTIVITY** Wildlife encounter **FITNESS/EXPERTISE LEVEL** Not required. **WHY NOW?** Darwin has just come out of its wet season. **DESCRIPTION** Australia's Top End is no place for a casual swim, with its rivers and coast home to crocodiles up to 6m in length. But that needn't preclude you from a nose-to-snout meeting with such a beast. At Darwin's Jurassically named Crocosaurus Cove, visitors can climb into the so-called Cage of Death, a transparent, 4cm-thick acrylic cage that is then lowered into the enclosure of an adult crocodile, including that of a 5m snapping handbag that starred in the movie *Crocodile Dundee*. You then spend 15 minutes in the cage, and whether the reptile views you with boredom or as something on which to try to sharpen its teeth, is up to it. www.crocosauruscove.com

Finally the diver claps his hands, crosses his arms and leans forward. The vines abruptly stop his downward rush. Only his hair will touch the soil, to fertilise the yam crop. The crowd roars its appreciation, dancing, stomping and whistling in tribute. If it sounds vaguely familiar, it is; *naghol* was the inspiration for bungee jumping.

South Pentecost has many land-diving sites. Land-dive towers are erected in Lonorore and on the hills between Panas and nearby Wali.

While you won't be allowed to make a land dive, you don't have to leave all the fun to the locals in Vanuatu. The country has several volcanoes, including the world's most accessible (very) active one, Mt Yasur, on Tanna. A night visit is recommended for sound effects and fireworks displays. Walkers can enjoy Ambrym, where the Benbow and Marum volcanoes breathe smoke and ash over an unbelievably desolate landscape; Marum had locals ready for evacuation throughout 2005.

Vanuatu is a snorkelling and diving paradise. In addition to countless coral reefs, there is terrific wreck diving: Espiritu Santo boasts the world's largest diveable WWII shipwreck: the SS *President Coolidge*. http://vanuatu.travel

[ABOVE] ↗
The air may be thin, your legs may be jelly, but the veiws of Everest are spectacular.

[TOP RIGHT] ↗
The Wadi Mujib Gorge enters the Dead Sea at 400m below sea level – considered to be the lowest point on the surface of the earth.

[BOTTOM RIGHT] ↗
Plunge into the turquoise depths of the Poor Knight Islands to discover an underwater wonderland.

DO: CYCLE THE FRIENDSHIP HIGHWAY

REGION Tibet/Nepal **TYPE OF ACTIVITY** Cycle touring

FITNESS/EXPERTISE LEVEL Moderate fitness and good acclimatisation required.

WHY NOW? To see Mt Everest at its best as you cycle past.

DESCRIPTION See the best of Tibet as you ride between Lhasa and Kathmandu on the Friendship Hwy. This ideal cycling route takes in most of Tibet's main sights, offering superb scenery and (for those leaving from Lhasa) featuring a spectacular roller-coaster ride down from high La Lung-la (5124m) into the Kathmandu Valley. The journey is without doubt one of the most spectacular in the world. At the energy-depleting altitudes of the Tibetan desert plateau, most of which is above 4000m, it might also be one of your slowest rides.

The entire trip is just over 940km (though most people start from Shigatse, Tibet's second-largest city, about 300km west of Lhasa, knocking out the busiest section of the highway) and will take a minimum of two weeks, although to do it justice and include stopovers at Gyantse, Shigatse and Sakya, it's better to allow 20 days.

The Friendship Hwy can be cycled comfortably during several months of the year, but this is the time to ride if you want to see Tibet's star natural feature – the north face of Mt Everest – at its clearest. If you've come with a mountain bike, you can detour to Everest Base Camp, turning off the highway at Shegar. From here it's about a two-day ride to Rongphu Monastery, said by some to have the finest of all Everest views. Base camp is just a few kilometres on, and at this time of year you might arrive with the first of the season's mountaineers. You can vary the return ride from base camp to the highway by taking the road to Tingri.

⬈DO: CANYON AT WADI MUJIB

COUNTRY Jordan **TYPE OF ACTIVITY** Canyoning **FITNESS/EXPERTISE LEVEL** Good fitness and swimming skills required. **WHY NOW?** The gorge is open April to October; come before the sun boils your brain. **DESCRIPTION** Stretching from the Desert Hwy to the Dead Sea (over 70km) is the vast and beautiful Wadi Mujib, sometimes called the 'Grand Canyon of Jordan'. There are four main walking trails in Mujib Nature Reserve, but the one through the gorge offers the most adventure. This trail follows the river as it slices through the earth, the cliffs narrowing at times to make it a slot canyon. You'll abseil down a 20m-high waterfall, and at times you'll be swimming, or submerging to squeeze under rock barriers – after high water levels in 2005, ropes were fastened to the gorge walls beside some of the longer swims. The canyon trail can take up to 12 hours and can only be done with a guide from the Royal Society for the Conservation of Nature. The number of people allowed into the gorge is limited. www.rscn.org.jo

⬈DO: DIVE THE POOR KNIGHTS ISLANDS

COUNTRY New Zealand **TYPE OF ACTIVITY** Scuba diving **FITNESS/EXPERTISE LEVEL** Snorkellers to advanced divers. **WHY NOW?** Visibility can reach to 50m in autumn. **DESCRIPTION** Rated by the late Jacques Cousteau as one of the world's 10 best dive sites, the Poor Knights Islands are the remnants of ancient volcanoes. Swept by the East Auckland current, which brings warm waters from the Coral Sea, you'll find fish-filled caves, archways and underwater cliffs that offer spectacular diving against a backdrop of colourful invertebrate life. And with virtually no runoff from the islands, visibility is excellent. The range of depths and dive sites promises something for everyone, including good snorkelling at most sites. Experienced divers will be drawn to Northern Archway, where schools of up to 30 large kingfish sometimes cruise through. Landing on the uninhabited, predator-free islands is prohibited. The tuatara, a reptile that roamed with the dinosaurs, and the giant weta, a fearsome-looking insect, are a couple of the unique species found here. Charter boats to the islands leave from Tutukaka.

⬈DO: TAKE TO THE WATER AT GIZO

COUNTRY Solomon Islands **TYPE OF ACTIVITY** Diving/surfing **FITNESS/EXPERTISE LEVEL** From snorkellers to submariners. **WHY NOW?** Diving is best in April and May, while April is also the tail end of the surfing season. **DESCRIPTION** Reefs and wrecks combine to make the Solomon Islands a diving wonderland – Honiara has probably the best diving of any capital city in the world, with a fantastic collection of WWII wrecks lying offshore in an area known as Iron Bottom Sound. The town of Gizo offers some of the best diving, even if some sites were damaged by a 2007 tsunami. Most dives are less than a 20-minute boat ride from town and include wrecks and reef dives. Diving isn't new to the area but surfing is. At Gizo you can be guaranteed almost virgin waves. There's excellent point surfing off Pailongge, with the October-to-April swell rising to 2m or more. There's a great left-hander nearer Titiana village, with a long paddle out to the reef's edge. Bring your own boards. www.divegizo.com

⬈ **Tampa Bay Marathon Swim**
www.distancematters.com
A 38km ocean swim across Florida's Tampa Bay.

⬈ **Oxfam Trailwalker Melbourne**
www.oxfam.org.au/trailwalker/melbourne
Run or walk (or both) through 100km of Australian bush in less than 48 hours.

⬈ **Flèche Vélocio**
www.audax-club-parisien.com (in French)
Easter cycling event, with teams selecting their own 24-hour (360km minimum) route, converging at a finish point in southern France.

⬈ **Arctic Circle Race**
www.acr.gl
Ski 160km across the Greenland Arctic in three days.

GO: PANTANAL, BRAZIL

(ABOVE) ↗
Hop from lilypad to
lilypad as you follow the
diverse birdlife of the
Pantanal wetlands.

(RIGHT) ↗
With access limited to
just 10 people a day,
you're sure to get the
'Wave' to yourself.

WHY NOW? ONE OF THE AREA'S TWO DRY SEASONS RUNS FROM APRIL TO MAY

The Amazon may attract more fame and glory, but the vast Pantanal wetlands in the centre of South America are a better place to see wildlife. They contain the greatest concentration of fauna in the New World, and while the Amazon's dense foliage hides its animals, the Pantanal's open spaces make the wildlife visible to the most casual observer.

The Pantanal is more than half the size of France – 230,000 sq km – of which most is in Brazil (around 100,000 sq km is in Bolivia and Paraguay). It has few people and no towns. Distances are so great and ground transport is so poor that people get around in small airplanes and motorboats. The only road that runs deep into the Pantanal is the Transpantaneira. This raised dirt road, sectioned by 118 small wooden bridges, was supposed to stretch to the Bolivian border but two-thirds of the intended route has

↗ DO: CANYONEER IN PARIA CANYON

COUNTRY USA **TYPE OF ACTIVITY**
Canyoneering/canyoning **FITNESS/
EXPERTISE LEVEL** Canyoneering experience
recommended. **WHY NOW?** Hit the slots in
spring to avoid the prospect of summer or
winter flash floods. **DESCRIPTION** Much of
Southwest USA's most stunning beauty is
within serpentine corridors of stone. Some
of these narrow to become slot canyons,
and offer some of the best canyoneering
anywhere, with technical climbing, swimming
in pools and shooting down waterfalls. Paria
Canyon, on the Arizona–Utah border, is one
of the most beautiful canyons, and features
highly in postcards in Utah giftshops. Paria's
biggest attraction is Buckskin Gulch, a deep,
19km-long canyon only 5m wide for most of
its length. Wire Pass and Buckskin are the
popular trailheads, and serious canyoneers can
tackle the five-day, 61km trek through to Lees
Ferry, Arizona, through this, the longest and
most flash-flood-prone canyon in the world.
www.blm.gov/az/st/en/arolrsmain/paria.html

been left incomplete for lack of funds and ecological
concerns.

April and May form one of the Pantanal's two dry
seasons, which are the best times to visit the World
Heritage–listed wetlands. The area floods in the wet
season from October to March, replenishing the
soil's nutrients, which would otherwise be very poor
due to the excessive drainage. The waters teem
with fish, and the ponds provide excellent niches for
many animals and plants. Enormous flocks of wading
birds gather in rookeries several square kilometres
in area. Later in the dry season, the water recedes,
the lagoons and marshes dry out and fresh grasses
emerge on the savannah. Hawks and alligators
compete for fish in the remaining ponds.

Guides can be arranged in the towns of Cuiabá
(in Mato Grosso), Corumbá or Campo Grande
(Matto Grosso do Sul). There's no obligation to use
a guide, but a good one can enhance your Pantanal
experience by spotting and identifying animal
and bird species, especially rarer animals such as
anteaters, anacondas, otters, iguanas and jaguars. A
guide who's familiar with the area will also know the
location of nests of rare birds in the world's largest
contiguous wetland.

(ABOVE) ↗
The only way is up. At Paklenica there are spectacular routes for all grades of climber.

(TOP RIGHT) ↗
Fly down the black ash slopes of Cerro Negro on a volcano board.

(BOTTOM RIGHT) ↗
It's been suggested that human and chimp DNA is so similar, we may be in the same genus.

DO: CLIMB AT PAKLENICA PARK

COUNTRY Croatia **TYPE OF ACTIVITY** Rock climbing
FITNESS/EXPERTISE LEVEL Beginner routes to big-wall epics.
WHY NOW? Spring is the best climbing season, with this week coinciding with an annual international climbers' meeting in the park of Alpinists.

DESCRIPTION Rising high above the Adriatic Sea, the stark peaks of the Velebit Massif stretch for 145km in a dramatic landscape of rock and sea. Paklenica National Park covers 36 sq km of the range, circling around two deep gorges, Velika Paklenica (Great Paklenica) and Mala Paklenica (Small Paklenica), which scar the mountain range like hatchet marks, with cliffs over 400m high.

This karst landscape makes for one of Europe's premier climbing venues, offering a tremendous variety of routes from beginners' level to borderline suicidal. The firm, occasionally sharp limestone offers graded climbs, including 72 short sports routes and 250 longer routes.

You'll see the beginners' routes at the beginning of the park near Marasovići, with cliffs reaching about 40m, but the best and most advanced climbing is on Anića Kuk, which offers more than 100 routes up to a height of 350m. Nearly all routes are well equipped with spits and pitons, except for the appropriately named Psycho Killer route. The most popular climbs here are Mosoraški (350m), Velebitaški (350m) and Klin (300m).

The best base for exploring the park is Starigrad, the site of the national park office and the town with the most restaurants and accommodation options. It's also near the entrance to Velika Paklenica, which offers the most varied climbs of the two gorges.

Come this week and you'll experience the added excitement of a big-wall speed climbing competition run in conjunction with an annual international climbers' meeting in the park, held at Paklenica. www.paklenica.hr

↗ DO: **VOLCANO BOARD ON CERRO NEGRO**

COUNTRY Nicaragua **TYPE OF ACTIVITY** Volcano boarding
FITNESS/EXPERTISE LEVEL Snowboarding skills an asset.
WHY NOW? Come just outside Nicaragua's peak tourist season but still inside its dry season. **DESCRIPTION** Nicaragua has an enviable reputation as a surfing destination but for landlubbers, the surf need not mean the sea. On Cerro Negro – Black Mountain – near the city of León, you can slip into an orange jumpsuit and board your way down the black rubble of the volcanic cinder cone that is Central America's youngest volcano – try not to think about the fact that it's erupted more than 20 times in the 160 years since its creation. After a short practice run, you will skim downhill across the rubble at what seems like breakneck speed – some boarders have reached almost 70km/h. Expect a fair bit of gravel rash if it doesn't go to plan. www.bigfootnicaragua.com/adventure.html

↗ DO: **WATCH CHIMPANZEES AT GOMBE STREAM**

COUNTRY Tanzania **TYPE OF ACTIVITY** Wildlife watching
FITNESS/EXPERTISE LEVEL Not required.
WHY NOW? The chimps are often easier to find during the rainy season between about February and June. **DESCRIPTION** With an area of only 52 sq km, Gombe Stream is Tanzania's smallest national park. It's also the site of the longest-running study of any wild animal population in the world. British researcher Jane Goodall arrived in 1960 to begin a study of wild chimpanzees, and her research is now entering its sixth decade. Gombe Stream's 100-or-so chimps are accustomed to humans, so you can sometimes get to within 5m of them. Accommodation in the park is a matter of extremes: a run-down hostel, a basic rest house or a luxury tented camp. You can also camp on the beach near the centre of the park, although park staff don't recommend it because of the danger from baboons. Children under seven and anybody with indications of illness are not allowed into the park. If you're really interested in chimpanzees, allow at least two days at Gombe. www.tanzaniaparks.com/gombe.html

↗ DO: **HIKE THE SOUTH WEST COAST PATH**

COUNTRY England **TYPE OF ACTIVITY** Hiking
FITNESS/EXPERTISE LEVEL Good fitness and endurance required.
WHY NOW? It's a long walk, so get started early in the season.
DESCRIPTION Britain's National Trail system is unequalled. Its 15 long-distance paths cover 4400km, and it's said that wherever you might stand on the island, there's a national trail within 80km. The longest, and arguably best, of the trails is the South West Coast Path, rounding Britain's spectacularly rugged southwest peninsula and crossing through three counties – Devon, Cornwall and Dorset. Walk for seven or eight weeks and you can cover its entire 1014km length. The distance is only half the battle; the peninsula's coast is decidedly hilly and following the path involves a *lot* of steep descents into valleys where rivers meet the sea, then just as many steep climbs out. Ascents along the route total 27,000m, or about three times the height of Mt Everest. www.southwestcoastpath.com

↗ Patrouille des Glaciers
www.pdg.ch
Biannual ski-mountaineering competition – telemark 53km from Zermatt to Verbier.

↗ Endorphin Fix
www.oarevents.com
Promising the 'toughest three-day race in the USA', this multisport event passes through the Appalachian Mountains and along the New River.

↗ Atlantic Coast Conquest
www.pangeaadventureracing.com
30-hour Florida adventure race where alligators are just one of the obstacles.

↗ Trento Film Festival
www.trentofestival.it
The world's oldest adventure film festival, running since 1952.

GO: HIGH ATLAS,
MOROCCO

[ABOVE] ↗
Trek deep into the High Atlas range through remote villages nestled in the mountainside.

[RIGHT] ↗
Take the high road through one of the deepest gorges in the world.

WHY NOW? IN MAY ALPINE FLOWERS WILL BE IN BLOOM AND DAYTIME TEMPERATURES ARE USUALLY PLEASANTLY WARM

The highest mountain range in North Africa, the High Atlas runs diagonally across Morocco, from the Atlantic coast northeast of Agadir all the way to northern Algeria, a distance of almost 1000km. There are several summits higher than 4000m and more than 400 peaks above 3000m in the range. The Toubkal region contains all the highest peaks, and is only two hours from Marrakesh and easily accessible by public transport.

Despite the wealth of high peaks it's the tallest, Jebel Toubkal (4167m), that monopolises trekking attention. From Imlil, the most popular trailhead in Morocco, it's a five-hour trek to the base of Jebel Toubkal. From here the mountain is a challenging walk rather than a climb. Most trekkers dash up and down it in two days, but you can also stretch the experience

↗ DO: HIKE TIGER LEAPING GORGE

COUNTRY China **TYPE OF ACTIVITY** Hiking
FITNESS/EXPERTISE LEVEL Moderate
fitness required. **WHY NOW?** For hillsides afire
with plants and flowers. **DESCRIPTION** After
making its first turn at Shígǔ, the mighty Yangzi
River surges through Tiger Leaping Gorge,
one of the deepest gorges in the world. The
entire gorge measures 16km in length, and it's
a giddy 3900m from the floor of the gorge to
the mountain tops above. There are two trails
through the gorge – the higher route is older
and is known as the 24-bend path (although
it's more like 30), while the lower route is a
new road replete with belching tour buses.
Needless to say, only the high trail is really
worth hiking. The town of Lìjiāng, 160km north
of the provincial capital, Dàlǐ, is the best base
for the hike.

out to a rewarding week by trekking around Toubkal,
passing through Berber villages as you go.

With the High Atlas streaked with old trading
routes and well-used mule trails, it's become the
site for some of the world's best mountain biking,
whether circumnavigating Toubkal or traversing the
range to the edge of the Sahara at Ouarzazate.

For climbers, the 300m-high walls of Todra Gorge
provide some of Africa's best routes. There are some
sublime climbs here, many around French grade 5,
some of them bolted. Pillar du Couchant, near the
entrance to the gorge, offers classic long climbs,
while the Petite Gorge is better for novice climbers
with some good short routes. You'll even find a
selection of hotels inside the gorge.

It's possible to trek throughout the year in the High
Atlas, though temperatures can drop below freezing
above 2000m between November and May, when
snow covers the higher peaks and passes. Therefore,
late April to late June is the ideal time to visit.

[ABOVE] ↗
Put on your Sunday best and join the Feria del Caballo (Horse Fair) in Jerez de la Frontera.

[TOP RIGHT] ↗
Phenomenal desert panoramas are one of the rewards of a trek along the ridges of the West MacDonnell Ranges.

[BOTTOM RIGHT] ↗
Catch some gnarly swells at the legendary Bells.

DO: HORSE RIDE IN ANDALUCÍA

COUNTRY Spain **TYPE OF ACTIVITY** Horse riding

FITNESS/EXPERTISE LEVEL All horse-riding abilities catered for.

WHY NOW? To be in Jerez for Feria del Caballo.

DESCRIPTION Andalucía is steeped in equestrian tradition. The horse has been part of rural life for time immemorial and Andalucía is the chief breeding ground of the elegant and internationally esteemed Spanish thoroughbred horse, also known as the Cartujano or Andalusian. Countless good riding tracks crisscross Andalucía's marvellous landscapes, and an ever-growing number of *picaderos* (stables) are ready to take you on a guided ride, be it for an hour or a week. Many of the mounts are Andalusians or Andalusian-Arab crosses – medium-sized, intelligent, good in traffic and, as a rule, easy to handle and sure-footed.

The provinces of Sevilla and Cádiz have perhaps the highest horse populations and concentrations of stables, but there are riding opportunities throughout the region. Among the many highlight experiences, standouts are trail rides in the Alpujarras and Sierra Nevada, and beach and dune riding just out of Tarifa.

One of Andalucía's biggest festivals, Feria del Caballo is a celebration of all things equine. Colourful parades of horses pass through the Parque González Hontoria fairgrounds in the town's north, the aristocratic-looking male riders decked out in flat-topped hats, frilly white shirts, black trousers and leather chaps, their female *crupera* (sideways pillion) partners in long, frilly, spotted dresses. It makes a tremendous end or beginning to a few days of riding through the baked Andalucían mountains.

The website www.andalucia.org has a directory of over 100 stables and other equestrian establishments.

↗ DO: HIKE THE LARAPINTA TRAIL

COUNTRY Australia **TYPE OF ACTIVITY** Hiking
FITNESS/EXPERTISE LEVEL Good fitness and endurance required.
WHY NOW? May is about as comfortable as it gets in this desert – average temperature of 23°C and almost no rainfall.
DESCRIPTION The Larapinta Trail is one of the world's great desert treks, stretching 223km across the Australian outback from the Alice Springs Telegraph Station to shapely Mt Sonder. Covering the virtual length of the West MacDonnell Ranges, one of the oldest mountain chains in the world, the trail switches between quartzite ridges, spinifex plains and the gorges that so characterise the West MacDonnells. The trail has an excellent infrastructure, with water sources no more than 33km apart and camp sites well spaced along its course. If you can brave their chill, there are even plenty of gorges for a dip. Allow between 12 and 16 days for a comfortable trek. Trek notes and printable maps can be found on the Northern Territory Parks and Wildlife Commission website (www.nt.gov .au/nreta/parks/walks/larapinta.html).

↗ DO: SURF AT BELLS BEACH

COUNTRY Australia **TYPE OF ACTIVITY** Surfing
FITNESS/EXPERTISE LEVEL High skill level and experience required.
WHY NOW? The most reliable time for Bells' waves.
DESCRIPTION For a beach with such enormous raps, Bells is surprisingly small, snuggled into the cliffs that line Australia's most famously scenic road, the Great Ocean Road. But almost nobody comes for the beach; Bells is all about waves. The powerful right-hand point break – the wave, not the movie – at Bells is a thing of surfing legend, especially when a 4m southwest swell is motoring in from the Southern Ocean. If you don't know your board from your Bells, you can always build up to this point break by taking lessons at nearby Torquay or Anglesea, or you can just wander through Surfworld, the world's largest surfing museum, in Torquay.

↗ **Great Saunter**
www.shorewalkers.org
A 51km walk around the rim of Manhattan.

↗ **Addo Elephant Trail Runs**
www.extrememarathons.com
Dodge Addo Elephant National Park's 300 elephants as you run 160km, 80km or 40km.

↗ **Diamond Quest Ireland**
http://diamondquestireland.com
Run, bike and paddle through the Mourne and Coolie mountains to win £10,000 in diamonds.

↗ **Dirt Works**
www.maxadventure.com.au/dirtworksclassic
A 100km mountain-bike event through Yengo National Park, north of Sydney.

↗ DO: SAIL THE BERMUDA TRIANGLE

COUNTRY Bermuda **TYPE OF ACTIVITY** Sailing
FITNESS/EXPERTISE LEVEL Good sailing skills required.
WHY NOW? A time of smooth seas, barring the paranormal.
DESCRIPTION Throw caution to the Atlantic Ocean wind and tack into the Bermuda Triangle, the name given to a notorious section of the Atlantic that's bound by Bermuda to the north, Florida to the west and Puerto Rico to the south. It's thought that as many as 100 ships and planes have vanished in the triangle, with mysterious disappearances dating back to the mid-19th century. Many of the vessels have gone down without so much as emitting a distress signal, and with no subsequent trace of the craft ever appearing. In other cases, ships have reappeared intact months after disappearing, but with no trace of the crew ever found. If you're still game, you can rent a sailboat at several places in Bermuda, or you can set sail from various points in Florida.

↗ **MAY**
WEEK.02

GO:
RÉUNION

[ABOVE] ↗
Take to the skies to fully appreciate the lush, tropical beauty of Réunion.

[RIGHT] ↗
Smooth sailing in the South Pacific – cruise through calm waters in the comfort of a well-equipped yacht.

WHY NOW? RÉUNION'S DRY SEASON RUNS FROM APRIL THROUGH OCTOBER, WITH MAY AND JUNE THE BEST TIMES TO HIKE

With its pavement cafes serving coffee and croissants, its French postal vans and its beret-clad bowls players, Réunion is like a slice of mainland France relocated lock, stock and wine barrel to an island in the middle of the Indian Ocean.

And what an island! Sheer and lush, this overseas department of France appears to have risen dripping wet from the deep blue sea. Like Hawaii, Réunion has breathtaking natural landscapes, a live volcano and a subtly tropical climate – but on arrival, you're likely to be offered a baguette and a cup of strong black coffee rather than a palm skirt and a garland of flowers.

For many visitors, hiking is the *raison d'être* for a trip to Réunion. The island boasts more than 1000km of hiking trails, the best of which take

REGION Pacific Ocean **TYPE OF ACTIVITY** Sailing **FITNESS/EXPERTISE LEVEL** Good sailing skills required. **WHY NOW?** Set sail at the start of the season. **DESCRIPTION** Between May and October the harbours of the South Pacific swarm with cruising yachts from around the world. If you have your own yacht, you've got the most flexible system for threading between the multitude of islands, but there are also options to charter or join the crew of someone else's yacht. Almost invariably, yachts follow the favourable winds west from the Americas towards Asia, Australia or New Zealand. Popular routes from the US west coast take in Hawaii and Palmyra Atoll before following the traditional path through the Samoan Islands, Tonga, Fiji and New Zealand. If you're looking to crew a yacht, ask at local yacht clubs and look at noticeboards at marinas and yacht clubs. Because of the cyclone season, which begins in November, hoist the sails now so you've got a few months in which to savour the journey.

you through an awe-inspiring landscape of jagged mountain crests, forested valleys, tumbling waterfalls and surreal volcanic tuff. Vast swaths of the interior of the island are accessible only on foot. As a result, the natural environment is remarkably intact, with a huge variety of flora, from tropical rainforest to gnarled thickets of giant heather.

There are two major hiking trails, known as Grande Randonnée Route 1 (GR R1) and Grande Randonnée Route 2 (GR R2), with numerous offshoots. The GR R1 does a tour of Piton des Neiges, passing through Cilaos, the Forêt de Bélouve, Hell-Bourg and the Cirque de Mafate. The GR R2 makes an epic traverse across the island all the way from St-Denis to St-Philippe via the

three cirques, the Plaine-des-Cafres and Piton de la Fournaise.

In recent years Réunion has also seen an explosion of interest in mountain biking. More than 1400km of special biking trails have been established, winding through forests and scooting down mountainsides. They are graded like ski runs, according to level of difficulty.

If you're au fait in French, you can make your hiking and biking preparations online at www.reunion -nature.com, buying maps, booking mountain lodges and checking general information. www.la-reunion -tourisme.com

[ABOVE] ↗
Don't lock horns
over which way to see
Kruger – there are
several trails to choose
from, each offering a
unique experience.

[TOP RIGHT] ↗
There's no place like
home – be blown away
by the power of a twister
as it carves up the road
in front of you.

[BOTTOM RIGHT] ↗
Pilgrimage and
adventure: the Unesco
World Heritage–listed
Camino de Santiago.

DO: HIKE KRUGER WILDERNESS TRAILS

COUNTRY South Africa **TYPE OF ACTIVITY** Watching wildlife/hiking
FITNESS/EXPERTISE LEVEL Moderate fitness required.
WHY NOW? In May, Kruger averages around 25˚C with almost negligible rainfall.

DESCRIPTION With its vast savannahs, abundant wildlife and long conservation history, Kruger National Park is one of the world's best safari destinations. It's reputed to have the greatest variety of animals of any African park, with lions, leopards, elephants, Cape buffaloes and black rhinos (the big five), plus cheetahs, giraffes, hippos and antelopes. There are 147 recorded mammal species and 507 bird species in the park.

The best way to get personal with this roll-call of critters is on one of Kruger's wilderness walking trails, which are a major attraction of the Southern African safari experience. They are done in small groups (maximum eight people), guided by highly knowledgeable armed guides and offer a superb opportunity to get a more intimate sense of the bush than is possible in a vehicle.

There are seven wilderness trails in the park, each with its unique attractions. The Napi Trail is known for the opportunities it offers for seeing the big five; the Bushmans Trail features treks to San rock paintings; the Nyalaland Trail is most memorable for its beauty and its wilderness ambience, and is a paradise for birders; while the highly rewarding Sweni Trail is near Satara rest camp, where many lions are attracted to the herds of wildebeests, zebras and buffaloes.

The walks are not particularly strenuous, covering about 20km per day at a modest pace. The itinerary of each walk is determined by the interests of the group, the time of year and the disposition of the wildlife. The wilderness-trail walks last two days and three nights, with departures on Wednesday and Sunday afternoon. The walks are extremely popular, so book well in advance. www.sanparks.org/parks/kruger

↗ DO: STORM CHASE IN TORNADO ALLEY

COUNTRY USA **TYPE OF ACTIVITY** Natural phenomena
FITNESS/EXPERTISE LEVEL Not required.
WHY NOW? May is peak tornado season. **DESCRIPTION** Tornado Alley stretches between the Rocky and Appalachian Mountains, covering central US states such as Oklahoma, Colorado, Arkansas, Texas and Nebraska. Spring here is not the time of flowers, but of tornadoes, spinning wildly with winds up to 500km/h. In May it's not uncommon for Tornado Alley to experience more than 400 twisters, which makes it probable that you will witness a twister if you join one of the growing number of tornado-chasing tours. Typically, tornado tours run for six days, beginning in twister-central Oklahoma City. Using satellite radar imaging, your guides will trace and chase the big storms across Tornado Alley, delivering you to a box-seat view of twisters or giant thunderstorms. You probably are in Kansas now, Dorothy.

↗ DO: WALK THE CAMINO DE SANTIAGO

COUNTRY Spain **TYPE OF ACTIVITY** Hiking/pilgrimage
FITNESS/EXPERTISE LEVEL Moderate fitness and good endurance required. **WHY NOW?** Long days matched by visual splendour – full rivers, hillsides bursting with wildflowers and swaying green cereal crops.
DESCRIPTION For more than 1000 years Europeans have taken up the age-old symbols of the Camino de Santiago (Way of St James) – the scallop shell and staff – and set off on foot to reach the tomb of James, the apostle, in the Iberian Peninsula's far northwest. Today, this magnificent long-distance walk is an appealing mix of pilgrimage and adventure, heading 783km through Spain's north from Roncesvalles, on the border with France, to Santiago de Compostela in Galicia. Testament to its importance is the fact that the walk is both a Unesco World Heritage listing and Europe's first proclaimed 'Cultural Itinerary'. If you walk every day, expect to be in pursuit of St James for one month.

Moonride
www.moonride.co.nz
Don't be afraid of the dark, mountain bike through it in Rotorua's Whakarewarewa Forest for 24 hours.

Isle of Wight Walking Festival
www.isleofwightwalkingfestival.co.uk
The largest of the UK's 20-plus annual walking festivals.

Red Centre MTB Enduro
www.rapidascent.com.au
Five-day mountain-bike race through the desert heart of Australia; stages range from less than one minute to 90km.

↗ DO: VISIT RIO'S FAVELAS

COUNTRY Brazil **TYPE OF ACTIVITY** Adventure travel
FITNESS/EXPERTISE LEVEL Not required.
WHY NOW? The best time to visit Rio is between May and August, when it's cooled by balmy trade winds and the average temperature hovers around 30°C. **DESCRIPTION** Rio de Janeiro's first *favela* (slum), Morro da Providência, was founded more than 100 years ago. Today, Rocinha is indisputably the largest *favela*, with over 127,000 inhabitants. Once one of the most dangerous parts of the city, Rocinha has mellowed considerably in recent years and in many ways is a normal, safe and welcoming place, a reality underlined by the tours that stroll through the *favela*, led by the pioneer of *favela* tourism, Marcelo Armstrong. The itinerary includes an explanation of the architecture and social infrastructure of the *favela* – particularly in relation to greater Rio de Janeiro. The trip also includes a walk through the streets, and a stop at both a community centre and a handicraft centre where visitors can purchase colourful artwork made by locals. www.favelatour.com.br

↗ **MAY**

WEEK.03

GO: WADI RUM, JORDAN

[ABOVE] ↗
Scale the *jebels* (hills) and follow in the camel prints of Lawrence of Arabia in kaleidoscopic Wadi Rum.

[RIGHT] ↗
Rio combines grunt and great views, with around 350 climbs near the city.

WHY NOW? BLAZING IN SUMMER, AND WITH COLD WINDS HOWLING DOWN FROM CENTRAL ASIA IN WINTER, NOW IS THE TIME TO DISCOVER THIS DESERT

Made famous by the presence of the Arab Revolt and TE Lawrence in the early 20th century, Wadi Rum offers some of the most extraordinary desert scenery you'll ever see. Its myriad moods and dramatic colours, dictated by the changing angle of the sun, make for a memorable scene, but it's a place to be experienced as much as it is to be seen. Blazing in summer, and with cold winds howling down from Central Asia in winter, now is the time to discover this desert.

Wadi Rum is a series of valleys about 2km wide, stretching north to south for about 130km. Among the valleys is a desert landscape of sand and rocks, punctuated by towering *jebels* (hills) that have eroded into soft sandstone over a period of up to 50 million years. These *jebels* offer some challenging rock climbing, equal to anything in Europe. While climbing is

↗ DO: CLIMB IN RIO DE JANEIRO

COUNTRY Brazil **TYPE OF ACTIVITY** Rock climbing **FITNESS/EXPERTISE LEVEL** Beginners to human spiders. **WHY NOW?** With winter nearing you'll find the rock suitably cool. **DESCRIPTION** Better known for its dancing and prancing, Rio is also said to be the city with the highest number of rock-climbing routes in the world. Within an hour's drive of the city, there are around 350 documented climbs, including routes on Rio's two most famous landmarks, Sugarloaf and Corcovado, the site of the Christ the Redeemer statue. Corcovado's south face offers some of Rio's longest multipitch routes, combining grunt with great views over the city. Rio de Janeiro state is blessed with further climbs if you prefer a complete escape from the city. Parque Nacional da Serra dos Órgãos, about 50km from Rio, is Brazil's climbing capital, and here you'll find the spire of Dedo de Deus (God's Finger), the country's classic piece of rock. www.climbinrio.com

still a nascent industry in Wadi Rum, and you'll need to bring your own gear, the situation has improved in recent years. There are at least several accredited climbing guides, most of whom have been trained in the UK. One of the more popular climbs for amateur climbers is up Jebel Rum (1754m), Jordan's highest peak. Minimal gear is needed and it's close to the Rest House in Rum village, although a guide is still required to find the best route and to help with the climb. There are also a number of sites north of the road to Diseh.

Excursions into the desert can be made by camel or 4WD. If you have the time, travelling around Wadi Rum by camel is highly recommended, enabling you to experience the desert as the Bedouin people

have for centuries and to really appreciate the silent gravitas of the desert. You can ride out and back from Rum village, cross to the famed archaeological site at Petra (about five nights), or follow in Lawrence of Arabia's camel prints to Aqaba on the Red Sea coast (three to six nights).

(ABOVE) ↗
Cycle touring is laid-back in Denmark – the highest peak is a mere 173m above sea level.

(TOP RIGHT) ↗
Squeeze between rocks to get a glimpse of ancient life – and death.

(BOTTOM RIGHT) ↗
Tiptoe through the tulips as you cross the rolling hills of the Aksu-Dzhabagly Nature Reserve.

DO: CYCLE IN DENMARK

COUNTRY Denmark **TYPE OF ACTIVITY** Cycle touring
FITNESS/EXPERTISE LEVEL Moderate fitness required.
WHY NOW? Roll into summer in the flattest kind of way.

DESCRIPTION Denmark is a superb country for cycling, with relatively quiet roads and an attractively undulating landscape. Here, cyclists enjoy rights that, in most countries, are reserved for motorists. There are bike lanes along major city roads, road signs are posted for bicycle traffic, and drivers are so accommodating that riding is an almost surreal experience.

There are 11 major bike routes in Denmark, all in immaculate condition. In addition to these each county has an extensive network of bike routes that enables you to explore every inch of the country. One classic ride, combining both national and local bike routes and taking in six islands, involves a loop of the Zealand Islands, using three of the 11 national bike routes and taking between 10 days and three weeks.

It begins by taking Route 9 south out of Copenhagen and along Zealand's east coast, passing through the historic port town of Køge, the yacht-infested Præstø and the medieval stronghold of Vordingborg. When you reach the southern tip, cross the bridge to Falster and ride around the northwest of the island before crossing another bridge to the pastorally rich island of Lolland. Once on Lolland, take in the towns of Sakskøbing and Maribo before switching onto Route 8 and heading west through Nakskov to the ferry terminal at Tårs. Sail to Spodsbjerg and cut a quick lap of Langeland island or make a beeline for Tåsinge and the island of Funen.

On arrival at Funen head north, hugging the east coast, to the town of Nyborg, passing through a number of pretty villages and gently rolling hills. Leave Funen at Nyborg, crossing back to Zealand by train at Korsør. From here it's a couple of days riding on Route 6 back to the capital. For route maps, see www.trafikken.dk.

↗ DO: CAVE AT ACTUN TUNICHIL MUKNAL

COUNTRY Belize **TYPE OF ACTIVITY** Caving
FITNESS/EXPERTISE LEVEL Basic swimming skills required.
WHY NOW? The end of the dry season assures low water levels and smooth tubing. **DESCRIPTION** One of the most unforgettable and adventurous tours you can make in Belize, the trip into 'ATM' takes you deep into the underworld of this 5km-long cave. After a 45-minute hike to the cave, your subterranean journey begins with a frosty swim across a 6m-deep pool. You then walk, climb, twist and turn your way through the cave to a massive opening, where you'll see hundreds of pottery vessels and shards, along with the skeletal remains of 14 humans (seven of them children) who were almost certainly sacrificial victims. They're believed to have been offerings to the rain god Chac (who dwelt in caves) at a time of drought in the 9th century. In view of the unique value and the fragility of the cave's contents, visits are strictly controlled and permitted only with trained guides from San Ignacio–based companies.

↗ DO: HORSE TREK IN AKSU-DZHABAGLY NATURE RESERVE

COUNTRY Kazakhstan **TYPE OF ACTIVITY** Horseback riding
FITNESS/EXPERTISE LEVEL Not required.
WHY NOW? To tiptoe/horseshoe through the tulips.
DESCRIPTION The Aksu-Dzhabagly Nature Reserve is a beautiful 1319-sq-km patch of valleys and mountains climbing to the Kyrgyz and Uzbek borders east of Shymkent. At the west end of the Talassky Alatau range, stretching from the edge of the steppe at about 1200m up to 4239m at Pik Sayram, it's a region best explored on horseback. One of the best rides spends about three days climbing to a set of 2000 stones with petroglyphs up to 900 years old, below a glacier descending from the 3800m peak Kaskabulak. More demanding treks will take you over 3500m passes with nights in caves. Aksu-Dzhabagly is promoted as the home of the tulip, and in April and May its alpine meadows are dotted with the wild bright-red Greig's tulip.

↗ DO: RAFT THE TARA RIVER

COUNTRY Montenegro **TYPE OF ACTIVITY** White-water rafting
FITNESS/EXPERTISE LEVEL Not required.
WHY NOW? The Tara is in full flow.
DESCRIPTION Slicing through the mountains of Durmitor National Park, the Tara River forms a canyon that drops to 1300m at its deepest point – the Grand Canyon is only 200m deeper. Rafting the river has become one of the most popular activities in Montenegro, with trips operating from May to October – in May the melting snow has the river at its greatest flow. The 82km section that is raftable starts from Splavište, south of the impressive 150m-high Tara Bridge, and ends at Šćepan Polje on the Bosnian border. The classic two-day trip heads through the deepest part of the canyon on the first day, stopping overnight at Radovan Luka. Most of the day tours from the coast traverse only the last 18km. You'll miss out on the canyon's depths, but it's still a beautiful stretch that includes most of the rapids.

↗ **Great Wall Marathon**
www.great-wall-marathon.com
A 42km run along and beside the Great Wall of China.

↗ **Green Belt Relay**
www.greenbeltrelay.org.uk
Teams of 11 run around London, beginning at Hampton Court Palace and, 350km later, finishing just down the road.

↗ **Explore Sweden**
www.exploresweden.se
Eight-day, 1000km adventure race across Sweden's high alpine country.

↗ **Bimbache Extrem**
www.meridianoraid.com
Spain's major adventure race, featuring the usual disciplines plus occasional 'treats' such as white-water rafting.

GO: MT EVEREST, NEPAL/CHINA

(ABOVE) ↗
Almost 9km and rising – Everest's peak gets 2.5cm higher every year.

(RIGHT) ↗
Leap tall mountains in a single bound on your way to complete the epic Trans Canada Trail.

WHY NOW? THIS WEEK IS THE MOST LIKELY OPENING OF THE SO-CALLED 'EVEREST WINDOW'

The word 'Himalaya' is Sanskrit for 'Abode of Snows', and Nepal's stretch of the Himalaya has eight peaks over 8000m, including the highest of them all, mighty Mt Everest (8848m). Known to Tibetans as Qomolangma and to Nepalis as Sagarmatha, the world's highest place was the overpowering attraction for Nepal's first modern tourists – the mountaineers.

This week is the conclusive one in the Everest climbing calendar, being both the anniversary of the first ascent in 1953 by Edmund Hillary and Tenzing Norgay, and the most likely opening of the so-called 'Everest window'. This pause in winds on Everest's summit, brought about by monsoon conditions further south, allows in an expectant draft of climbers, creating the busiest time of the year on the mountain – in 2008, for

⬈ DO: HIKE THE TRANS CANADA TRAIL

COUNTRY Canada **TYPE OF ACTIVITY** Hiking/cycling/horse riding **FITNESS/EXPERTISE LEVEL** Epic endurance required. **WHY NOW?** With such an epic distance ahead, best get started ahead of the summer. **DESCRIPTION** Got a couple of years to spare? Then get started on hiking the Trans Canada Trail, which, with 14,500km of trail constructed by 2009, is well on its way to becoming the world's longest recreational path. Beginning at North America's most easterly point, Cape Spear, this work in progress will reach to Victoria on Vancouver Island, crossing through every Canadian province on its way. At a completed length of around 21,500km, it will be half as long as the earth is round, and if you walk at a decent clip of about 30km a day it will take almost exactly two years to finish. If you're in a hurry, grab a bike or horse for this multiuse path. www.tctrail.ca

instance, 387 of the year's 422 Everest summiteers reached the top between 20 and 28 May.

If you're contemplating becoming one of the 1300-plus people to have stood atop Everest, your first piece of training should be to test the weight of your bank account. Mountaineers on the most popular route, the Southeast Ridge, pay upwards of US$10,000 per person for the permit alone.

If you lack the skills, lungs, money or inclination for this bit of high-altitude mountaineering, you can still share part of the mountaineering experience by trekking to either of Everest's two base camps, one in Nepal, the other in Tibet. The camp on the Nepali side, on the Khumbu Glacier, is by far the most popular of the two trekking destinations. Most treks into the Khumbu now begin at Lukla, passing through the Sherpa village of Namche Bazaar, Tengboche monastery and on to base camp, at 5340m, about 11 days later.

Across the range in Tibet, the walk to the northern base camp has traditionally begun on the Friendship Hwy near Shegar, and involves a four-day trek past Rongphu monastery, but the construction of a road to the base camp (and the world's highest post box!) has dulled much of its trekking appeal.

(ABOVE) ↗
Marvel at the terraced ruins of Huiñay Huayna on the Inca Trail.

(TOP RIGHT) ↗
Leave the 4WD in the carpark for this unique safari.

(BOTTOM RIGHT) ↗
A moveable feast – tornadoes of sardines tempt dolphins, sharks and orcas.

DO: HIKE THE INCA TRAIL

COUNTRY Peru **TYPE OF ACTIVITY** Hiking

FITNESS/EXPERTISE LEVEL Moderate fitness required.

WHY NOW? The vegetation is beautifully green and the June crowds have yet to arrive.

DESCRIPTION Run a straw poll across the globe and the Inca Trail would almost certainly win as the world's best-known hiking trail. South America's most fabled adventure attracts so many trekkers that the government has heavily regulated it in recent years – now you can only walk the trail with a guide or tour, and trekker numbers are limited to 200 per day. The famous El Camino Inca is not the only Inca trail to the archaeological site of Machu Picchu, but it is the only one that winds its way past three major Inca sites in good repair. Any one of Sayacmarca, Phuyupatamarca or Huiñay Huayna would be considered a great day trip out of Cusco if they were easily accessible by road, but none can be reached without hiking all or part of the Inca Trail.

The trail is only 38km long but has steep ascents, especially to Warmiwañusca (Dead Woman's Pass), followed by swooping descents into the cloudforests bordering the Amazon Basin.

The elevation ranges from under 2000m at Aguas Calientes (the trail's end) to 4198m at Warmiwañusca, and so vegetation varies from montane rainforest, cloudforest and high-altitude *quenua* woodlands to bare *puna* grasslands. The lower reaches are a riot of different flower species, and the bird life is varied and prolific.

Curiously, the trail's end goal – Machu Picchu – is both the best known and the least known of the major Inca sites. It is not mentioned in the chronicles of the Spanish conquistadors, and archaeologists today can only speculate on its function. It is mysterious, beautifully located, extensive and expertly built, and despite its remoteness, it attracts many thousands of visitors. Savvy trekkers know to time their visit to Machu Picchu for the early morning and late afternoon, when it is relatively empty.

↗ DO: CYCLE SAFARI AT MASHATU GAME RESERVE

COUNTRY Botswana **TYPE OF ACTIVITY** Cycling/wildlife watching
FITNESS/EXPERTISE LEVEL Moderate fitness required.
WHY NOW? The best wildlife and weather is from May to September.
DESCRIPTION Pinched between Zimbabwe and South Africa, Mashatu Game Reserve is one of the largest private wildlife reserves in Southern Africa, and an excellent place to view big cats and elephants (over 1000 have been counted here). The reserve is only available for viewing by prebooked guests staying at one of two accommodation options, among the most luxurious in Botswana. Once here, however, you have the opportunity to add a unique twist to the traditional safari genre by touring the 250-sq-km park on a bicycle. Morning and afternoon mountain bike safaris range out from the accommodation centres, following elephant paths in the company of reserve rangers.
www.mashatu.com/adventure_cycle.htm

↗ DO: SNORKEL THE SARDINE RUN

COUNTRY South Africa **TYPE OF ACTIVITY** Snorkelling
FITNESS/EXPERTISE LEVEL No special requirements.
WHY NOW? To observe a seasonal ocean wonder.
DESCRIPTION Between late May and early July millions upon millions of sardines gather along South Africa's east coast in a mass said to be visible even by satellite. From their spawning grounds off Cape Agulhas, the sardines thread a 1600km path, riding a countercurrent north along the coast. In turn, each and every predator in the oceanic food chain follows this moving feast. Dolphins, sharks, seabirds, game fish and even orcas all join the fracas. Visitors who witness the feeding frenzy will long remember the adrenaline rush as huge whales breach metres away from the boat and dolphin pods ride the bow-wave. Snorkellers score ringside views of the spectacular action, though diving should not be attempted amid the sardine shoals, as hungry predators could pose a risk to sport divers.

↗ Tenzing Hillary Everest Marathon
www.everestmarathon.com
A 42km run from Everest Base Camp to Namche Bazaar.

↗ 100km del Passatore
www.100kmdelpassatore.it
Run 100km, from Florence to Faenza, within 20 hours.

↗ Yak Attack
www.yak-attack.co.uk
Run or mountain bike out from Kathmandu and around the Annapurna Circuit, including a crossing of 5416m Thorung La.

↗ Wild, Wonderful 24 Hour
www.oarevents.com
Trek, mountain bike and raft (up to grade 5 rapids) through the New River Gorge in West Virginia.

↗ DO: RAFT THE SHUBENACADIE TIDAL BORE

COUNTRY Canada **TYPE OF ACTIVITY** White-water rafting
FITNESS/EXPERTISE LEVEL Not required.
WHY NOW? Come on the cusp of summer.
DESCRIPTION The Bay of Fundy gets the world's highest tides, rising up to 15m daily. As a result of these extreme tides, a tidal wave or bore flows up the feeder rivers when high tide comes in. At the mouth of the Shubenacadie River in Nova Scotia this has led to the creation of tidal-bore rafting trips, with powered Zodiacs riding the collision of water as the river's outflow meets the blasting force of the incoming Fundy tides. Wave heights are dependent on the phase of the moon, and will dictate whether your experience is mild or wild. Be prepared to get very wet.
www.shubie.com; www.tidalborerafting.com

GO: PEAK DISTRICT, ENGLAND

(ABOVE) ↗
Clamber over ridges
blanketed in snow
for superb vistas
of Europe's busiest
national park.

(RIGHT) ↗
Shaken, not stirred?
Follow in James Bond's
footsteps at the 220m-
high Verzasca Dam.

WHY NOW? BEGIN THE NORTHERN SUMMER IN ONE OF THE HEMISPHERE'S PREMIER NATIONAL PARKS

So what if the Peak District takes its name from an early British tribe, the Picts, and not because of any towering summits. Or that its highest point is just 636m above sea level. Or that it's the busiest national park in Europe, and supposedly the second-busiest in the world (after Mt Fuji), receiving 22 million visitors (or more than the population of Australia) every year. If you can forgive this Midlands national park its crowds and its grandiose name, you'll be treated to some of Britain's wildest, most beautiful scenery.

Britain's first national park spills across six counties, and is surrounded by Midlands' industry. The park's own industry is adventure, much of which takes place out of sight, beneath the limestone coating, where cavers burrow through the earth in both caves and former mines. More than 100 caves and mines have been explored by spelunkers,

↗ DO: BUNGEE JUMP AT VERZASCA DAM

COUNTRY Switzerland **TYPE OF ACTIVITY**
Bungee jumping **FITNESS/EXPERTISE LEVEL**
Not required. **WHY NOW?** Crack open the
northern summer with the world's highest
bungee jump. **DESCRIPTION** The enormous
Verzasca Dam, in Switzerland's Italian-
speaking province of Ticino, holds more than
water. From its 220m-high lip you can also
make one of the world's highest bungee
jumps, one made famous by James Bond.
In the movie *GoldenEye*, 007 plunged from
this dam, a stunt that was once voted the
greatest in movie history. Thinking of yourself
as a suave secret-service agent may be about
the only thing that will give your legs the
spring they need as you stand on the lip of
the dam eyeballing a drop that looks more like
kilometres than metres. Cheer up; in another
7.5 seconds you'll be bouncing around at the
base of the dam. www.trekking.ch

and there are show caves open to the public in
Castleton, Buxton and Matlock Bath. At Poole's
Cavern, near Buxton, you'll find England's longest
stalactite, while Speedwell Cavern at Castleton
is a unique flooded tunnel that you travel along
by boat to reach an underground lake called the
'bottomless pit'.

The Peak District's second piece of adventuring
fame is as the southern terminus for Britain's
oldest, second-longest and arguably most famous
national trail, the Pennine Way. Beginning in Edale,
in the national park, the trail follows the Pennine
Range for 416km into Scotland. If you haven't the
time or the ticker for that, try the Limestone Way;
the original route (now altered and extended but still

walkable) covers a marathon-length chunk of the
national park.

The Peak's outdoors trinity is complete with a
climb. Graced with rock stacks and tors, the Peak
offers thousands of routes on gritstone edges
and limestone. Popular climbing areas include
Millstone Edge and Stanage Edge (gritstone) and
the limestone cliff at High Tor. Burbage South offers
the unlikely combination of the Peak's most difficult
climbs and some of its gentlest bouldering.
www.peakdistrict-npa.gov.uk;
www.visitpeakdistrict.com

[ABOVE] ↗
A striped stalker approaches a tourist-laden jeep.

[TOP RIGHT] ↗
No snow? No problem. Sand never melts.

[BOTTOM RIGHT] ↗
Take in some of the surrounding scenery before you get swept away by the Çoruh currents.

DO: TRACK TIGERS IN INDIA

COUNTRY India **TYPE OF ACTIVITY** Wildlife watching
FITNESS/EXPERTISE LEVEL Not required.
WHY NOW? The tail end of the dry season offers the most likely tiger sightings.

DESCRIPTION Corbett National Park was India's first national park, and is now home to around 10% of the country's estimated 1500 tigers. Its high forests and dense understorey make tiger sightings unreliable, but by visiting now you stand the best chance because the forest has died back, waterholes are scarce and the grass cover is minimal after winter burn-offs.

Most visitors to Corbett stay in the main camp, Dhikala, overlooking the elephant-grazed flood plains of the Ramganga River. From here safaris through the park take two forms: jeep and elephant-back. The jeeps range further, heading across to pools in the Ramganga in which tigers can sometimes be seen cooling themselves from the 40°C heat, but the elephants move more quietly, grazing on the cannabis that grows naturally and prolifically in the park. Try to arrange both if you can, though Dhikala's few elephants are in high demand.

If you miss out on sighting a tiger, you'll be appeased by a field guide worth of other creatures. Corbett is home to around 50 species of mammals, including leopards, elephants and 600 species of birds. The most commonly seen animals include langur monkeys, elephants, the ubiquitous rhesus macaques, and a variety of deer. To reach Corbett, take the overnight Ranikhet Express from Delhi to Ramnagar, where permits and accommodation must be arranged at the Project Tiger office. Jeep drivers hang about the office each morning, so don't worry about your prospects of finding a ride. Try to get a petrol vehicle as the noisier diesel jeeps can blast away any chance you have of spotting shy wildlife such as tigers. http://projecttiger .nic.in/corbett.htm

↗ DO: **SANDBOARD IN OREGON**

COUNTRY USA **TYPE OF ACTIVITY** Sandboarding
FITNESS/EXPERTISE LEVEL Not required.
WHY NOW? Open March to January, the Sand Master Park offers its finest weather now.
DESCRIPTION The snows may have gone for the season but there's always sand, so head to the Oregon town of Florence to turn yourself into sandpaper at the world's first sandboarding park, set in the Oregon Dunes National Recreation Area, the largest expanse of oceanfront dunes in the United States. Sandboarding is like snowboarding for the sun worshipper – the only 'down' you need worry about at the 40-acre Sand Master Park is not in your clothing but in the descents you make through this gritty version of powder. Board rental is available at the park, as is instruction for boarding novices. www.sandmasterpark.com

↗ DO: **RAFT THE ÇORUH RIVER**

COUNTRY Turkey **TYPE OF ACTIVITY** White-water rafting
FITNESS/EXPERTISE LEVEL Not required.
WHY NOW? Fed by snowmelt, the river is at its churning best.
DESCRIPTION Çoruh River in eastern Anatolia is one of the world's best rafting rivers, offering grade four to five rapids with welcoming names such as King Kong and High Tension. But the river's great joy is the scenery – tear your eyes from the rapids and you'll see 1500m gorge walls and snapshots of traditional village life. Various local operators run day trips out of the town of Yusufeli into the river's frothing Yusefeli Gorge (where King Kong awaits you), while other companies operate longer trips. To run the river's 300km length will take around a week, culminating at Yusufeli Gorge. Don't procrastinate about rafting this river; by August there's usually not enough water to raft.

↗ DO: **CLIMB THE 100 FAMOUS MOUNTAINS**

COUNTRY Japan **TYPE OF ACTIVITY** Hiking/climbing
FITNESS/EXPERTISE LEVEL Good fitness and endurance required.
WHY NOW? If you want to climb 100 mountains, it's going to be a long Japanese summer, so best get started.
DESCRIPTION In 1964 noted alpinist and author Fukada Kyūya released his book *Hyakumeizan*, in which he chose his 100 Famous Mountains of Japan, selecting them for a variety of reasons – height, history, shape and character. It was his wish that keen Japanese hikers would choose their own 100 and set out to climb them in their lifetimes. It didn't quite work out that way. His 100 Famous Mountains are now the accepted 100, and they have become almost every hiker's target, whether they can manage them all in one year or 30 years. The mountains stretch from Yaku-shima, an island off the southern tip of Kyūshū, to Rishiritō, an island off the northern tip of Hokkaidō.

↗ **Corsica Raid**
www.corsicaraid.com
Europe's first adventure race, with an electoral roll of disciplines.

↗ **Big Five Marathon**
www.big-five-marathon.com
Running race through a habitat populated by Africa's 'big five' animals; thinking about the lions will make you run faster.

↗ **Banff Jasper Relay**
www.bjr.ca
Teams race 258km along Canada's spectacular Icefields Parkway.

↗ **Mud Run**
www.mudrun.ca
A 10km Toronto cross-country run over climbing walls, through tunnels and into, yes, lots of mud.

GO: THE SERENGETI, TANZANIA

[ABOVE] ↗
Witness the annual
migration of wildebeests
in the Grumeti.

[RIGHT] ↗
Coast to coast across
the USA in six days.
Could this be cycling's
ultimate challenge?

**WHY NOW? THE MIGRATING WILDEBEESTS ARE MOST
LIKELY TO CROSS THE GRUMETI RIVER IN JUNE**

Africa's most famous park is a place that guarantees immersion
in the quintessential African landscape. Here, an estimated 2800 lions
roam alongside 250 cheetahs and 9000 spotted hyenas. There are zebras,
giraffes, antelopes and, most famously, there's a seething mass of
endlessly migrating wildebeests.

The annual migration of one million wildebeests is not a single event
but a continuous cycle of movement that varies from season to season.
One thing is unchanging: to cross through the Serengeti towards Kenya's
Masai Mara National Reserve, the wildebeests must run the gauntlet of
the Grumeti River. It's the most spectacular moment of the migration,
with gigantic Nile crocodiles preying on the weakest of the beasts. This
chancy crossing doesn't adhere to numbers on the calendar. It can occur
anytime between May and July, though June is the likely month.

↗ DO: **RACE ACROSS AMERICA**

COUNTRY USA **TYPE OF ACTIVITY** Endurance cycling **FITNESS/EXPERTISE LEVEL** Superior fitness and endurance required. **WHY NOW?** To boast about racing in arguably the planet's toughest event. **DESCRIPTION** Pedalling your bike 5000km across the United States may sound like an enjoyable sort of cycle tour, but to do it in around nine days (there's a 12-day cut-off limit) breeds the sort of race that *Outside* magazine once declared the world's toughest event. Solo cyclists in this event will ride for up to 22 hours a day, covering around 550km each day; teams ride around the clock, averaging speeds of around 37km/h for almost six days. To compete as a solo rider, you must qualify at one of the events held by the UltraMarathon Cycling Association (www.ultracycling.com).
www.raceacrossamerica.org

The Grumeti crossing takes place in the Serengeti's Western Corridor, where there are several accommodation options, including luxury tent camps at Kirawira and Grumeti River Camp. It's also easily accessed from the park centre at Seronera.

Even if you miss the drama in the Grumeti River you'll still be treated to a Serengeti show by visiting at this time of year. Wildlife concentrations in the park are greatest from December to June, and the park is one of the best places in Africa to observe big cats. The Wandamu River area in Seronera is said to hold the world's greatest density of cheetahs, and without the obstruction of trees it's almost certain that you'll see them on the plains. You'll definitely sight lions, which spend most of their time laying

about in shade with their paws in the air, so search the shady patches along watercourses and the shadows of big trees – chances are your driver will be listening on the radio and know where the cats are.

North of Seronera, seek out hippos at Retima Hippo Pool, where you can get out of your car and picnic. If there's been recent rain, scout about for tracks of leopards and other animals and wonder what it might be like to be the picnic and not the picnicker. www.serengeti.org

[ABOVE] ↗
One of the planet's great rivers, the densely populated Sepik is a conduit to a world of myth, magic and ritual.

[TOP RIGHT] ↗
Ease yourself into the waves at Kuta before heading out on the ultimate surfari experience.

[BOTTOM RIGHT] ↗
Follow in the footsteps of shipwreck survivors along Vancouver Island's West Coast Trail.

DO: CRUISE THE SEPIK RIVER

COUNTRY Papua New Guinea **TYPE OF ACTIVITY** Adventure travel
FITNESS/EXPERTISE LEVEL Not required.
WHY NOW? It's best to visit early in the dry season because the mosquitoes are less numerous and the river's full.

DESCRIPTION The Sepik is one of the world's great rivers, and is to PNG as the Congo is to Africa and the Amazon to South America. However, the Sepik is more than just a river – it's also a densely populated repository of complex cultures, and produces the most potent art in the Pacific. While cruising on the river, you'll still see naked kids poling dugout canoes, woven fish traps and the towering facades of spirit houses.

The Sepik is 1126km long and is navigable for almost its entire length, though a few days on the river is enough for many people. Locals prefer to travel in faster, more manoeuvrable motorboats, but most travellers favour the long dugout motor-canoes. There's nothing quite like cruising along the river sitting below the waterline in the bottom of a 20m dugout. It takes hours to get anywhere and the experience is quite calming and meditative, once you've accepted that the canoe won't tip over rounding a corner.

The most artistic villages are concentrated on the Middle Sepik and the most spectacular scenery is on the lakes or tributaries. Canoes aren't superbly comfortable but the biggest drawback is uncertainty – you can arrive at the river and find there are no canoes available for days. Motor-canoes can be hired in Ambunti, Pagwi and Angoram, though it's better to arrange this beforehand in Wewak or, better still, before you come to PNG. River traffic is reasonably constant, and if you have an open-ended schedule and a lot of time, you can catch rides in locals' boats and with traders moving up and down the river. This is the cheapest way to go but you might be stuck somewhere for a few days waiting for a lift.

↗ DO: **SURF BALI**

COUNTRY Indonesia **TYPE OF ACTIVITY** Surfing
FITNESS/EXPERTISE LEVEL From surf learners to surf legends.
WHY NOW? June offers the best surf conditions. **DESCRIPTION** Like a dream-catcher, Bali's southern Bukit Peninsula droops into the Indian Ocean, picking up swells that have journeyed across the globe just to tumble onto its holiday beaches. From Ulu Watu, near the peninsula's southwestern point, to Canggu, north of Seminyak, the midyear brings trade winds from the southeast for warm water and epic waves. And you won't have to run the gauntlet of territorial hard-heads. Kuta is Bali's surfing nursery, with gentle beach breaks and tubes. Canggu has a good right-hander at high tide, while a 2.5m swell at Balangan can be a classic wave. Kuta is also the place to broaden your Indonesian surf experience, with one-week 'surfaris' on offer to other parts of the country, including the legendary Grajagan (G-Land) on eastern Java. You'll find surfboards and boogie boards for rent at Kuta, with variable quality and prices.

↗ DO: **HIKE THE WEST COAST TRAIL**

COUNTRY Canada **TYPE OF ACTIVITY** Hiking
FITNESS/EXPERTISE LEVEL Good fitness required.
WHY NOW? This week is the last before permits are required to hike the trail. **DESCRIPTION** The 75km West Coast Trail on Vancouver Island was originally constructed as an escape route for shipwreck survivors, following a century of horrific maritime accidents. It's a stunning hike that takes between five and seven days, passing through virgin spruce, cedar and hemlock forests, across cliff tops and over suspension bridges, along stretches of deserted beaches punctuated by clear tidal pools, and up and down steep gullies and waterways. And every kilometre must be earned. You'll climb hundreds of rocky steps, cross streams on slippery logs, scale cliffs on rock-face ladders, and plough through knee-deep mud. Heavy fog and torrential rain are *de rigueur* (as are chance encounters with bears and even cougars). The trail is open from May through September, and walker numbers between 15 June and 15 September are controlled by a strict permit system. www.pc.gc.ca

↗ DO: **CLIMB DAMAVAND**

COUNTRY Iran **TYPE OF ACTIVITY** Trekking/mountaineering
FITNESS/EXPERTISE LEVEL The summit doesn't require any technical gear but it does require good fitness. **WHY NOW?** The climbing season is from June to September, or May to October for experienced mountaineers. **DESCRIPTION** Shaped like Mt Fuji, Mt Damavand (5671m) is the highest mountain in the Middle East. Its image is one of the most recognisable icons in Iran, appearing on the IR10,000 note. From a technical point of view, Damavand is basically a walk-up, and climbing too far too quickly is the most dangerous aspect of this climb. The ascent starts in Reyneh, and Damavand can be climbed in two or three days, though the three-day option is preferable as it allows more time for acclimatisation and means fewer headaches. The first day you walk to Camp 2, and then on to Camp 3 at around 4250m the next day, before heading for the summit. Nights are freezing on the mountain and it can be -10°C at the summit.

↗ **Finke Desert Race**
www.finkedesertrace.com.au
Race a motorbike or buggy 230km from Alice Springs to Finke (and return) in central Australia.

↗ **Triangle Race**
www.royaltorbayyc.org.uk
Biannual, two-week sailing (and partying) race from Torquay (England) to Kinsale (Ireland), Treguier (France) and back.

↗ **GeoQuest Adventure Race**
www.gar.com.au
A 48-hour nonstop multisport event in New South Wales.

↗ **Manhattan Island Marathon Swim**
www.nycswim.org
Swim 46km to circumnavigate Manhattan.

GO:
NAMIBIA

(ABOVE) ↗
Cracked mud flats
in the Namib Desert
imitate the waves of
the neighbouring South
Atlantic.

(RIGHT) ↗
Caught in the spotlight.
Manta rays wing their
way towards dive lights.

**WHY NOW? COME NOW AND YOU'LL FIND WILDLIFE
BEGINNING TO CLUSTER AROUND DRYING WATERHOLES**

Wedged between the vast Kalahari and the chilly South Atlantic,
Namibia has attractions that are unparalleled anywhere. Stretching more
than 2000km along its central coast is the Namib Desert, with its vast dune
seas and the surprising oasis of Sossusvlei. This large ephemeral pan is set
amid red sand dunes that tower up to 200m above the valley floor. If you
experience a sense of déjà vu here, don't be surprised – Sossusvlei has
appeared in many films and advertisements worldwide, and nearly every
story ever written about Namibia features a photo of it. The best way to get
the measure of this sandy sprawl is to climb a dune, as most people do.

In the south, the immense Fish River Canyon dominates the stark
landscape. Nowhere else in Africa will you find anything quite like this
160km-long chasm. Up to 27km wide, the dramatic inner canyon reaches
a depth of 550m, forming the setting for a trekking treasure little known

↗ DO: NIGHT DIVE WITH MANTA RAYS

COUNTRY USA **TYPE OF ACTIVITY** Diving/ wildlife watching **FITNESS/EXPERTISE LEVEL** Good diving skills recommended. **WHY NOW?** Smooth seas and few storms in June. **DESCRIPTION** Manta Ray Village, located on the Big Island's Kona coast, is the most popular night dive in Hawaii. Night-dive operators shine powerful lights on the water, which attracts plankton, which in turn attracts manta rays. Divers have seen up to 10 mantas 'performing' their spectacular underwater show, though it's more common to find only a couple at a time. Although there is no guarantee that mantas will show up on any particular night, dives during the new moon seem to be the best bets for encounters. Spanish dancers, sleeping parrotfish, sleeping goatfish and beautiful cowries can all also be found here. Manta Ray Village is in the middle of a boat channel and diving here from shore isn't recommended, not only because of possible boat traffic but also because entering the water over the sharp lava rocks can be extremely dangerous.

outside Southern Africa. The 85km Fish River Hiking Trail follows the sandy riverbed past a series of ephemeral pools – in June you'll probably be treated to the river in flow. Due to flash flooding and heat, the route is open only from mid-April to mid-September.

Other hiking routes can be found in the Naukluft Mountains and Waterberg Plateau, and a growing number of private ranches have established wonderful routes for their guests.

Namibia is where you'll also find a 'dead' plant that has lived for 1200 years, fields of apparently lifeless lichen that can be resurrected with a drop of water, and lonely beaches shared by hyenas, gemsboks, flamingos, penguins and sea lions.

Overshadowing everything is Etosha National Park, one of the world's pre-eminent wildlife areas. The name of this vast park means 'Great White Place of Dry Water'. Come now and you'll find wildlife beginning to cluster around drying waterholes. You might observe elephants, giraffes, Burchell's zebras, springboks, red hartebeests, blue wildebeests, gemsboks, elands, kudus, roans, ostriches, jackals, hyenas, lions and even cheetahs and leopards. www.namibiatourism.com.na

DO: **CLIMB ELBRUS**

(ABOVE) ↗
Surprisingly easy to climb, the Colossus of the Caucasus rises 5642m.

(TOP RIGHT) ↗
Sail into the blue off Turkey's coast.

(BOTTOM RIGHT) ↗
Want to bag all of Britain's highest peaks in a single day?

COUNTRY Russia **TYPE OF ACTIVITY** Mountaineering/hiking

FITNESS/EXPERTISE LEVEL Good fitness required.

WHY NOW? The climbing season is from around June to September.

DESCRIPTION If you've long believed that Mont Blanc is the highest mountain in Europe, allow us to introduce you to a peak named Elbrus, on the border of Russia and Georgia. A volcanic cone with two peaks – the western at 5642m and the eastern at 5621m – Elbrus bulges from the Caucasus Ridge, the geographical border between Europe and Asia, and is nearly 1000m above anything else in the vicinity. Its upper slopes are said to be coated in ice up to 200m thick, and numerous glaciers grind down its flanks. Several rivers, including the Kuban, start here.

The climb to Elbrus' summit is not technically difficult, and its beginning is made even easier by the Azau cable car, which rises in two stages, from 2350m to the Mir Bar at 3500m. A chairlift continues to 3800m. You then walk for about 1½ hours – fairly easy but slow because of the altitude and crevasses – up to Camp 11. To stay here in the peak season, you'll need to make arrangements in advance through a tour operator, or contact the rescue post. Staff here may be able to advise you.

Acclimatising at Camp 11, the final assault is made in a day – about eight hours up and eight hours down. Testament to its accessibility is the fact that in the 1980s, the Soviet regime, showing off for propaganda purposes, had groups of up to 400 climbers reaching the peak at one time. The ascent and descent have since been done in many ways: by ski, light aircraft, hang glider and paraglider, as well as by a motorcycle with skis and, in 1997, a Land Rover.

↗ DO: **SAIL THE BLUE VOYAGE**

COUNTRY Turkey **TYPE OF ACTIVITY** Sailing
FITNESS/EXPERTISE LEVEL Sailing experience required for bareboat charter. **WHY NOW?** For a summer sail on the Mediterranean and Aegean Seas. **DESCRIPTION** Between the wars, writer and painter Cevat Şakir Kabaağaç wrote an account of his idyllic sailing excursions along Turkey's southern Aegean and western Mediterranean coasts, an area then untouched by tourism. Kabaağaç called his book *Mavi Yolculuk* (Blue Voyage), a name that has come to represent all sailing journeys along these shores. *Gülets* (wooden yachts) now sail two routes here with great frequency. Most popular is a four day, three-night cruise between Fethiye and Kale (Demre); the less-popular route between Marmaris and Fethiye, also taking four days and three nights, is said by aficionados to be much prettier. Experienced sailors can opt for a bareboat charter and do the crewing (and cooking) themselves. Bareboats sleep between six and 11 passengers. Marmaris and Fethiye are good places to ask around about charters.

↗ DO: **TAKE THE THREE PEAKS CHALLENGE**

COUNTRY Britain **TYPE OF ACTIVITY** Walking/fell running/sailing
FITNESS/EXPERTISE LEVEL Good fitness required. **WHY NOW?** To compete in the Three Peaks Yacht Race. **DESCRIPTION** To drive between the highest peaks in Scotland, England and Wales – Ben Nevis (1344m), Scafell Pike (978m) and Snowdon (1085m) – takes around 10 hours, which helped spawn the idea that all three could be climbed in a single day. Today, it's one of the premier hill challenges in the United Kingdom, embraced as a charity event and coveted by walkers and runners. At a casual pace it's difficult to meet the 24-hour challenge, so you'll need a spring in your step across the ridges. If you want to make things more difficult still, enter the Three Peaks Yacht Race, held this week. Beginning in Barmouth at the foot of Snowdon, teams sail, cycle and run to the three summits, concluding in Fort William beneath Ben Nevis.
www.threepeaksyachtrace.co.uk

↗ DO: **DIVE AT BAZARUTO ARCHIPELAGO**

COUNTRY Mozambique **TYPE OF ACTIVITY** Diving
FITNESS/EXPERTISE LEVEL Come PADI-equipped.
WHY NOW? For the best dive conditions.
DESCRIPTION Mozambique's Bazaruto Archipelago is the quintessential tropical paradise and most people who come here treat it as such by doing little more than lazing on the beaches. But the five main islands of this archipelago also offer clear, turquoise waters filled with colourful fish, with excellent diving and snorkelling. Since 1971 much of the archipelago has been protected as a national park and thanks to this protected status – and to the archipelago's relative isolation from the ravages of war on the mainland – nature bursts forth here in full force. Dolphins swim through the waters, along with 2000 types of fish, plus loggerhead, leatherback and green turtles and, most impressive, elusive dugongs, which spend their days foraging among sea-grass meadows. The wildlife parade doesn't stop in the water. You'll see dozens of bird species, including soaring fish eagles and graceful pink flamingos. There are also red duikers, bushbucks and Nile crocodiles.

↗ **London to Brighton Bike Ride**
www.bhf.org.uk/events
Get lost in the crowd as 27,000 cyclists ride 93km from the capital to the coast.

↗ **Lowe Alpine Mountain Marathon**
www.lamm.co.uk
Spend a night in the Scottish wilds during this two-day mountain run.

↗ **Comrades Marathon**
www.comrades.com
Run about 90km in this South African ultramarathon between Durban and Pietermaritzburg; the 'big five' here are hills.

↗ **National 24 Hour Challenge**
www.n24hc.org
Quite simply, cycle as far as you can through Michigan in 24 hours; 809km if you fancy the record.

GO: BOVEC,
SLOVENIA

(ABOVE) ↗
It's like shooting through
a washing machine.

(RIGHT) ↗
Adrenaline junkies unite
for BASE jumping.

**WHY NOW? COME AS SUMMER SHRUGS THE ALPS FREE OF
SNOW, AND PUMPS WATER INTO THE SOČA RIVER**

Aspiring to become a Queenstown of the north, the small
Slovenian town of Bovec has a great deal to offer adventure-sports
enthusiasts. With the Julian Alps above, the Soča River below and Triglav
National Park at the back door, you could spend a week propelling yourself
through the outdoors without ever doing the same thing twice.

There are up to a dozen adventure companies organising all kinds of
sporting activities in Bovec, including ice and rock climbing, skydiving,
potholing, bungee jumping and, in winter, sleighing. But the holy
adventuring trinity here is undoubtedly rafting, hiking and skiing.
The rafting season on the beautiful 96km-long Soča River runs from April
to October. Rapids on this river, which is coloured a deep, almost unreal,
turquoise, range from easy to extreme (grades one to six). Rafting trips
last for about 1½ hours and cover a distance of 10km. You can also go it

COUNTRY Norway **TYPE OF ACTIVITY**
BASE jumping **FITNESS/EXPERTISE LEVEL**
Minimum of 20 BASE jumps required.
WHY NOW? To witness (and participate in)
Extremesports Week. **DESCRIPTION** The town
of Voss, 100km east of Bergen, is the de facto
capital of Norway's Hardangerfjord region and
also one of Norway's adventure hotspots. In
the final week of June it hosts Extremesports
Week, which attracts adrenaline junkies with
a range of activities and competitions, with
most events open to public participation. Most
notable of the events is a BASE jump from
the 350m Nebbet cliff, open to experienced
jumpers – this imposing cliff is not a place to
indulge your curiosity about BASE jumping.
Other activities in Extremesports Week
include rafting, climbing, mountain biking,
skydiving and paragliding. Even if you miss
Extremesports Week, Voss' cliff-lined fjords
offer great BASE jumping, though they're all
suited only to experienced leapers.
www.ekstremsportveko.com

solo by hiring canoes or kayaks and doing what you
can to keep your nose pointed straight in the rapids.

Hikes out of Bovec range from a two-hour stroll
south to Čezsoča and the protected gravel deposits
in the Soča, to an ascent of Rombon (2208m), five
hours away. The most popular walk in the area is
to Boka Waterfall, 5.5km southwest of Bovec. The
waterfall drops 106m from the Kanin Mountains
into the valley and is almost 30m wide – it's an
impressive sight, especially now with the last of the
snowmelt.

Paragliders need not go without in Bovec, with
the best offering being from the Mangrt Saddle
(2072m) between June and September. Skiiers who
feel they've long missed the season are closer than
they imagine. The Kanin ski centre in the mountains
northwest of Bovec has runs up to 2200m – the only
real altitude alpine skiing in Slovenia. As a result, the
season can be long, with good spring skiing in April
and even May. It has 17km of pistes and a similar
amount of cross-country runs. www.bovec.si

↗ JUNE
WEEK.04

(ABOVE) ↗
Conquer Britain from toe to top, and celebrate at John o'Groats with a bottle of bubbly.

(TOP RIGHT) ↗
Hang 10 in Munich during the river-surfing season.

(BOTTOM RIGHT) ↗
It takes nerves of steel to scale the two-horned Svolværgeita (Svolvær Goat).

DO: CYCLE END TO END

COUNTRY Britain **TYPE OF ACTIVITY** Cycle touring

FITNESS/EXPERTISE LEVEL Moderate fitness required.

WHY NOW? The weather favours a summer ride, with June the best month for quiet roads.

DESCRIPTION Travelling from Land's End to John o'Groats – from the extreme southwest tip to the northeast corner of the British mainland – is an ambition harboured by many, and a route cycled by around 3000 people every year. It can be cycled along numerous routes, most totalling around 1600km in length. The Cyclists' Touring Club (www.ctc.org.uk) produces a route information pack for end-to-enders, available as a download (to club members) on the website.

Most cyclists do the trip in two to three weeks, though if you're short on time the record stands at a smidge over 41 hours. If you're not hurried, make provisions to stretch it out a little – Land's End to John o'Groats may be the United Kingdom's epic ride but there's plenty to enjoy, with the possibility of riding past places such as Dartmoor, Glastonbury, Cheddar Gorge, the Lake District and Loch Ness, and across some gruelling Grampians passes.

For the most favourable conditions, begin in Land's End and ride to John o'Groats (even if heading south to north is psychologically uphill – at least if you believe north is higher than south). Riding in this direction, the winds are more likely to be favourable and there'll be no riding into the midday sun.

Raising money for charity is very common among end-to-enders – it's estimated that around 80% of those undertaking the trip (most of them locals) are doing it in aid of a charity.

↗ DO: **SURF IN MUNICH**

COUNTRY Germany **TYPE OF ACTIVITY** River surfing
FITNESS/EXPERTISE LEVEL Basic surfing skills required.
WHY NOW? Time your visit to coincide with the Munich Surf Open.
DESCRIPTION Landlocked Munich hasn't let geography get in the way of
a good surf. At the southern tip of the Englischer Garten, in the centre of
the city, there's an artificially created wave located in a deep-chilled creek
known as the Eisbach, where surfers practise their moves. The sport was
introduced here after WWII by an American GI who knew how to cruise on
a primitive waxed plank, and is now an inland fix for those who can't bear
the thought of being hundreds of kilometres from a decent wave. A little
further out from town you'll find a gentler standing wave just a stroll from
the tents at popular Campingplatz Thalkirchen. In the last week of June
the Eisbach wave hosts the Munich Surf Open, the conclusion to the river
surfing season.

↗ DO: **CLIMB SVOLVÆRGEITA**

COUNTRY Norway **TYPE OF ACTIVITY** Rock climbing **FITNESS/EXPERTISE**
LEVEL Climbing experience (and a head for heights) required. **WHY**
NOW? Who wants to climb this far north at any time other than summer?
DESCRIPTION The small but modern port town of Svolvær is as busy as it
gets on Norway's Lofoten Islands, and much of the activity centres on a
pinnacle of rock. Svolværgeita, (the Svolvær Goat), is one of the symbols
of Lofoten, a distinctive two-pronged peak that towers above the town.
Climbing it is claimed as one of Norway's great adrenaline rushes, not so
much for the climb but for the challenge once you reach its top. Having
scaled the Goat, it's almost compulsory that you then jump from one
'horn' to the other. Nearly anyone can get to the base of Svolværgeita, but
reaching the horns, Storhornet and Lillehornet, requires a 40m technical
climb before you make the 1.5m jump between them, a leap made even
more difficult after a section of rock fell away in 2008. www.lofoten.info

↗ DO: **GOBI MARCH**

COUNTRY China **TYPE OF ACTIVITY** Endurance running **FITNESS/**
EXPERTISE LEVEL Superior fitness and endurance required. **WHY NOW?**
To race through a vast Asian desert. **DESCRIPTION** A week-long run
through the Gobi Desert in the Chinese province of Xīnjiāng. Each day
you'll run or walk between 20km and 80km, covering a total of 250km
across ankle-twisting rock, through slot canyons and over 300m-high
dunes at altitudes certain to suck the oxygen from your lungs and energy
from your thighs. As a bonus prize you can expect seasonal sand storms
and temperatures nudging beyond the century (38°C). You'll also be almost
fully self-reliant, carrying your own food, clothes and equipment – water
and tents are supplied. Sound like a bundle of fun?
www.racingtheplanet.com/gobimarch

↗ **Tal-total**
www.taltotal.de (in German)
Cyclist heaven, with 60km of highway closed
along the Rhine River for a day of pedalling.

↗ **Rat Race Bristol Urban Adventure**
www.ratraceadventure.com
Adventure race through the city of Bristol;
your chance to cycle down stairways or
abseil from buildings.

↗ **RAW Scandinavia**
http://scandinavia.runacrosstheworld.com/
Nonstop 177km run along Sweden's famed
Kungsleden trail; 46-hour time limit.

↗ **Lapland Ultra**
www.laplandultra.nu
A 100km run through the midnight sun
of northern Sweden.

↗ JUMP

In 1987 a New Zealander named AJ Hackett leaped from the Eiffel Tower with an elastic rope tied around his ankles. It was another 'one small step, one giant leap' moment, introducing the world to a seemingly crazy pursuit named bungee jumping.

Hackett was not the first to jump like this. On the Vanuatu island of Pentecost (p64-5), locals have been leaping from towers, their feet tied to vines, for centuries to try to ensure decent yam crops. Inspired by this *naghol* (land diving), the Oxford University Dangerous Sports Club tinkered with bungee jumping during the 1970s. But it was Hackett and his audacious, illegal leap from the Eiffel Tower that popularised the activity.

The world's first commercial bungee jump was established at the Kawarau Suspension Bridge in Queenstown, New Zealand (p6-7), in 1988, offering a 43m leap towards the glacial waters of the Kawarau River. That pioneering jump site continues in business today but it's far from alone, with hundreds of bungee jump opportunities now sprinkled around the world. At the upper end, they well and truly dwarf the original Kawarau leap.

The world's highest commercial bungee jump is from the Macau Tower, with bungee jumpers leaping 233m towards Macau's sea of casinos. Once a year, at the Go Fast! Games in Canon City, Colorado, even this is eclipsed with a bungee cord set up on the Royal Gorge Bridge (the world's highest suspension bridge), a massive 321m above the river bed.

Before the Macau Tower jump opened in 2006, highest honours went to the 220m-high jump at Verzasca Dam (p89) – if it was Hackett that brought notoriety to bungee jumping, it was this dam that produced its cinematic fame when James Bond plunged from Verzasca's lip in the movie *GoldenEye*.

Bungee jumping's evolution continues apace. Not only can you leap from bridges, city towers and concrete dams, but also from cliff tops at Puerto Vallarta in Mexico; from a parasail (p137) in the Norwegian fjord town of Voss; and from a cable car in the activity's ancestral home of Queenstown (p6-7). Most insanely of all, you can jump from a helicopter into the smoking crater of a Chilean volcano (p191).

For those who want the jump but not the elastic, there's the major step up into BASE jumping. An acronym for Buildings, Antennas, Spans and Earth – the four types of fixed objects you can leap from – BASE jumping is, simply put, like skydiving without the plane or the altitude. BASE jumpers leap from bridges, buildings and cliffs, freefalling for seconds before deploying their parachutes. The highest BASE jump was made in 2006 by two Australians, who leaped from the 6604m summit of Meru Peak in northern India. BASE jumping's dangers (more than 130 people have been killed in the last 20 years) have led to it being banned at many locations, with a lot of its most memorable leaps being made illegally, such as a 2008 BASE jump from the Burj Dubai, the world's tallest building.

Legal jumping sites include the fjord cliffs around Voss (p101) and at events such as Colorado's Go Fast! Games and Bridge Day (p167) in the West Virginian town of Fayetteville – on this one day, 450 BASE jumpers pile over the edge of the New River Gorge Bridge. If you prefer just to sample BASE jumping with a little security attached, Auckland's Skyjump (p187) offers a cable-controlled leap of nearly 200m that has you plummeting for about 20 seconds towards the rooftops of the city.

WEEK.01

GO:
GREENLAND

[ABOVE] ↗
Experience endless ice, infinite space, clear Arctic air and year-round winter sports.

[RIGHT] ↗
Don't get bogged down with life in the office. Instead, jump into a 60m-long mud trench and get snorkelling.

WHY NOW? IN THIS ARCTIC LAND, SPRING BEGINS IN JULY; WATCH AS THE FLOWERS BURST THROUGH THE MELTING SNOWS

The world's largest island (2.1 million sq km) has vast swathes of beautiful, unfenced wilderness that give adventurers unique freedom to wander at will whether on foot, by ski or by dog-sled.

Greenland's dominant feature is its ice cap, the world's second-largest, covering around 80% of the island and so heavy that Greenland's interior has sunk into an immense concave basin depressed just below sea level. Very experienced cross-country skiers can emulate Fridtjof Nansen and join expeditions across the ice cap, organised every year by a couple of expedition tour companies. With just white infinity ahead for three exhausting weeks, some claim it's like meditation, others that it's wanton masochism. Some crossings are accompanied by dog-sled, on others you drag your own supplies. If you cross the ice cap in the far south the chore

↗ **DO: BOG TRIATHLON**

COUNTRY Wales **TYPE OF ACTIVITY** Bog snorkelling/triathlon **FITNESS/EXPERTISE LEVEL** Good fitness for a good placing. **WHY NOW?** The mud is ready. **DESCRIPTION** There is evolution in the bog. What began as the pretty basic sport of bog snorkelling has grown a couple of extra legs to become an annual triathlon through the mud. Competitors in this event at the Waen Rhydd Bog – the Wembley or Madison Square Garden of bog sports – must run 12km, mountain bike 30km and, in between, snorkel two lengths of the 60m-long mud trench in Waen Rydd Bog. Come a day earlier and you can also compete in the World Mountain Bike Bog Snorkelling Championship, racing on lead-filled bikes with water-filled tyres through a 1.8m-deep trench of mud. Racers wear a weight belt to stop them floating off the bike and a snorkel so they can breathe while in the muck. www.green-events.co.uk

is much shorter (though still very tough) and can be combined with trekking through more aesthetically appealing landscapes.

Away from the ice cap, Greenland offers some of the world's most marvellous trekking for those seeking a total-wilderness experience. Except for a few farm tracks in South Greenland, almost all walking is on unmarked routes. Views are magnificent and the purity of light is magical, with a profound silence generally broken only by ravens, trickling streams or the reverberating thuds of exploding icebergs.

Kayakers will find themselves in something of a paddling heartland, though if you've never kayaked before this is not the place to start. Greenland *qajaq*

are the precursors of modern kayaks and few places in the world are more mind-bogglingly beautiful for sea kayaking than Greenland's inner fjords. Great accessible areas to paddle include Tasermiut Fjord, Nuup Kangerlua and the sheltered sounds around Aasiaat. The Ilulissat area is also superb but perhaps a little too crowded with icebergs. One-way drop-off rentals mean the lovely Narsaq-to-Narsarsuaq route is especially popular.

For traditional rock climbing, Greenland's southern tip is a remarkable paradise of nearly pristine vertical granite. Walls and spires, many still unclimbed, rival those of Yosemite or Patagonia, yet are unusually accessible once you have a boat. www.greenland-guide.gl

[ABOVE] ↗
Wilderness and white
water await in Canada's
far north.

[TOP RIGHT] ↗
Lights out, goodnight.
Sleep in a cold hole on a
hot summer's night.

[BOTTOM RIGHT] ↗
Do red bobsleds go
faster on the
Innsbruck track?

DO: PADDLE THE SOUTH NAHANNI

COUNTRY Canada **TYPE OF ACTIVITY** Canoeing/kayaking

FITNESS/EXPERTISE LEVEL Grade-four experience if paddling independently.

WHY NOW? The river is navigable from June to September, with July the warmest month (17˚C average in Fort Simpson).

DESCRIPTION Perched just below the Arctic Circle, Nahanni National Park Reserve – Canada's first World Heritage–listed site – is a wild place that embraces its namesake, the epic South Nahanni River. Untamed and pure-blooded, the river tumbles more than 500km through the jagged Mackenzie Mountains, including a 125m drop over 200m-wide Virginia Falls. You can't get to the park by road, yet each year about 1000 people visit. Half of them are paddlers on epic white-water expeditions.

Paddling trips on the South Nahanni begin at either Rabbitkettle Lake or below Virginia Falls, simply because that's where planes can land. For the 118km from Rabbitkettle to the falls, the river meanders placidly through broad valleys. After the falls, it's another 252km to Blackstone Territorial Park, first through steep-sided, turbulent canyons and then along the broad Liard River. Moose, wolves, grizzly bear, Dall sheep and mountain goats patrol the landscape. The lower-river trip requires seven to 10 days. From Rabbitkettle it's around 14 days.

If you plan to paddle independently, you should be a capable white-water paddler (in grade-four rapids). This is no pleasure float; people have died here. Canoes are best for people with basic experience; rafts are more relaxing and are suitable for all ages. If you intend to paddle with an outfitter, trips should be prebooked, preferably months in advance.

A list of accredited outfitters is available at the park website: http://www.pc.gc.ca/pn-np/nt/nahanni. To access the park independently, you'll need to charter an airplane by contacting a flightseeing company.

⤴ DO: **OVERNIGHT IN HELL'S HOLE**

COUNTRY Switzerland **TYPE OF ACTIVITY** Caving
FITNESS/EXPERTISE LEVEL Not required.
WHY NOW? Escape the summer heat underground.
DESCRIPTION Want an adventure you can do indoors…kind of? In central
Switzerland's Muotha valley, Hoelloch – or Hell's Hole – is one of the
world's longest cave systems, said to contain almost 200km of tunnels
and chambers. A big hole requires a big commitment, and here you can
not only do the usual spelunking exploration, you can also sleep the night.
Bivouac tours into the cave last for two or three days, which are spent
exploring the cave system, while nights are spent bedded down in a
bivouac, though in this darkness who can tell the difference between night
and day? Come rugged up; the cave temperature is a constant 6°C.
www.trekking.ch

⤴ DO: **SUMMER BOBSLED AT IGLS**

COUNTRY Austria **TYPE OF ACTIVITY** Bobsledding
FITNESS/EXPERTISE LEVEL Not required.
WHY NOW? Summer bobsled runs begin this week (running until early
September). **DESCRIPTION** In 1976 the Olympic Winter Games journeyed
to the Austrian city of Innsbruck where, high above the city in the ski
resort of Igls, a bobsled track snaked like plumbing across the Alpine
slopes. A few days of competition and the world moved on, ostensibly
leaving Igls and its bobsled track to slide into history. After all, what does
a city do with a slightly used bobsled track? In the case of Innsbruck and
Igls, it throws it open to the public. Bobsled runs behind professional
drivers quickly became a winter favourite in the Tyrolean city. And more
recently, summer visitors to Innsbruck have also been able to climb
aboard bobsleds, with wheels replacing runners for two months of the
year. What's unchanged is the speed and the G-force thrill of banking and
bending through a 1270m blur of Alpine country.
www.knauseder-event.at

⤴ DO: **SWIM THE ENGLISH CHANNEL**

COUNTRIES England and France **TYPE OF ACTIVITY** Swimming
FITNESS/EXPERTISE LEVEL Strong swimming ability and
endurance required.
WHY NOW? Be first out of the blocks on the Channel swimming season,
which runs from July to September. **DESCRIPTION** Sure, you can cross
the English Channel by ferry or Chunnel, but why not swim across to the
Continent? Cover yourself in grease (the water temperature is only about
15°C), dive into the sea at Shakespeare's Cliff near Dover, roll your arms
over for 32km, then step onto French soil at Cap Gris Nez to complete the
world's classic marathon swim. You won't be alone in the Channel, since
you'll be accompanied by a registered pilot and you'll pass through one of
the world's busiest shipping lanes, with around 600 tankers alone using
the Channel each day. If you think you're quick, the record time is just
under seven hours. Only swims registered with the Channel Swimming
Association are recognised as official Channel crossings.
www.channelswimmingassociation.com

⤴ **Wife-Carrying World Championships**
www.sonkajarvi.fi
Carry your wife (or somebody else's) through
a 253m obstacle course to win her weight in
beer; in Finland.

⤴ **Explore Sweden Monster**
www.exploresweden.se
One of the world's longest (1060km) and most
varied - trekking, mountaineering, kayaking,
hydrospeed, rafting, zip-lining, mountain
biking, in-line skating and rappelling –
adventure races.

⤴ **BC Bike Race**
www.bcbikerace.com
Seven-day singletrack mountain-bike dash
from Vancouver to Whistler.

GO: **KAMCHATKA PENINSULA, RUSSIA**

(ABOVE) ↗
Far from the beaten
track, spectacular
Kamchatka is blessed
with an abundance
of volcanoes and wild
animals.

(RIGHT) ↗
Enduring love in Death
Valley – one last kiss
before facing the world's
toughest foot race.

**WHY NOW? KAMCHATKA DANGLES JUST BELOW THE
ARCTIC CIRCLE; COME IN MIDSUMMER FOR ENDLESS DAYS
AND THE FINEST WEATHER**

Closer to Los Angeles than Moscow, and dubbed the 'land of fire and ice',
Kamchatka is one of Russia's least-explored but most spectacular regions.
A 1000km-long peninsula separated from the mainland by the Sea of
Okhotsk, this hyperactive volcanic land bubbles, spurts and spews in a
manner that suggests Creation hasn't yet finished. The region claims more
than 200 volcanoes in varying degrees of activity. Some are long extinct
and grassed over, with aquamarine crater lakes, while 20 or more rank
among the world's most volatile.

The volcanoes are often surrounded by lava fields, and these lunar-like
cinder landscapes served as the testing grounds for Russia's moon
vehicles. The thermal activity deep below the earth's surface also
produces numerous hot springs, heated rivers and geysers. The most

↗ DO: BADWATER ULTRAMARATHON

COUNTRY USA **TYPE OF ACTIVITY**
Ultramarathon **FITNESS/EXPERTISE LEVEL**
Supreme fitness and endurance required.
WHY NOW? To discover that madness is a
foot race. **DESCRIPTION** Billed as the world's
toughest foot race, the Badwater Ultramarathon
puts the 'deathly' back into Death Valley.
Beginning at Badwater, the lowest point in the
Western Hemisphere (85m below sea level)
in Death Valley's navel, the race crosses three
mountain ranges to the Mt Whitney Portals,
the trailhead to the summit of the highest peak
in the contiguous United States. Not content
to inflict 217km of running and 4000m of
ascent on its competitors, the race is held in
midsummer, a time when Death Valley once
suffered the second-highest temperature on
record: 56.7˚C. If you're still keen, you must
pass a rigorous selection process. All applicants
are ranked on a scale of zero to 10, according
to their previous ultramarathon achievements,
with the 90 highest-ranked runners accepted
into the race. www.badwater.com

spectacular examples are found in the Valley of the Geysers, where around 200 fumaroles sporadically blast steam, mud and water from the canyon floor.

Away from the volcanoes, Kamchatka is covered by large areas of mixed forest and plains of giant grasses that are home to a vast array of wildlife, including between 10,000 and 20,000 brown bears and the sable, the animal that provided much of the impetus for early Russian explorations of the peninsula.

The entry point to Kamchatka is the town of Petropavlovsk-Kamchatsky, which is reasonably well served by air from other parts of Russia. It's possible to hike up mountains Avachinskaya and Koryakskaya, the two volcanoes that loom over Petropavlovsk-

Kamchatsky. An ascent of Avachinskaya should take about four to six hours, and you should watch for fissures in the glaciers, high winds and the thick fog that often covers the steep upper slopes in the late afternoon. Koryakskaya is more difficult and shouldn't be attempted by inexperienced climbers.

The Valley of the Geysers is 150km north of Petropavlovsk-Kamchatsky but is an expensive excursion as the only access is by helicopter, and special permission is required. If you go, the best place to touch down is the otherworldly Uzon Caldera, a 10km crater that features steaming lakes, enormous mushrooms and prolific berry bushes that are well-attended by bears.

[ABOVE] ↗
Need some motivation
for your morning run?
Head to Pamplona
for Sanfermines.

[TOP RIGHT] ↗
Hold onto your hat –
the Ring Racer has
twice the acceleration
of an F1 car.

[BOTTOM RIGHT] ↗
Rough-riding the
Bitches is not for
the faint-hearted.

DO: RUN WITH THE BULLS, PAMPLONA

COUNTRY Spain **TYPE OF ACTIVITY** Adventure travel/sprinting for your life
FITNESS/EXPERTISE LEVEL Bull-dodging skills handy.
WHY NOW? The bulls are about to be released.

DESCRIPTION In the Basque city of Pamplona, all hell breaks loose as Spain's best-known bull fest, Sanfermines, kick-starts a frenzy of drinking and mayhem. For visitors, the festival is best known for the chance to run with (or, more precisely, run from) the bulls as they charge through the city to the bullring.

Every morning from 7 July to 14 July, six bulls are let loose from the Coralillos de Santo Domingo to charge across the square of the same name (a good vantage point if you're not running). They continue up the street, veering onto Calle de los Mercaderes from Plaza Consistorial and then onto Calle de la Estafeta for the final charge to the ring. *Mozos* (the brave or foolish, depending on your point of view) race madly with the bulls, aiming to keep close – but not too close. The total course is 850m long and lasts a little over three minutes.

The majority of those who run are full of bravado (and/or drink), but have little idea what they're doing. It's difficult to recommend this activity, but plenty of people (mostly Spaniards) participate anyway. Try to run with someone experienced, and above all don't get caught near bulls that have been separated from the herd – a lone, frightened 500kg bull surrounded by charging humans makes for an unpredictable and dangerous animal. Keeping ahead of the herd is the general rule. As part of your preparation, familiarise yourself with the course.

To participate, you must enter the course before 7.30am from Plaza de Santo Domingo and take up your position. Around 8am two rockets are fired: the first announces that the bulls have been released from the corrals; the second lets you know they're all out and running. www.pamplona.net

↗ DO: RIDE THE WORLD'S FASTEST ROLLERCOASTER

COUNTRY Germany **TYPE OF ACTIVITY** Rollercoaster
FITNESS/EXPERTISE LEVEL Not required.
WHY NOW? To coincide with the German Formula One Grand Prix at the venue.
DESCRIPTION In July, Germany's Nurburgring hosts the fastest drivers in the world at the German Formula One Grand Prix, but from 2010 they will no longer be the fastest people at the track. What blows the doors off the F1 cars (if they had doors) is Ring Racer, the world's fastest rollercoaster, beginning and ending beside the track's start/finish line and reaching a speed of 217km/h in just 2.5 seconds – or about twice the acceleration of an F1 car. Watch this space, however. On Abu Dhabi's Yas Island – also the scene of a Formula One Grand Prix – the new Ferrari World indoor theme park is aspiring to surpass Ring Racer for the title of world's fastest rollercoaster. www.nuerburgring.de/en/ringwerk/ringracer.html

↗ DO: KAYAK THE BITCHES

COUNTRY Wales **TYPE OF ACTIVITY** White-water kayaking
FITNESS/EXPERTISE LEVEL Superior kayaking skills required.
WHY NOW? If you're going to roll in the Welsh sea, do it in summer.
DESCRIPTION As the daily tide rolls in across a line of reef and rock between Ramsey Island and the Welsh mainland, it creates a tidal race that has become a favourite with rough-riding kayakers. Named for its habit of destroying ships, the Bitches can create standing waves up to 3m in height as the tide rushes in and over the shallow reef. Kayakers surf the waves or perform manoeuvres (what's known as playboating) in the holes created around the waves. The Bitches are about 800m off the coast of St Justinian, and most kayakers set out three hours before high tide for their piece of water rodeo. To even contemplate tackling the Bitches, you should be competent in grade-four water.

↗ DO: CYCLE THE DANUBE TRAIL

COUNTRIES Germany, Austria and Slovakia **TYPE OF ACTIVITY** Cycle touring **FITNESS/EXPERTISE LEVEL** Not required.
WHY NOW? Enjoy summer sun as you pedal through Central Europe.
DESCRIPTION Following the Danube River for more than 365km from Passau to Bratislava, the Danube Path is perhaps Europe's most popular bike route. The path is flat, the scenery (especially in the Wachau region) impressive and most towns and hotels cater well to cyclists. For most of the journey you ride along Europe's second-longest river on dedicated bike paths. Many cyclists ride only between Passau and Vienna, allowing six comfortable days to cross through northern Austria. Free booklets are available along the way, but for something with more detail, pick up Esterbauer's *Danube Bike Trail*, which contains maps, instructions and a smattering of practical tourist information.

↗ **International Climbers' Festival**
www.climbersfestival.org
Head to Lander, Wyoming, for lectures, tips, slide shows and a bit of climbing.

↗ **Fireweed 400**
www.fireweed400.com
Cycle 640km through wilderness Alaska, climbing 8500m...about the height of Everest.

↗ **Gigathlon**
www.gigathlon.ch (in German and French)
Race 320km in 24 hours by cycling, mountain biking, swimming, in-line skating and running.

GO:
FRENCH ALPS

(ABOVE) ↗
A whirr of wheels and a
blur of lycra herald the
heroes of Le Tour.

(RIGHT) ↗
Southern exposure –
taking snow angels
to the extreme.

WHY NOW? FOR A FEW DAYS IN MID-JULY THE TOUR DE FRANCE ROLLS INTO THE FRENCH ALPS

The French Alps form the highest and most spectacular mountains in Western Europe. Their icy spikes, needles and snowy peaks have inspired Roman generals, Romantic poets and madcap mountaineers alike, and for a few days in the middle of July they inspire the world's greatest cyclists.

When the Tour de France rolls its annual show into the French Alps, most everything else is forgotten. Pelotons grind out enormous climbs, then plummet like bobsledders, reaching speeds approaching 100km/h. In the hours before they arrive you can see what all the sweat is about by riding the climbs ahead of the racers (or you can just join the majority and paint riders' names across the road).

The climb that defines the Tour's Alpine stages is the Alpe d'Huez. This 13.8km lung-searing climb has an average grade of 8.5%, includes 21

↗ DO: JOIN THE 300 CLUB

CONTINENT Antarctica **TYPE OF ACTIVITY** Nude ice running **FITNESS/EXPERTISE LEVEL** Willingness to be very cold required. **WHY NOW?** When else will it hit -73˚C (-100˚F)? **DESCRIPTION** If you ever find yourself wintering at the South Pole station, keep a careful eye on the thermometer because when it hits -73˚C (-100˚F) you'll have the opportunity for an outdoor experience about which very few people can boast. After steaming in a 93°C (200°F) sauna, you run naked (but for shoes) out of the station onto the snow. Some people push on even further, going around the Ceremonial Pole. While some claim that the rime of flash-frozen sweat acts as insulation, if you fall, the ice against your reddened skin will feel as rough as rock. Induction into the club requires photographic documentation. On completion, you join the elite in the 300 Club, so named for the 300˚F drop in temperature between the sauna and the Pole.

numbered hairpin bends and is ranked *hors categorie* (above categorisation, ie *very* steep). The day the Tour visits Alpe d'Huez is a grand celebration of people, colour and sounds. Nearly 500,000 fans line the route, in touching distance of the riders in most places. Preceding this, a snake of chrome and colour inches its way to the summit as hundreds of riders painstakingly make their way to the top. Enthusiastic French spectators are usually on hand to dole out free samples of *pastis* (a liqueur) to kick riders along.

What the Alpe d'Huez is to cyclists, the Chamonix Valley is to hikers, who have their own tour of sorts. The 10-day Tour du Mont Blanc passes along the northern side of the Chamonix Valley and circuits the Alps' highest mountain in one of the world's top

treks. Elsewhere in the valley, more than 300km of trails provide opportunities for walks of all difficulties. The extremely rugged Aiguilles Rouges provide some of Chamonix's classic routes, while the Grand Balcon Nord and the Montagne de la Côte take walkers as high into the mountains as they can go without becoming mountaineers.

The French Alps are at their busiest and best during July and August, when the popular trails attract tremendous numbers of walkers.

[ABOVE] ↗
Take a hike and
tackle the Munros,
Corbetts and Donalds
of Scotland.

[TOP RIGHT] ↗
Take two wheels to
the top of challenging
Khardung La.

[BOTTOM RIGHT] ↗
Glide through pristine
waters as 'Eric' gets
behind your sails.

DO: **BAG SOME MUNROS**

COUNTRY Scotland **TYPE OF ACTIVITY** Hiking

FITNESS/EXPERTISE LEVEL Good fitness and endurance required if climbing all 283 peaks.

WHY NOW? Summer is the most practical time to be bagging Munros.

DESCRIPTION In 1891 Sir Hugh Munro, a member of the recently founded Scottish Mountaineering Club (SMC), published a list of more than 500 Scottish summits over 900m (3000ft), a height at which they apparently became 'real' mountains. Sir Hugh differentiated between 283 'mountains in their own right' (those with a significant drop on all sides or well clear of the next peak) and their satellites, now known as 'tops'. In 1901 all of the 'Munros' were climbed for the first time, initiating a pastime known as Munro bagging. This has grown to a national passion – there are books, CD-ROMs and even a Munro board game.

Munro's original list has since been revised by the SMC and, after revision in September 2009, again totals 283 summits, all of which are located north of the Highland Boundary Fault, which runs from Stonehaven, on the west coast, to Helensburgh, west of Glasgow on the shore of Gare Loch. More than 4000 people have completed the full round of Munro summits, thus earning themselves the title of Munroist.

For some, the elongated task of ticking off all 283 summits is not enough: the full round has been completed in less than 49 days; they've been done in a single winter; and they've been walked in alphabetical and height order. And once you've bagged all the Munros, there are other collections of summits you might want to tackle: the Corbetts (Scottish 'hills' over 762m/2500ft with a drop of at least 152m/500ft on all sides) and the Donalds (lowland 'hills' over 610m/2000ft). Rack them all up together and you have an outing of more than 500 peaks. That ought keep you busy for a summer. www.smc.org.uk

↗ DO: RIDE TO KHARDUNG LA

COUNTRY India **TYPE OF ACTIVITY** Cycling/motorcycling
FITNESS/EXPERTISE LEVEL Good fitness and acclimatisation required.
WHY NOW? It's a short snow-free season at 5600m.
DESCRIPTION Winding into the Himalaya from the Ladakhi city of Leh, the road to Khardung La (5602m) is the highest motorable road in the world (though there's now contention that the pass might only be around 5300m and pumped up for the purposes of claiming the title of 'highest'), which has made it a favourite challenge among cyclists and motorcyclists. The pass is occupied by a grubby military camp and stacks of oil drums, but none of this detracts from gawking at the distant vistas and the thrill of cycling to the highest point you're ever likely to take a bike. Nor will it help the inevitable altitude aches, even if you have spent a few days acclimatising in Leh, 2100m below. The road is open for one-way traffic only: Leh to Khardung La in the morning and Khardung La to Leh in the afternoon.

↗ DO: WINDSURF AT VASILIKI BAY

COUNTRY Greece **TYPE OF ACTIVITY** Windsurfing
FITNESS/EXPERTISE LEVEL Wind and waves to suit all levels.
WHY NOW? 'Eric' is a summer creature.
DESCRIPTION Windsurfing is the most popular water sport in Greece, and little wonder when Vasiliki Bay, on the south coast of the Ionian island of Lefkada, is considered *the* place to windsurf in Europe. Nor are conditions here elitist, with many people reckoning that Vasiliki Bay is one of the best places in the world to learn the sport. You'll find a wide, sheltered bay just waiting for the afternoon winds – known locally as 'Eric' – to blow in. Along the pebbly beach, numerous windsurfing companies have staked prominent claims with flags, equipment and their own hotels. They offer all-inclusive tuition and accommodation packages. If they've got spare gear, some will willingly rent it to the independent enthusiast for a day or two. www.lefkada-greece.biz

↗ DO: SURF AT JEFFREY'S BAY

COUNTRY South Africa **TYPE OF ACTIVITY** Surfing
FITNESS/EXPERTISE LEVEL Surfing learners to the surfing learned.
WHY NOW? June to September is the best time for experienced surfers, with July also bringing the Billabong Pro championship to town.
DESCRIPTION Once a sleepy seaside town, 'J Bay' is now South Africa's foremost centre of surfing and surf culture. Boardies from all over the planet flock here to ride waves such as the famous Supertubes, once described as 'the most perfect wave in the world'. Development is raging at a furious pace in the Eastern Cape town, with clothes shopping almost overtaking surfing as the main leisure activity, but so far the local board-waxing vibe has been retained. Most beachgoers come to J Bay in December and January, handing the strong Atlantic swells to surfers in winter. Keep your eye on the low-pressure systems – anything below 970 millibars and you'll be in heaven. www.gardenroute.co.za

↗ **Transalp Challenge**
www.bike-transalp.de
Eight-stage, 750km mountain-bike race for pros and amateurs, crossing the European Alps from north to south.

↗ **Rocky Mountain 1200**
www.randonneurs.bc.ca
Four-yearly randonnée (2012 and 2016) through the Canadian Rockies; cycle 1200km in 90 hours.

↗ **Vermont 100 Endurance Run**
www.vermont100.com
Run 161 hilly kilometres within 30 hours.

↗ **St Olavsloppet**
www.st-olavsloppet.com
Four-day, 332km relay run from Östersund (Sweden) to Trondheim (Norway).

GO: BALTISTAN,
PAKISTAN

(ABOVE) ↗
A stairway to heaven –
Baltistan's ice highways
lead the way to seven of
the world's 25 highest
summits.

(RIGHT) ↗
He's just checking out
the daily special.

WHY NOW? MID-JUNE TO SEPTEMBER IS THE OPTIMAL
TREKKING SEASON IN BALTISTAN, AND THE ONLY TIME
YOU'LL BE ABLE TO TRAVERSE GLACIERS AND CROSS PASSES

A journey through northern Pakistan is heaven for mountain lovers, a place
where you can walk for days on even the most popular routes without
seeing another trekker. Foremost among the trekking regions is Baltistan,
the centre of the Karakoram's glaciers, peaks and rock towers, where
villages are oases in a vertical wilderness of rock and ice. Five of the
biggest glaciers – Biafo (65km), Baltoro (62km), Chogo Lungma (44km),
Panmah (42km), and Kaberi and Kondus (36km) – offer the longest glacier
traverses outside the sub-polar zones.

The ultimate in Karakoram trekking is to traverse the length of one
of these Karakoram glaciers. Two treks epitomise this experience: the
Hispar La trek to Snow Lake, and the Baltoro Glacier trek to K2 Base
Camp. Both take you up massive ice highways lined with magnificent

COUNTRY South Africa **TYPE OF ACTIVITY** Diving/wildlife watching **FITNESS/EXPERTISE LEVEL** Diving certificate usually required. **WHY NOW?** The sharks are active in their feeding patterns. **DESCRIPTION** Cage diving to view the ocean's fiercest resident, the great white shark, is one way to get your blood flowing faster as you travel through South Africa's Western Cape. Gansbaai's tourist star has risen almost entirely on the basis of cage dives, with nine operators (many of them based in nearby Hermanus) offering the chance to experience what it feels like to be tinned tuna. There's no doubting the activity's popularity, but it doesn't come without controversy. Operators use bait to attract the sharks, so these killer fish are being trained to associate humans with food. It's not a pleasant idea, especially if you're a surfer. While most of the operators require that you have an internationally recognised diving qualification, some allow snorkellers. www.gansbaaiinfo.com/experiences/sharkcage.html

peaks and towers into the very heart of the Karakoram.

The Hispar La is a glaciated pass that links the Biafo and Hispar Glaciers, the Karakoram's second- and fifth-longest glaciers. Together they form the longest continuous stretch of glacier (114km). At the base of the Hispar La is Lukpe Lawo, commonly called Snow Lake, one of the world's largest glacial basins. More than a dozen 7000m peaks tower above these glaciers. To cross this technical pass is to walk through what both Francis Younghusband and HW Tilman called the finest mountain scenery in the world. The trek is extreme in its difficulty, but anyone who takes on the challenge is awed by the experience of travelling in this glacial wilderness.

Baltoro, the Karakoram's third-longest glacier, leads into the most extensively glaciated high mountain terrain on the planet. Seven of the world's 25 highest peaks rise above the glacier, including K2 (8611m), second only to Everest. All along the lower Baltoro Glacier are monumental, sheer rock walls and granite towers – Uli Biaho, the Trangos, the Cathedrals – that draw elite climbers from around the world. The trek is demanding, but is glacier travel at its best. Far and away, it is northern Pakistan's most popular trek.

(ABOVE) ↗
Alaskan brown bears
pick up some takeaway.

(RIGHT) ↗
Hang on tight to those
rusty chains as you
make the perilous trek
up sacred Huá Shān.

DO: WATCH BEARS, MCNEIL RIVER

COUNTRY USA **TYPE OF ACTIVITY** Wildlife watching

FITNESS/EXPERTISE LEVEL Not required.

WHY NOW? July is the prime month for seeing what happens when bear meets fish.

DESCRIPTION The McNeil River State Game Sanctuary, just north of Katmai National Park and Preserve on the Alaska Peninsula and 400km southwest of Anchorage, was created in 1967 to protect the world's largest concentration of brown bears. This spot is renowned among wildlife photographers, and just about every great bear-catches-salmon shot was taken either here or on the Brooks River. Often 20 brown bears will feed together at McNeil River Falls, and up to 72 have congregated here at one time. The majority of the bears congregate 1.5km upstream from the river mouth, where falls slow the salmon, providing an easy meal.

The Alaska Department of Fish and Game has set up a viewing area and allows 10 visitors per day for a four-day period to watch the bears feed. From a camp, park guides lead a 3km hike across sedge flats and through thigh-deep Mikfik Creek to the viewing area on a bluff. There you can watch the bears feed less than 20m away in what is basically a series of rapids and pools where the salmon gather between leaps.

The season begins in June, when viewing is done at Mikfik Creek. Viewing switches to the bigger McNeil River in July, the prime season.

Visits to the sanctuary are by permit only, and these are issued by lottery. Your odds of drawing a permit are less than one in five, so large are the number of applications. For an application, contact the Alaska Department of Fish and Game (www.wildlife.alaska.gov); return it by 1 March. You must come to the sanctuary self-sufficient, with camping equipment and food, and the entry fee, supposing you make it through the ballot, is US$350 for non-Alaskans.

↗ DO: HIKE THE WORLD'S MOST DANGEROUS TREK

COUNTRY China **TYPE OF ACTIVITY** Hiking
FITNESS/EXPERTISE LEVEL Steel for blood an asset.
WHY NOW? Come in the midst of summer for the safest and best conditions.
DESCRIPTION Treks around the globe jostle for the title of world's best, but few aspire to be known as the most dangerous. By design or fluke, that 'honour' seems to have fallen squarely on China's sacred mountain Huá Shān in Shaanxi province, near to the city of Xī'ān. This hike is a high-wire act without a net, scaling a massive cliff face on chains. Huá Shān has five peaks, and it is the route up the South Peak that some suggest claims dozens of lives every year. Planked paths hang precariously from the mountain, with rusting hand chains the only thing holding you to the rock and away from a massive drop from the cliff. This is not the time to get an itchy nose or, worse yet, vertigo. If that all sounds a little too precarious, there's always the cable car.

↗ DO: HIKE ON CROAGH PATRICK

COUNTRY Ireland **TYPE OF ACTIVITY** Hiking/pilgrimage
FITNESS/EXPERTISE LEVEL Basic fitness sufficient.
WHY NOW? Come for Reek Sunday.
DESCRIPTION Croagh Patrick (764m) occupies a special place in Irish tradition as the country's most hallowed place of pilgrimage. It attracts tens of thousands of pilgrims to its summit every year, making it Ireland's most-climbed mountain. It has been a place of pilgrimage since at least the 12th century, and the last Sunday in July – Reek Sunday – is a national day of pilgrimage. It's the mountain's association with Patrick, the best known of Ireland's patron saints, that is Croagh Patrick's glory. It's believed that the saint fasted for 40 days and 40 nights on the mountain, emulating the biblical accounts of Moses and Christ. Legend also has it that Patrick famously evicted Ireland's snakes during his time on the mountain. The climb takes two to three hours, and concludes at the summit chapel.

↗ DO: PADDLE IN POLAND

COUNTRY Poland **TYPE OF ACTIVITY** Canoeing/kayaking
FITNESS/EXPERTISE LEVEL Basic paddling skills required.
WHY NOW? Let the rivers relieve the summer heat.
DESCRIPTION The Polish towns of Augustów and Olsztyn have no great lure for tourism, but they do serve as bases for two great river trips. From Augustów, the most popular of several paddling routes is along the Czarna Hańska River. The traditional route starts at Lake Wigry and follows the river downstream through the Augustów Forest to the Augustów Canal, a trip taking six to eight days. The most spectacular section is the 25km stretch between Frącki and Jałowy Róg. Out of Olsztyn, a 103km route runs along the Krutynia River, beginning at Stanica Wodna PTTK, 50km east of Olsztyn. The trip ends at Ruciane-Nida and is considered Poland's top paddling trip.

↗ **Mongolia Sunrise to Sunset**
www.ultramongolia.com
Immodestly calls itself the world's most beautiful 100km run.

↗ **London-Edinburgh-London (LEL)**
www.londonedinburghlondon.co.uk
The UK's premier randonnée, held every four years (2013, 2017); cycle 1400km within 118 hours.

↗ **Traversée internationale du Lac Saint-Jean**
www.traversee.qc.ca
Plunge into a 32km swimming marathon in Quebec.

↗ **AuSable River Canoe Marathon**
www.ausablecanoemarathon.org
Race a canoe 190km along this Michigan River; expect to take about 16 hours.

GO: IUYBASDVILUB,
ICELAND'S INTERIOR

[ABOVE] ↗
In search of
remoteness? Find it
here in the Land
of Fire and Ice.

[RIGHT] ↗
Only the most intrepid
of 4WDers take on
the challenge of the
Canning, the world's
longest stock route.

WHY NOW? THE INTERIOR IS ONLY REALLY ACCESSIBLE IN JULY AND AUGUST

Iceland's vast, barren interior is one of Europe's great wilderness areas. Gazing across the expanses, you could imagine yourself in Tibet, Mongolia or even on the moon – the Apollo astronauts held training exercises here before the 1969 lunar landings. The interior is only really accessible in July and August, and this is seriously remote country. There are practically no services, accommodation, bridges, mobile-phone signals, and no guarantees if things go wrong. In 2008 much of the area was turned into Europe's largest national park – Vatnajökull National Park – covering 12,000 sq km, or about 11% of Iceland's total land area, swallowing up the existing Skaftafell and Jokulsargljufur National Parks and much of the Vatnajökull icecap.

There are four main routes through the interior – the Kjölur, Sprengisandur, Öskjuleið and Kverkfjöll Routes – and historically, they

↗ DO: DRIVE THE CANNING STOCK ROUTE

COUNTRY Australia **TYPE OF ACTIVITY** 4WDing **FITNESS/EXPERTISE LEVEL** Mechanical knowledge and 4WDing skills vital. **WHY NOW?** The coolest and best time to be on the Canning. **DESCRIPTION** The world's longest and most remote stock route doubles as the most difficult road journey in Australia. Stretching more than 1700km across the arid heart of Western Australia, between Wiluna in the south and Halls Creek in the north, it crosses through uninhabited but vegetated desert country, pushing across more than 800 sand dunes. People have walked the Canning, including the eponymous Alfred Canning, and there have been rare crossings by bicycle, but it's predominantly a route for the hardiest of 4WDers. Travelling the Canning in the Australian summer is suicide. It usually begins to see the first adventurers in late April or early May. By the middle of October the season is coming to a close.

were places of terror to be traversed as quickly as possible. Today they are attracting hardy visitors to such sights as Herðubreið (1682m), Iceland's most distinctive mountain, described variously as a birthday cake, a cooking pot and a lampshade; and Askja, a 50-sq-km caldera created by a colossal explosion of tephra in 1875 and containing Iceland's deepest lake as well as a hot crater lake where the water (around 25°C) is ideal for swimming.

Also here is one of the world's finest, yet least known, trekking routes: the Landmannalaugar to Þórsmörk trek. Usually passable from mid-July to September, most people walk the trail in three to four days, though it can be stretched to six days by continuing to Skógar. The route crosses lava flows and a black pumice desert, passes belching fumaroles, makes foot-numbing stream crossings and offers views of torrential waterfalls. Most trekkers walk from north to south, losing altitude rather than gaining it. There are several huts along the course of the trek, operated by the Iceland Touring Association (Ferðafélag Íslands; www.fi.is), so that you needn't brave Iceland's notoriously ferocious winds in a tent. Due to the trek's popularity, however, it's wise to book and pay hut fees in advance.

Any travel in the interior requires high-clearance 4WD vehicles, and it's recommended that vehicles travel in pairs. www.vatnajokulsthjodgardur.is

[ABOVE] ↗
Kayak alongside magnificent creatures of the deep.

[TOP RIGHT] ↗
If you've ever wanted to windsurf a river, head to Columbia River Gorge.

[BOTTOM RIGHT] ↗
Feast your eyes on wildflowers near the sacred lake of Hem Kund.

DO: **PADDLE WITH ORCAS**

COUNTRY Canada **TYPE OF ACTIVITY** Kayaking/wildlife watching
FITNESS/EXPERTISE LEVEL Not required.
WHY NOW? To get among the orcas as they cruise through Johnstone Strait.

DESCRIPTION With salmon spawning now in full swim along Canada's west coast, a host of creatures follow hungrily behind, including pods of orcas. Whale-watching boats tail along viewing these beautiful animals, but the most intimate way to watch the so-called killer whales is from a kayak. Paddling trips operate in Johnstone Strait, a narrow funnel of water above a canyon-like ocean floor that plunges about 500m below the ocean's surface. At this time of year it is also home to up to 250 resident killer whales, which cruise about picking off salmon as they head for the Fraser River near Vancouver. Orca downtime is spent rubbing their bellies against the pebbly beach in Robson Bight, the only spot in the world where they are known to do this. Paddling into the exclusion zone around the bight is banned, but most multiday kayaking trips base themselves nearby, in view of the whales as they head for the bight. At time the paddling itself is redundant, with the killer whales cruising past camp along the kelp line, just a few metres from the shore.

Most trips use base camps among the rocky beaches and dense forest that plunges to the shores of the strait. From here, there's good kayaking along the Vancouver Island coast or across the strait to islands such as Sophia or West Cracroft. Along the way you might also see Steller sea lions, Dall's porpoises, bald eagles and perhaps even a minke whale, before you bed down to the sound of orcas swimming and surfacing past your tent.

And, fear not. Resident killer whales eat only fish.

↗ DO: **WINDSURF THE COLUMBIA RIVER GORGE**

COUNTRY USA **TYPE OF ACTIVITY** Windsurfing
FITNESS/EXPERTISE LEVEL Beginners to pros.
WHY NOW? The winds are only suitable in summer.
DESCRIPTION In the Columbia River Gorge, forming the border between Oregon and Washington State, the 1.6km-wide river has carved a 1000m-deep chasm through the Cascade Range. What has formed (beyond a spectacular array of waterfalls) is a natural wind tunnel, with 30-knot winds pushing through the gorge from the cool, coastal west in summer. These westerlies, which directly oppose the river's flow, create optimal windsurfing conditions, and are generally strongest at the eastern end of the gorge. Experienced windsurfers head for a couple of heavy-duty sites near Maryhill, while the Wall is a small launch spot that attracts expert windsurfers who can handle huge swells. If you're new to windy ways, you'll find windsurfing schools in the town of Hood River.
www.fs.fed.us/r6/columbia

↗ DO: **HIKE TO THE VALLEY OF FLOWERS**

COUNTRY India **TYPE OF ACTIVITY** Hiking
FITNESS/EXPERTISE LEVEL Moderate fitness required.
WHY NOW? For the valley's full floral display.
DESCRIPTION In 1931 British mountaineer Frank Smythe wandered into the Himalayan Bhyundar Valley to find many hundreds of species of wild flower carpeting the earth. He named the place – and it remains – the Valley of Flowers. Begin trekking from near the Uttaranchal town of Joshimath, a long, uncomfortable drive into the Himalaya from the yoga centre of Rishikesh, and follow the crowded pilgrims' trail towards the holy lake of Hem Kund. Branching away from the trail 6km before the lake, you enter the Valley of Flowers, which is about 10km long and 2km wide. At this time of year it's also a palette of colour. To protect the valley, camping is not allowed, but accommodation is available in Ghangaria, on the Hem Kund path, about 7km from the Valley of Flowers.

↗ DO: **VISIT CHORNOBYL**

COUNTRY Ukraine **TYPE OF ACTIVITY** Adventure travel
FITNESS/EXPERTISE LEVEL Not required.
WHY NOW? Do it in sun not snow.
DESCRIPTION It's the world's weirdest day trip; a visit into the Chornobyl exclusion zone, the site of the world's worst nuclear disaster on 26 April 1986. Tours to the site were launched in 2001 and, despite the inevitable fear factor, most scientists agree that visitors will receive no more radiation in three hours in the exclusion zone than they would on a New York–London flight. The two 'highlights' of the tour are visits to the infamous reactor No 4, where the disaster occurred (you can't go inside without special permission and a special protective suit) and the ghost town of Prypyat, still home to around 350 people.

↗ **RAW Britain**
http://britain.runacrosstheworld.com/
Six-day, 320km run through the Scottish Highlands.

↗ **Descenso Internacional del Sella**
www.descensodelsella.com
Race a canoe 20km down the Sella River in northern Spain.

↗ **Avon Descent**
www.avondescent.com.au
Paddling and power-dinghy race along 134km of Western Australia's Avon and Swan Rivers.

↗ **Boston Light Swim**
www.bostonlightswim.org
USA's oldest marathon swim; stroke 13km across Boston Harbour.

GO LADAKH,
INDIA

(ABOVE) ↗
Ladakh will leave you
breathless however you
choose to explore its
high-altitude landscape.

(RIGHT) ↗
Bike down the
Amazon – the best
view may well be from
the seat of your
trusty treadly.

**WHY NOW? THE POPULAR LEH TO MANALI ROAD IS
USUALLY ONLY OPEN FROM MID-JULY TO MID-SEPTEMBER**

Ladakh, literally 'the land of high passes', separates the peaks of
the western Himalaya from the vast Tibetan plateau. Opened to tourism
in 1974, Ladakh is often called 'Little Tibet', due to the similarities in
topography and culture.

Access to Leh (3505m), the Ladakhi capital, is via one of two very
different experiences: you can take a 75-minute flight from Delhi for
one of the most spectacular air journeys in the world, or you can drive
for two days from Manali or Srinagar across high Himalayan passes.
The popular Leh to Manali road is usually only open from mid-July to
mid-September but dates depend on the passes being clear of snow. If
you fly in, prepare to be greeted by altitude sickness. Take it easy for a
couple of days, drinking water and not alcohol. At the end of this time
you should be twitching to explore the desert foothills and snowcapped

↗ DO: CYCLE FROM BAÑOS TO PUYO

COUNTRY Ecuador **TYPE OF ACTIVITY** Cycling **FITNESS/EXPERTISE LEVEL** Moderate fitness required. **WHY NOW?** The highlands' dry(ish) season – June to September – offers the most comfortable cycling conditions. **DESCRIPTION** When it comes to incredible views of the upper Amazon Basin, it doesn't get much better than the stretch of road from Baños to Puyo in the central highlands of Ecuador. The bus ride is great, but taking in the views from the seat of a mountain bike is even better. It's mostly downhill – the road follows the Río Pastaza canyon as it drops steadily from Baños, at 1800m, to Puyo, at 950m – but there are some definite climbs, so ready those legs for the 60km ride. Along the way you'll pass Pailón del Diablo, one of Ecuador's most impressive waterfalls. Parts of the road are unsealed, and there's passport control at Shell, so carry your documents. From Puyo (or earlier), you can simply take a bus back to Baños, putting your bike on the roof. Several companies in Baños rent mountain bikes.

peaks that enclose this side chamber of the mighty Indus Valley.

Mountain trekking is king in Ladakh, where you can wander over passes and between the Buddhist *gompas* (monasteries) that balance atop sharp-edged rocky spurs. You'll find myriad trekking agencies in Leh willing to guide you through this starkly beautiful land. Most enticing of the trekking opportunities is the ancient kingdom of Zanskar, cut off from the rest of Ladakh by frozen passes for eight months of the year and a haven for trekkers. Beautiful and dramatic, the high altitude will leave you short of breath in more ways than one.

White-water rafting trips on the Indus and Zanskar Rivers are possible from July to September. A popular taster is the three-hour thrill from Phey to Nimmu (grade two to three rapids), or you can arrange longer, customised trips.

Cyclists have also discovered Ladakh as the springboard for one of the great touring routes. Although only 475km in length, the raw and elemental road between Leh and Manali crosses four high passes (including Taglang La at 5328m), with high-altitude scenery that will most certainly astound and impress. Riding from Leh to Manali (2050m) means a net loss of altitude, but cycling from Manali means you can work on acclimatising as you ride. Take your pick.

[ABOVE] ↗
Bears, whales and seals will be the only ones to share the glory of Glacier Bay National Park with you.

[TOP RIGHT] ↗
First-timer or kiteboard king, Kanaha Beach has a spot for you.

[BOTTOM RIGHT] ↗
Squelch your way through the mud flats of Groningen.

DO: **KAYAK IN GLACIER BAY**

COUNTRY USA **TYPE OF ACTIVITY** Sea kayaking
FITNESS/EXPERTISE LEVEL Newcomers to experts.
WHY NOW? Cold seas, warm summer.

DESCRIPTION Ten tidewater glaciers that spill out of the mountains and fill the sea with icebergs of all shapes, sizes and shades of blue have made Glacier Bay National Park and Preserve an icy wilderness renowned worldwide. It's also a kayakers' paradise, despite the expense of getting there.

Using the the daily summer tour boat to drop you and your kayak off means your paddling options around Glacier Bay are extensive because you can be put ashore at one of several spots up bay. The landing sites are changed periodically in order to avoid habituating bears to human presence at any one spot.

Sebree Island, near the entrance of Muir Inlet, is a good spot to be dropped off because it allows you to avoid the long paddle from the park headquarters at Bartlett Cove. Many kayakers then travel the length of the inlet to McBride, Riggs and Muir Glaciers at the north end before returning to Sebree Island for a pickup. Such a trip would require five or six days of paddling. Those with more time but less money can book a drop-off and then paddle back to Bartlett Cove, an eight- to 10-day trip. A round-trip paddle out of Bartlett Cove to the glaciers of Muir Inlet is a two-week adventure for most people. However your paddle, keep a watch for humpback whales, which are migratory residents here over summer.

The most dramatic of Glacier Bay's eponymous blocks are in the West Arm, but the upper areas of this inlet are usually closed to campers and kayakers due to seal-pupping and brown bear activity.
www.nps.gov/glba

↗ DO: **KITEBOARD ON MAUI**

COUNTRY USA **TYPE OF ACTIVITY** Kiteboarding
FITNESS/EXPERTISE LEVEL Kite kids to kite kings.
WHY NOW? Expect the best winds from June to September.
DESCRIPTION Kiteboarding has become so popular at the western end of Kanaha Beach on Maui's north shore that they've renamed the place 'Kite Beach'. There are even areas set aside solely for kiteboarders. A little like skateboarding or snowboarding on water, kiteboarding is actually a form of surfing. While it may be impressive to watch, it's hard to master. Instruction is available at Kite Beach in three-hour lessons. First you learn how to fly the kite, then you practice body-dragging (letting the kite pull you across the water) and finally you step on board. A reef keeps waters near the shore flat for beginners, while the more experienced can head beyond the reef for breaking waves.

↗ DO: **MUDWALK IN GRONINGEN**

COUNTRY Netherlands **TYPE OF ACTIVITY** Mud walking
FITNESS/EXPERTISE LEVEL Moderate fitness required.
WHY NOW? Buried knee-deep in a sea of mud, you're going to want a warm time of year.
DESCRIPTION At low tide in the northern Dutch province of Groningen, mud flats stretch from the coast all the way to the Frisian Islands. Undeterred by this sloppy mess, the locals have turned it to their advantage, creating the unique activity of *wadlopen* (mud walking). Treks of up to 18km from the mainland to the islands are possible, though the 16km walk to Schiermonnikoog is among the most popular. The centre for *wadlopen* is the tiny village of Pieterburen (22km north of Groningen), where you'll find several groups of trained guides. Don't head out without a skilled guide as it's easy to get lost on the mud flats, and without a good knowledge of the tides you can end up under water, permanently. www.wadlopen.net

↗ DO: **HIKE THE KOKODA TRAIL**

COUNTRY Papua New Guinea **TYPE OF ACTIVITY** Hiking
FITNESS/EXPERTISE LEVEL Good fitness required.
WHY NOW? The coolest, driest and best months to trek are from May to September.
DESCRIPTION Every one of the steep, slippery steps you take on the Kokoda Trail's 96km natural rollercoaster requires concentration. Imagine, then, how tough it must have been carrying a pack, rifle and ammunition, constantly ill with dysentery and waiting to be ambushed by enemy troops. Such was the trail's origin, with Japanese troops attempting a sneak attack on Port Moresby, repelled eventually by Australian forces and Papua New Guineans. Today, the trail attracts hundreds of hikers a year, many to honour its history and many simply for a damn good hike. You should use local guides and carriers, never walk with less than four people, and allow between six and 11 days.

↗ **TransRockies**
www.transrockies.com
Week-long, 600km mountain-bike event, with around 12,000m of climbs.

↗ **Primal Quest Badlands**
www.ecoprimalquest.com
One of America's major adventure races: 970km of running, cycling and paddling over 10 days.

↗ **Sierre-Zinal**
www.sierre-zinal.com (in French)
A 31km mountain run through the Swiss Alps, with views on to five 4000m peaks.

↗ **Leadville Trail 100**
www.leadvilletrail100.com
Mountain bike 161km through the Colorado Rockies, or come a week later to run the same course.

GO: CENTRAL TIAN SHAN,
KYRGYZSTAN

[ABOVE] ↗
Kyrgyzstan is home
to the highest and
most beautiful peaks
of the Tian Shan
mountain range.

[RIGHT] ↗
A humpback whale gets
to know her calf, off
Tonga's Vava'u islands.

WHY NOW? **MOST HIGH-ALTITUDE TREKS OR CLIMBS TAKE PLACE IN JULY OR AUGUST**

This highest and mightiest part of Central Asia's Tian Shan mountain system is at the eastern end of Kyrgyzstan. It's an immense knot of ranges, with dozens of summits above 5000m, which culminates in Pik Pobedy (Victory Peak, 7439m) and Khan Tengri (7010m) – it's one of the most beautiful peaks in the world, and is often likened to the Matterhorn.

The best selection of treks is out of the town of Karakol. The Terskey Alatau range that rises behind the town offers a fine taste of the Tian Shan. Of numerous possible routes that climb to passes below 4000m, the best of them take in the alpine lake Ala-Köl above Karakol, and the Altyn Arashan hot springs above Ak-Suu.

Of the Tian Shan's thousands of glaciers, the grandest is 60km-long Inylchek, rumbling westward from both sides of Khan Tengri. Across the

↗ DO: SWIM WITH HUMPBACK WHALES

COUNTRY Tonga **TYPE OF ACTIVITY** Swimming/wildlife watching **WHY NOW?** Humpbacks visit Tongan waters between July and November. **DESCRIPTION** Whale-watching tours are offered throughout the world, but only on the Tongan island group of Vava'u can you actually swim beside the whales. Tonga is an important breeding ground for humpbacks, and from June or July to November they can be seen bearing young in the calm reef-protected ocean, caring for new calves, and engaging in elaborate mating rituals. Visitors to the town of Neiafu can board boats, cruise up to the whales and snorkel around them. It's a controversial practice, which some say disturbs the mothers and calves just when they are most vulnerable, and may force them to abandon the area before they are ready. Whale-watching operators should take their cue from the whales: if they seem disturbed and want to get away from the boat, then they should not be pursued.

glacier's northern arm, where it joins the southern arm, a huge, iceberg-filled lake – Lake Merzbacher – forms at 3300m every summer. Some time in early August, the lake bursts its ice-banks and explodes into the Inylchek River below.

The most common walking route to the Inylchek Glacier is a remote and wild five- or six-day trek from Jyrgalang. You'll need the support of a trekking agency to guide you over the glacier, keep you in supplies and let you stay in its base camps. With an experienced guide it's possible to continue over the glacier for one long day to Lake Merzbacher and continue the next day to the camps. Most groups take in a stunning helicopter route around the valley and out to Inylchek town.

Nearby Lake Issyk-Kul is arguably Kyrgyzstan's biggest attraction. At 170km long, 70km across and a maximum depth of 695m, it's the second-largest alpine lake, after South America's Lake Titicaca, and has an astonishing array of ecosystems, from desert and semidesert to steppe, meadow, forest, subalpine and glacial. The lake is also the centre of a biosphere reserve larger than Switzerland and covering around one-fifth of Kyrgyzstan.

The best walking season is June through to September, with most high-altitude treks or climbs taking place in July or August.

[ABOVE] ↗
Sink into sharkdom
off Cocos Island.

[TOP RIGHT] ↗
Coasteering – the
cliff-hanging adventure
sport that calls the
Pembrokeshire coast in
Wales its home.

[BOTTOM RIGHT] ↗
Need a good shake up?
Take to the bone-jarring
course of the
Tour de Timor.

DO: DIVE WITH HAMMERHEAD SHARKS

COUNTRY Costa Rica **TYPE OF ACTIVITY** Diving/wildlife watching
FITNESS/EXPERTISE LEVEL Experienced divers only.
WHY NOW? For the sharks, school is in.

DESCRIPTION In the opening minutes of the film *Jurassic Park*, a small helicopter swoops over and around a lushly forested island with dramatic tropical peaks descending straight into clear blue waters. That island is Isla del Coco (Cocos Island), around 600km southwest of the Costa Rican mainland in the eastern Pacific Ocean. It's extremely wet, with about 7000mm of annual rainfall, and legend has it that a band of pirates buried a huge treasure here – despite more than 5000 treasure-hunting expeditions, it's never been found.

For divers, however, there is indeed a great treasure chest here, one reflected in the title of an IMAX film shot here: *Island of the Sharks*. This film wasn't fantasy; the waters around Cocos Island offer probably the best shark diving in the world and some of the most memorable underwater experiences on the planet.

Though it's the wet season in August in Central America, it's also the busiest time for sharks. Due to Cocos Island's isolation and the fact that you cannot stay on the island, live-aboard boats are your ticket to the sharks – two companies, Undersea Hunter and Okeanos Aggressor, operate 10- to 12-day diving trips out of San Jose. The customary first dive is in the protected waters around Manuelita Island, a shark cleaning station off the northern tip of Cocos, but it's the submerged mountain at Alcyone that is the great drawcard. Here the largest schools of hammerheads are found, white-tip reef sharks mill about like ants and whale sharks have been known to cruise by. You'll wonder if Jacques Cousteau was looking above or below the ocean surface when he described Cocos as the 'most beautiful island in the world'. www.aggressor. com; www.underseahunter.com

↗ DO: COASTEER IN PEMBROKESHIRE

COUNTRY Wales **TYPE OF ACTIVITY** Coasteering
FITNESS/EXPERTISE LEVEL Good swimming skills required.
WHY NOW? You're going to be leaping into the Irish Sea, so you want summer at full beam. **DESCRIPTION** Coasteering is Wales' private piece of adventuring, pioneered on the Pembrokeshire coast in the 1980s and still comfortably at home here. It's something of a superhero sport, like canyoning along a cliff-rimmed coast. Equipped with wetsuit, flotation jacket and helmet, you traverse along the coastal cliffs by a combination of climbing, traversing, scrambling, cliff jumping and swimming. Routes are graded, so you can choose your dunking according to the level of difficulty. Give coasteering a try around its birthplace, St Davids, or head north to Snowdonia. Your only regret will be that coasteering wasn't created in a place with warmer water.

↗ DO: CYCLE IN THE TOUR DE TIMOR

COUNTRY East Timor **TYPE OF ACTIVITY** Cycling
FITNESS/EXPERTISE LEVEL Good fitness and mountain-biking skills.
WHY NOW? To race around East Timor.
DESCRIPTION Inaugurated in 2009, the Tour de Timor is an effort to bring cyclists and visitors into East Timor and then, conversely, punish them once they are there. The five-stage race begins and ends by the Presidential Palace in the capital city, Dili, and covers around 450km, crossing and recrossing the mountainous island. Complicating the effort are the roads, with washouts and disrepair common on the mixed bitumen and dirt surfaces – if Tour de France riders complain about cobblestones, they should ride here for a few days. Stage one is the longest – 130km – and ends cruelly with a steep 500m climb, while stages two and four involve the cross-island hauls, ascending more than 1800m during the latter. Reward comes on the final day with a 1600m descent and flat sprint finish to Timorese glory. www.tourdetimor.com

↗ DO: DIVE TECTONIC PLATES AT SILFRA LAGOON

COUNTRY Iceland **TYPE OF ACTIVITY** Diving
FITNESS/EXPERTISE LEVEL Basic diving skills required.
WHY NOW? In 4°C water, you're going to want to come in summer.
DESCRIPTION In the middle of the Atlantic Ocean, the North American and Eurasian tectonic plates come together. Known as the Mid-Atlantic Rift, it passes through few islands but almost bisects Iceland. Here in Thingvellir National Park, it cuts a deep crack beneath Silfra Lagoon, offering a unique diving destination – to dive here is to literally enter into the earth. Perhaps the most striking thing about the diving (other than the cold) is the clarity of the water, with divers reporting being able to see further than 100m; at times it can be like swimming in air. www.thingvellir.is

↗ **Boston-Montreal-Boston (BMB)**
http://boston-montreal-boston.com
North America's major 1200km randonnée, with a 90-hour time limit.

↗ **Grand Raid Cristalp**
www.grand-raid-cristalp.ch
Mountain bike 131km while climbing around 4700m through the Swiss Alps.

↗ **Björkliden Arctic Mountain Marathon**
www.bamm.nu/en
Two-day (30km, 50km or 70km) mountain orienteering race 200km north of the Arctic Circle.

↗ **Pikes Peak Marathon**
www.pikespeakmarathon.org
Ascend almost 2400m over 21.5km to reach one of the USA's highest summits.

GO:
YUKON TERRITORY

(ABOVE) ↗
The ultimate Arctic
escape – slip on a pair
of snowshoes to
slush across the
Tombstone Range.

(RIGHT) ↗
¡Arriba! Take a ride on
the Mexican Pipeline.

WHY NOW? **TO CATCH THE BRIEF, GOLDEN BLUSH OF AUTUMN IN THE TOMBSTONE RANGE**

Straddling the Arctic Circle, Canada's Yukon Territory is a place where gold rushes have turned to adrenaline rushes. It is the home of the winter Yukon Quest, in which dog-sledders mush through 1600km of frozen wilderness; and also the summer Yukon River Quest, which, at 740km, is the world's longest annual paddling race. But it is in autumn that parts of the Yukon really shine. Right now the endless Arctic days are beginning to fade away into eternal night, but on the Tombstone Range, out of Dawson City, the colours are only getting brighter. Autumn here is almost subliminal, blowing in and out seemingly in a moment, but it is spectacular, with the Arctic tundra turning a variety of reds and golds, the vivid colours offset by the black granite peaks of the range. The hiking possibilities in the Tombstone Territorial Park are extensive, from day walks to remote backcountry epics.

↗ DO: SURF AT PUERTO ESCONDIDO

COUNTRY Mexico **TYPE OF ACTIVITY** Surfing **FITNESS/EXPERTISE LEVEL** Good surfing skills and experience required. **WHY NOW?** The May to September wet season brings the best waves. **DESCRIPTION** Mexico's Pacific coast has some awesome waves. Among the very best are the summer breaks at spots between San José del Cabo and Cabo San Lucas in Baja California, and the 'world's longest wave' on Bahía de Matanchén, near San Blas. Most famous and cherished are the barrelling waves at Puerto Escondido, a place that has become known as the 'Mexican Pipeline'. Escondido's barrels roll into long, straight Zicatela Beach, which doubles as the town's hip hang-out, with its enticing cafes, restaurants and accommodation. The heavy beach break here will test the mettle of most surfers. Celebrate a day of waves with a customary bit of Puerto partying.

For those who prefer their adventure on wheels, the park is cut through by the Dempster Hwy, a gravel hell-raiser that begins 40km out of Dawson City and rock 'n' rolls 747km north to Inuvik on the shore of the Beaufort Sea. It was once a dog-sled track, and services are few and far between. There's a service station at the southern start of the highway, and from there it's 370km to the next one. Ferries cross the Peel and Mackenzie Rivers or, if the freeze has already begun, they are crossed on ice bridges.

In Dawson City itself, the adventure of choice is a little more distasteful. Inside the Downtown Hotel, you can join the Sourtoe Club...once you pass the unusual initiation. To become a member you must drink a shot of whisky with an amputated toe in it, and the toe – which looks like petrified wood – must touch your lips. http://travelyukon.com

DO: **PARIS–BREST–PARIS**

COUNTRY France **TYPE OF ACTIVITY** Endurance cycling
FITNESS/EXPERTISE LEVEL Supreme endurance required.
WHY NOW? Grab the chance, for it comes around only once every four years.

DESCRIPTION The PBP, as it is affectionately known, is the most prestigious event in the world of non-competitive long-distance cycling, running since 1891. The 1200km event is held every four years (2011, 2015) in the last week of August and attracts around 5000 riders from all over the world.

The PBP starts at St Quentin-en-Yvelines, near Versailles, southwest of Paris, and meanders west through Normandy and Brittany on a convoluted series of tiny, hilly roads to Brest (613km) before returning to Paris.

Participants are required to finish the course within 90 hours, thereby averaging at least 13.3km/h. The large bunches charge off the starting line as if in a short time trial. Despite using roads open to normal traffic, the peloton often occupies the full width of the carriageway. If traffic appears from the opposite direction, the whole bunch suddenly squeezes on to the right-hand side, where riders on the outside can be squeezed off the bitumen, ending up ignominiously in a muddy ditch.

Cyclists ride for much of the day and night. The resulting sleep deprivation is a major hazard and a reason for many abandonments. Riders have been known to fall asleep, crash and be unable to continue.

Riders pass through around eight *contrôle* (checkpoint) towns, where the town's residents turn out to watch, cheer or set up unofficial wayside feeding stations, creating an atmosphere not unlike the Tour de France. Prospective participants must qualify by completing a series of Audax Club Parisien–sanctioned lead-up rides involving randonnées of 200km, 300km, 400km and 600km in the year prior to PBP. www.paris-brest-paris.org

↗ DO: HIKE THE KALALAU TRAIL

COUNTRY USA **TYPE OF ACTIVITY** Hiking
FITNESS/EXPERTISE LEVEL Good fitness required.
WHY NOW? Kauai is one of the world's wettest places, but August sees an average of just 45mm of rain in Lihue. **DESCRIPTION** By reputation, the Kalalau Trail is Hawaii's premier hiking trail. It's also a heartbreaking path, both beautiful and brutal, following an ancient Hawaiian footpath along the valleys of Kauai's famous Na Pali Coast. It passes hidden waterfalls, wild beaches and visions of traditional Hawaii, ending below the steep fluted *pali* (cliffs) of Kalalau, where the sheer green cliffs drop into brilliant turquoise waters. Though these cliffs aren't Hawaii's highest, they are indeed the grandest. The classic hike involves walking 18km into Kalalau Valley on the first day, camping at Kalalau Beach for two nights and then hiking back out the third day. Permits are required to hike the Kalalau Trail, and the campgrounds are often booked up months ahead, so apply for your permit as far in advance as possible (up to one year is allowed). www.hawaiistateparks.org/hiking/kauai

↗ DO: BUNGEE JUMP FROM A PARASAIL

COUNTRY Norway **TYPE OF ACTIVITY** Bungee jumping/parasailing
FITNESS/EXPERTISE LEVEL Not required.
WHY NOW? See out summer in curious style. **DESCRIPTION** In mega-adventure towns like Voss in southern Norway, activities are like a game of poker, with the ante continually on the up. So while you might have bungee jumped from a bridge, or a dam, or even a helicopter, you can only jump from a parasail here along the shores of Hardangerfjord. With a purpose-built platform suspended on webbing from the parasail, the so-called Parabungy sails along behind its boat until it rises to 180m above the fjord. At this point you step forward and leap. There's nothing but air for about three seconds, and then suddenly you're springing and bouncing about at the end of the elastic as the boat continues to zip across the waters. They call it the highest bungee jump in Europe, and it is surely also the strangest. www.nordicventures.com

↗ DO: HIKE ON MT OLYMPUS

COUNTRY Greece **TYPE OF ACTIVITY** Hiking
FITNESS/EXPERTISE LEVEL Good fitness required.
WHY NOW? For the most favourable mountain conditions.
DESCRIPTION Mt Olympus, chosen by the ancients as the abode of their gods, is Greece's highest and most awe-inspiring mountain and the country's first national park. It takes two days to climb to Olympus' highest peak, Mytikas (2918m), with one night spent in a refuge, though it's worth spending more time if you really want to explore the mountain. The village of Litohoro is the best base for Olympus; it has bus connections to Athens and Thessaloniki. The most popular trail up the mountain begins at Prionia, a tiny settlement 18km from Litohoro. Most people drive or take a taxi to Prionia, but you can trek there along an 11km marked trail, which follows the course of the Enipeas River. The strenuous 4½-hour trek is over sharply undulating terrain, but offers glorious views. From Prionia, it's a 2½-hour walk to Refuge A, which can accommodate 140 people.

↗ **Oxfam Trailwalker Sydney**
www.oxfam.org.au/trailwalker/sydney
Run or walk (or both) through 100km of Australian bush in less than 48 hours.

↗ **Birkebeinerrittet**
www.birkebeiner.no
Billed as the world's largest mountain-bike race; pedal 91km from Rena to Lillehammer.

↗ **Ultra Trail Mont Blanc**
www.ultratrailmb.com
Run 166km through three countries, ascending 9400m as you loop around Mont Blanc within 46 hours.

↗ SEPTEMBER

WEEK.01　　GO: DOLOMITES, ITALY

(ABOVE) ↗
The Dolomites' mighty stacks are studded with steel ladders and cables to help climbers.

(RIGHT) ↗
Get back to glorious nature in the Rila Mountains.

WHY NOW? VIE FERRATE ARE USUALLY ACCESSIBLE FROM ABOUT JULY TO OCTOBER

The spiky peaks of the Dolomites in northern Italy are, in fact, ancient coral reefs reconstituted as alpine peaks. Eroded by glaciers and normal atmospheric erosion, they have been shaped into fantastic and spectacular formations. Appropriately, such unique Alpine mountains have spawned a unique mountain pastime.

Via ferrata (iron way) is the Dolomites' gift to mountain lovers. Neither hiking nor mountaineering, it is, like scrambling, a middle ground for those who seek something more or less than these two common alpine pursuits. A *via ferrata* uses intriguing and often ingenious combinations of ladders, metal brackets, chiselled footholds and even bridges to allow progress on steep or vertical cliffs. Steel cable is bolted to the rock at waist level. The cable acts as both a handhold and security, with walkers clipping onto it with a lanyard and karabiner system.

↗ DO: HIKE IN THE RILA MOUNTAINS

COUNTRY Bulgaria **TYPE OF ACTIVITY** Hiking **FITNESS/EXPERTISE LEVEL** Good fitness recommended for Rila's steep slopes. **WHY NOW?** Catch the tail end of the summer hiking season. **DESCRIPTION** The Rila Mountains might be small (2629 sq km) but they are beautiful, boasting 180 perennial lakes and streams and numerous mineral springs (*rila* comes from the Thracian word for 'mountains of water'), and Mt Musala (2925m), the highest peak in the Balkans. The mountains are steep but the spectacular views, flora and fauna make the hard work worth it. One popular three-day hike starts at Maliovitsa, visits the magnificent Sedemte Ezera (Seven Lakes) and finishes at Rila Monastery, Bulgaria's largest and most renowned monastery. A more sustained seven-day outing involves a north–south crossing of the range from Klisura to Hizha Predel. *Hizha* (mountain huts) provide dormitory accommodation. Many serve meals but these can be basic, so it may be advisable to bring food: inquire first. www.rilanationalpark.org/en

The first *vie ferrate* were created as military tools to move troops and equipment quickly and safely over difficult terrain, and there are now dozens of routes through the Dolomites. The most popular is probably Ivano Dibona, a spectacular but technically straightforward route to the summit of Monte Cristallo above Cortina d'Ampezzo.

The standout *via ferrata*, however, is the Bocchette Alte (High Bocchette) in the Brenta Dolomites. This advanced route is considered the most difficult in the Brenta Dolomites, requiring basic alpine skills to cope with crossing steep snow gullies. The popular Bocchette Centrali offers an excellent intermediate route. It is well protected, featuring spectacularly exposed ledges and ladders. The Bocchette routes

can be accessed by cable car from Madonna di Campiglio.

The Dolomites can also be seen by more conventional methods. Hiking paths crisscross the mountains, including four Alte Vie (High Routes), each taking up to two weeks. These routes link existing trails and incorporate new trails that make difficult sections easier to traverse. Other summer pastimes include mountain biking, hang-gliding and rock climbing. www.dolomiti.org.

[ABOVE] ↗
Awake to a cacophony
of rainforest sounds,
including the call of
the squirrel monkey,
in Parque Nacional
Madidi.

[TOP RIGHT] ↗
Take the Roman road
less travelled en route
to Venice.

[BOTTOM RIGHT] ↗
Glide through crystal-
clear waters as you
kayak in Queensland.

DO: **PARQUE NACIONAL MADIDI**

COUNTRY Bolivia **TYPE OF ACTIVITY** Wildlife watching

FITNESS/EXPERTISE LEVEL Not required.

WHY NOW? Bask in the dry season.

DESCRIPTION The Río Madidi watershed is one of South America's most intact ecosystems. Most of it is protected by the 18,000-sq-km Parque Nacional Madidi, which takes in a range of habitats, from steaming lowland rainforests to 5500m Andean peaks. This little-trodden utopia is home to a mind-boggling variety of Amazonian wildlife, including 44% of all New World mammal species, 38% of tropical amphibian species, over 10% of the world's bird species and more protected species than any park in the world.

Most of the park is effectively inaccessible, which is why it remains such a treasure, but Madidi also has a special Unesco designation permitting indigenous inhabitants to use traditional forest resources. There's only one accommodation option in the park: Chalalán Ecolodge, on the idyllic oxbow lake, Laguna Chalalán. This simple but comfortable lodge, surrounded by relatively untouched rainforest, allows visitors to amble through the jungle and appreciate its incredible richness. Although the flora and fauna are lovely, sounds more than sights provide the magic here: the incredible dawn bird chorus, the evening frog symphony, the collective whine of zillions of insects, the roar of bucketing tropical rainstorms and, in the early morning, the thunder-like chorus of every howler monkey within a 100km radius.

If all this sounds too primeval, be comforted: Madidi is also home to the world's first dot-com animal. With the discovery of a new titi monkey in 2004, park authorities saw a unique fundraising opportunity – they auctioned the naming rights. An internet gaming company secured the rights for US$650,000, and the monkey's common name officially became GoldenPalace.com monkey. www.chalalan.com

↗ DO: **CYCLE THE VIA CLAUDIA AUGUSTA**

COUNTRIES Germany, Austria, Italy **TYPE OF ACTIVITY** Cycling
FITNESS/EXPERTISE LEVEL There are Alps about, so come with a decent fitness base.
WHY NOW? High season has gone but the warmth has not.
DESCRIPTION What have the Romans ever done for us? Apart from the aqueducts they also, ultimately, gave touring cyclists this magnificent Alpine bike route, following the course of the first Roman road into northern Europe. The 770km route connects Donauworth (Germany) with Venice (Italy), threading through Alpine valleys and across some of the range's lower passes – its highest point is a smidge over 1500m. Sections of the route through Austria remain a little agricultural – the Fernpass crossing is definite mountain-bike territory – but the bulk of the ride is on good paths and roads, offering views of the likes of Zugspitze and the edges of the Dolomites. In the Inn Valley, there's even the chance to see the wheel ruts of Roman chariots still imprinted into rock beside the track.
www.claudia-augusta.net

↗ DO: **SEA KAYAK IN QUEENSLAND**

COUNTRY Australia **TYPE OF ACTIVITY** Sea kayaking
FITNESS/EXPERTISE LEVEL Novice paddlers to old salties.
WHY NOW? Get here before the stingers do.
DESCRIPTION With the Great Barrier Reef as its headlining act, Queensland is a place that more than encourages water activity. Two areas stand out as kayaking destinations: the Whitsunday Islands and Hinchinbrook Island. In the Whitsundays you can paddle out from Airlie Beach, island hopping towards the luminous sands of Whitehaven Beach, or you can cut out the grind of the Whitsunday Passage by simply taking a shuttle to the outer islands and following the island ellipsis back to the mainland. Hinchinbrook is Australia's largest island national park and paddling along its east coast offers an armchair look at its kilometre-high mountains and fringe of rainforest and castaway beaches.

↗ DO: **SEE ANGEL FALLS**

COUNTRY Venezuela **TYPE OF ACTIVITY** Adventure travel
FITNESS/EXPERTISE LEVEL Not required.
WHY NOW? The best time to see Angel Falls is during the wettest months of August and September.
DESCRIPTION Angel Falls, the world's highest waterfall, has a total height of 979m and an uninterrupted drop of 807m, 16 times the height of Niagara Falls. It's in a distant wilderness without any road access. The village of Canaima, about 50km northwest, is the major gateway but it also doesn't have any overland link to the rest of the country. A visit to the falls is normally undertaken in two stages; flying into Canaima and then taking a light plane or boat to the falls. In the wet months of August and September the falls are voluminous and spectacular, though frequently covered by cloud.

↗ **Liffey Descent**
www.liffeydescent.com
Paddle 28km on Ireland's Liffey River; do it in earnest or just for the craic, but watch out for the Straffan Weir.

↗ **Maui Channel Swim**
www.mauichannelswim.com
Team relay swim, crossing the 15.3km channel between the Hawaiian islands of Lanai and Maui.

↗ **Durango MTB 100**
www.gravityplay.com/MTB100
Mountain bike 161km, climbing across the Colorado Rockies.

GO: **XĪNJIĀNG,
CHINA**

(ABOVE) ↗
In Xīnjiāng, northeast
China, a 1000km
expanse of desert
meets mighty
mountain ranges.

(RIGHT) ↗
Hot foot it past ancient
civilisations as you push
yourself to great heights
on the Inca Run.

WHY NOW? HIT THIS DESERT PROVINCE BETWEEN THE
BLAZE OF HIGH SUMMER AND THE BITE OF WINTER

Xīnjiāng is like a whole other country enclosed within China's
borders. Vast deserts stretch over 1000km before ending abruptly at the
foot of towering mountain ranges, and its extreme climate has been
a defining aspect of its culture throughout the centuries. Abandoned
Buddhist cities lie along the treacherous trade routes of times past, while
in newer oasis towns, Islamic monuments point the way to the future.

Gone are the trifling regional differences between Běijīng and
Guǎngzhōu – here the language is not just a different dialect, it's a
completely different linguistic family; it's no longer about whether you dip
your dumplings in soy sauce or vinegar, it's how you want your mutton
cooked. However you look at it, the province is a world apart, more
Central Asian than East Asian, but nevertheless with a fate that's always
been inextricably tethered to the Middle Kingdom.

↗ DO: **INCA RUN**

COUNTRY Bolivia **TYPE OF ACTIVITY** Adventure racing **FITNESS/EXPERTISE LEVEL** Superior fitness (and acclimatisation) required. **WHY NOW?** To race through the Andes at lung-shrinking altitudes. **DESCRIPTION** If running near sea level leaves you puffed, imagine a 160km foot race at altitudes of up to 5100m. That's the offering in the country where even flying into the capital city can bring on altitude sickness. The Inca Run begins on the shores of Lake Titicaca and ends four stages and a prologue later in the Andean town of Sorata. The 80 runners must be self-sufficient, carrying their own food and daily water, while set mountain camps (with tents, campfires and water) divide the stages. There can be few runs in the world with less oxygen at hand – these are the sort of heights that defeat many trekkers, let alone those running with packs on their backs. The longest stage is 55km. www.incarun.com

Xīnjiāng is China's most arid province; it contains the country's hottest and coldest places; it has the longest inland river, the Tarim; the largest desert; and the second-lowest lake in the world, Aydingkul Lake.

It's also a place from where you can set out to explore two of the world's great overland routes: the Karakoram Hwy and the Silk Road. The former heads south over high Khunjerab Pass, while the latter runs east from Kashgar, splitting into two in the face of the huge Taklamakan Desert. Within Xīnjiāng, this ancient route is marked by a ring of abandoned cities deserted by retreating rivers and swallowed by encroaching sands. Cities such as Niya, Miran and Yotkan remain covered by sand.

This is a great time of year to explore. You can fly to the provincial capital, Ürümqi, from Běijīng, or if you want an adventurous approach to an adventurous destination, follow the southern Silk Road in through Charklik to Ali in Tibet.

{ABOVE} ↗
Every year 22,000 eager adventurers take an adrenaline-pumping ride down the Colorado River.

{TOP RIGHT} ↗
Take the donkey work out of exploring Lesotho – ride through this vibrant land on a Basotho pony.

{BOTTOM RIGHT} ↗
A sacred site for many religions; Mt Kailash is circled by countless pilgrims each year in search of enlightenment.

DO: **RIVER RUN THE GRAND CANYON**

COUNTRY USA **TYPE OF ACTIVITY** White-water rafting
FITNESS/EXPERTISE LEVEL Not required for commercial trips; extensive experience needed for private trips. **WHY NOW?** Travel outside the peak summer season and you stand some chance of securing a place on a trip. **DESCRIPTION** If standing on the South Rim peering at the dark line of the Colorado River has you twitching for a more intimate canyon experience, join the 22,000-plus people who run the river in rafts and inflatable boats each year.

A run down the Colorado River is an epic, adrenaline-pumping adventure. 'Normal' rapids are rated one through five (with five being pretty damn tough), but the 160-plus rapids on the Colorado are rated one to 10, with many five or higher – two rapids merit a 10! The biggest single drop is at Lava Falls, which plummets 11 stomach-churning metres in less than 300m.

Rafting the Colorado independently is very popular. For short trips (two to five days) you can apply for permits up to a year in advance, and they are issued on a first-come-first-served basis. For longer, independent trips there's a lottery system each February for trips the following year.

Commercial trips fill up months (even a year) in advance and take three forms – oar, paddle or motorised. Motorised inflatable boats are the fastest and most stable, but the paddle trips are the most adventurous, with all people aboard the raft paddling – overturning at some point is almost guaranteed.

Given two or three weeks, you can run the entire 446km of river through the canyon. Three shorter sections (each 160km or less) take four to nine days. www.nps.gov/grca

↗ DO: PONY TREK IN LESOTHO

COUNTRY Lesotho **TYPE OF ACTIVITY** Pony trekking
FITNESS/EXPERTISE LEVEL Not required.
WHY NOW? Cool and comfortable trekking ahead of the wet season.
DESCRIPTION Pony trekking is one of Lesotho's top drawcards. It's done on sure-footed Basotho ponies, the result of crossbreeding between short Javanese horses and European full mounts. Lesotho's revered King Moshoeshoe the Great is recorded as having ridden a Basotho pony in 1830, and since that time these animals have become the preferred mode of transport for many villagers. Malealea is arguably the best pony trekking centre, with popular routes that include Ribaneng Waterfall (two days); Ribaneng and Ketane Waterfalls (four days); and Semonkong (five to six days). The Basotho Pony Trekking Centre, atop the delightfully named God Help Me Pass, is more no-frills and do-it-yourself, and the place to come if you want to ride away from the crowds for up to a week. For overnight treks, you'll need to bring food (stock up in the capital, Maseru), a sleeping bag and warm, waterproof clothing.

↗ DO: HIKE AROUND MT KAILASH

COUNTRY Tibet **TYPE OF ACTIVITY** Hiking/pilgrimage
FITNESS/EXPERTISE LEVEL Moderate fitness required.
WHY NOW? Get here before the winter snows do (usually October).
DESCRIPTION The 52km *kora* (circuit) of Mt Kailash (6714m) is one of the most important pilgrimages in Asia, holy to Hindus, Buddhists, Bon-pos and Jains. Tibetan Buddhists believe that a single circuit cleanses the sins of one life, while 108 circuits brings nirvana in this life. The hike isn't easy, since it crosses a 5630m pass, though some devout pilgrims walk it in a day. Four days is more comfortable, and if you think you're doing it tough, look out for the pious pilgrims who circuit by prostrating themselves – lying on the ground, standing and walking to the point their hands reached on the ground before lying down once again.

↗ DO: DIVE IN EAST TIMOR

COUNTRY East Timor **TYPE OF ACTIVITY** Diving
FITNESS/EXPERTISE LEVEL Some diving experience is best.
WHY NOW? For clear water and the prospect of manta rays and whale sharks. **DESCRIPTION** Scuba diving and snorkelling has been the most successful adventure activity to develop in East Timor since the country gained its independence in 2002. Coral reefs run close to shore, and divers only have to wade in and swim a few strokes to reach spectacular drop-offs. The reefs offer a colourful array of hard and soft corals with a vivid assortment of reef fish. Pelagics and open-water species such as tuna, bonito and mackerel are also regularly encountered, along with harmless reef sharks, manta rays, dolphins and dugongs. The water is clearest from April to September, with visibility typically 20m to 35m and water temperature around 26°C to 28°C. Dive operators can be found in the capital Dili, with some dive sites very close to the city. Atauro Island, 30km north from Dili, also has superb diving, and day trips can be made from Dili.

↗ **Everest Challenge**
www.everestchallenge.com
Two days, 330km of cycling, and 8850m of climbing in southern USA - a long way from Everest.

↗ **Three Peaks Alpine Run**
www.dreizinnenmarathon.com
A 17.5km run through the Dolomites, ascending 1350m in the shadow of the mighty Drei Zinnen.

↗ **Colorado Relay**
www.coloradorelay.com
Teams of five or 10 run 273km in a day.

↗ **Jungfrau Marathon**
www.jungfrau-marathon.ch
Marathon-length Swiss trail run from Interlaken to Kleine Scheidegg, ascending around 1500m.

⌐ SEPTEMBER

WEEK.03   GO: HOKKAIDŌ, **JAPAN**

[ABOVE] ↗
Step outside the stereotypes of modern Japan and trek wild Hokkaidō's land of volcanoes.

[RIGHT] ↗
Take pride (in your planet) by tracking the patterns of maneless Tsavo lions.

WHY NOW? **COME AT THE BEGINNING OF SEPTEMBER AND YOU CAN WITNESS THE BEGINNING OF THE WAVE OF AUTUMN COLOURS**

The northernmost of Japan's islands, Hokkaidō accounts for more than 20% of the country's land area yet it contains just 5% of the population. The real beauty of the island lies in its wilderness regions, where there are no cultural monuments but there is superb scope for outdoor activities.

There are 10 active volcanoes on Hokkaidō, and while some are occasionally closed to hikers, it can be an intriguing experience to scale a volcano with sulphur shooting out of cracks in the rocks.

Daisetsuzan National Park – Japan's largest national park – is both the island's crown and its jewel, covering Hokkaidō's highest peaks and dominating the tourist scene. Most visitors, however, only travel around its boundaries, riding the gondolas and taking little more than a glance at

↗ DO: **MONITOR TSAVO LIONS**

COUNTRY Kenya **TYPE OF ACTIVITY** Wildlife monitoring **FITNESS/EXPERTISE LEVEL** Not required. **WHY NOW?** It's warm and dry, bringing wildlife to the waterholes. **DESCRIPTION** Join Earthwatch for a scientific expedition gathering information about the maneless lions of Tsavo. You will identify individual lions, record their behaviour and study their prey in an effort to protect the livestock of the local people (and, ergo, protect the declining lion population). You will also record and film their behaviours and take photos of their whisker patterns, which is crucial to identification. If maneless lions aren't your thing (or you're troubled by their past reputation as man-eaters), you can pick from more than 100 other year-round, worldwide expeditions operated by Earthwatch, a nonprofit organisation that sponsors conservation research by placing paying volunteers alongside scientists. You might prefer to excavate an 11-century Tuscan castle or track jaguars in Brazil. www.earthwatch.org

its beauty. To really appreciate this landscape you must walk – a five-day traverse can take you across the summits of more than a dozen alpine peaks, including Hokkaidō's highest, the active volcano Asahi-dake (2290m).

Five more Hokkaidō national parks will continue to challenge any preconceived ideas you have about an urban, neon-powered Japan. In World Heritage-listed Shiretoko National Park you can choose your poison: the active volcano Iō-san, or Japan's highest concentration of brown bears. Akan National Park contains several volcanic peaks, and while there aren't many extended hikes, there are plenty of day-walk options and postcard-perfect crater lakes. Shikotsu-Tōya National Park offers an even more

personal look at volcanoes – Mt Usu erupted in 2000 – with fast and easy access to the island's major airport if you're in a hurry.

A welcome by-product of all this thermal indigestion is the presence of so many *onsen* (natural hot springs). Soaking in one is an activity as Japanese as sumo. You'll even find a spring at the end of your Daisetsuzan traverse.

Hokkaidō's relative sparseness also makes it a great cycling destination, as you can pedal 2500km around its perimeter roads.

The lively city of Sapporo is Hokkaidō's major centre, with good air and rail connections to Tokyo. www.visit-hokkaido.jp

[ABOVE] ↗
Shift into top gear for
a world-class cycling
adventure.

[TOP RIGHT] ↗
Dragons are alive and
well on Indonesia's
Komodo Island, in the
form of these 3m-long,
100kg beasts.

[BOTTOM RIGHT] ↗
Look out for relics from
Apocalypse Now on the
banks of the Pagsanjan
as you pit yourself
against the current.

DO: MOUNTAIN BIKE IN WALES

COUNTRY Wales **TYPE OF ACTIVITY** Mountain biking
FITNESS/EXPERTISE LEVEL Trainer wheels to disc brakes.
WHY NOW? Good weather, firm tracks.

DESCRIPTION Wales has become something of a mountain-biking mecca in recent years, with its trails once dubbed the best in the world by the International Mountain Bicycling Association. Stunning all-weather single-track radiates from seven excellent mountain-biking centres, five of which have world-class ratings.

In North Wales head for some of Britain's best purpose-built tracks at Coed Y Brenin Forest Park, and epic rides at Gwydyr Forest Park at the edge of outdoors-central Betws-y-Coed. Here you'll find the 28km Marin Trail, with some excellent single track and testing climbs.

Explore the wilds of Mid-Wales on some excellent networks by basing yourself at Machynlleth or Llanwrtyd Wells, two towns where mountain biking has almost become a way of life. Other good facilities in this area include wild Nant-y-Arian near Aberystwyth and the Hafren Forest near Llanidloes.

In South Wales, Afan Forest Park, east of Swansea, is also in the world-class rankings. Its newest offering, the White's Level Trail, has added rocky outcrops to the cycling challenge. There's also a superb specialist downhill course – the 15km Trwch Trail – at Cwmcarn, northeast of Caerphilly.

If you fancy cycling on a bit of horizontal as well as vertical, or perhaps even riding between your mountain-biking outings, consider riding 420km across Wales on Lôn Las Cymru, a cycle trail with a reputation as the most difficult on the UK's National Cycle Network. Starting from the Anglesey port of Holyhead, it passes through mountainous Snowdonia before hitting the green hills and mountains of rural Mid-Wales, and then on into the formerly industrial Welsh Valleys and finally to the capital, Cardiff. www.mbwales.com

↗ DO: VISIT THE KOMODO DRAGONS

COUNTRY Indonesia **TYPE OF ACTIVITY** Wildlife watching
FITNESS/EXPERTISE LEVEL Not required.

WHY NOW? Enjoy your reptiles in the dry season. **DESCRIPTION** Komodo
is a hilly, desolate yet beautiful island in eastern Indonesia with a name
all but usurped by its most famous inhabitants, the gargantuan monitor
lizards, 3m long and 100kg in weight, known as Komodo dragons. Dragons
also inhabit the islands of Rinca, Padar and coastal western Flores, but
there's still something undeniably attractive about seeing Komodo dragons
on Komodo itself. You're most likely to see dragons at Banu Nggulung,
a dry river bed about a 30-minute walk from the tourist accommodation
camp of Loh Liang. A little 'grandstand' overlooks the river bed where
the dragons gather. Spectators are fenced off from the dragons, so don't
expect to walk up to them and have them say 'cheese'. Ferries to Komodo
run from Labuhanbajo on the island of Flores.

↗ DO: CANOE THE RAPIDS OF PAGSANJAN

COUNTRY Philippines **TYPE OF ACTIVITY** White-water canoeing
FITNESS/EXPERTISE LEVEL Not required.

WHY NOW? The wet season (August to September) creates the best
rapids. **DESCRIPTION** Canoe rides through the rapids of the Pagsanjan
River, near Manila, are one of Luzon's major tourist attractions. The rides
begin with a paddle up to Magdapio Falls, with two *banceros* (boatmen)
guiding each canoe for about 1½ hours against the fearsome flow of
the river, through an awesome gorge hemmed by towering cliffs and
vegetation. Some of the final scenes of Francis Ford Coppola's epic
Vietnam War movie *Apocalypse Now* were filmed along this stretch of
river (a few relics from the movie can still be seen along the banks). At the
top, the *banceros* will take you under the 10m-high falls on a bamboo raft
(for an additional fee). From here, you let the water do the work. The trip
downstream is fast and exhilarating. Avoid weekends, when half of Manila
seems to descend on Pagsanjan.

↗ DO: HIKE IN JAPAN'S NORTH ALPS

COUNTRY Japan **TYPE OF ACTIVITY** Hiking
FITNESS/EXPERTISE LEVEL Moderate fitness required.
WHY NOW? Let summer melt the snows.
DESCRIPTION The hiking route from Tate-yama to Kamikōchi is Japan's
ultimate long hike. Running the length of the North Alps – Japan's hiking
hotspot – it's the one walk every Japanese walker wants on his or her
resumé, and although long, it's not especially difficult and no technical
skills or special equipment are required. The hike's start at Murodō (below
Tate-yama) is at 2450m, the maximum altitude reached is 3190m at
Oku-hotaka-dake (Japan's third-highest peak) and you won't drop below
2000m until you descend on the final day. In five or six days you'll cover
65km, and it's possible to stand atop more than 20 summits. The most
interesting way to reach Murodō is along the Tate-yama Kurobe Alpine
Route, a combination of train, cable car and bus from Toyama railway
station 30km away.

↗ **Mourne Mountain Marathon**
www.mourne2day.com
Two-day orienteering run through the
mountains of Northern Ireland.

↗ **Colorado Last Chance**
www.rmccrides.com/lastchance.htm
A 1200km randonnée out of Boulder and
crossing into Kansas.

↗ **Xtreme Terrain Triathlon**
www.allabouttriathlons.co.uk
A Surrey triathlon for the bush lover, with a lake
swim, mountain-bike ride and cross-country
run.

↗ **Terra Incognita**
www.adventurerace.hr
Five-day relay adventure race in Croatia.

↗ SEPTEMBER

WEEK.04 GO: CORSICA, FRANCE

(ABOVE) ↗
Corsica is crisscrossed with trails linking the coast with its mountainous interior.

(RIGHT) ↗
Swap your pinstripe suit for a thermal one and conquer the world's highest peak from above.

WHY NOW? THE HIGH TOURIST SEASON IS OVER, THE BAKING SUMMER HEAT IS ON THE SLIDE AND THE SEA'S AT A PLEASANT 23°C

For such a small island (less than 200km long and less than 90km wide), Corsica offers adventure in large doses. The lush mountains and multitude of well-marked trails are ideal for hiking and horse riding alike, while 1000km of coastline with clear warm waters and top diving makes it a water-lover's paradise.

As famous as Corsica itself is the trans-island GR20 trekking route, stretching 168km through the granite ridges of the island's interior. To walk its entirety you'll need at least two weeks, but if you fancy something shorter, you can try the selection of Mare e Monti (Sea to Mountains) and Mare e Mare (Sea to Sea) trails that crisscross the island. Although less publicised than the GR20, these routes take in some spectacular mountain and coastal scenery, with the added bonus of ending each day comfortably in a village.

↗ DO: SKYDIVE OVER MT EVEREST

COUNTRY Nepal **TYPE OF ACTIVITY** Skydiving
FITNESS/EXPERTISE LEVEL Not required
WHY NOW? The skydiving season over the world's tallest mountain is brief – September to October. **DESCRIPTION** In October 2008 three skydivers became the first to jump from a plane above Mt Everest, leaping at around 8992m (29,500ft) , using supplementary oxygen and special suits to counter the cold at such altitude. One year later Everest skydiving went commercial, with parachuting trips being offered above the roof of the world. Skydivers who are experienced in freefall can make solo jumps, while novice skydivers are offered tandem jumps strapped to an instructor. Apart from being the world's highest skydives, they are also the longest, with the programs lasting a fortnight and including four days of trekking to help with acclimatisation. At the end there are several days set aside for jumps, which are made at 8992m (29,500ft), with a drop zone on the slopes of Everest.
www.everest-skydive.com

The variety of landscapes in Corsica also makes it an ideal place to see on horseback. There are 1900km of bridle tracks open to riders, and whether you choose an hour-long trek or a two-week tour, there are a whole host of reputable riding schools to cater to most needs and abilities.

If you're a diver, Corsica will show you about as good a time as you'll find anywhere in the Mediterranean. The dramatically rugged landscape continues underwater in the form of more mountains and canyons, needles, sharp peaks, rocky masses and scree, while the sea bed is a handsome carpet of yellow flowering anemone, red coral and gorgonian. Of the island's 30 diving centres, the Golfe de Porto, with its granite walls plunging to abysses 800m beneath the surface and its teeming marine life, is Corsica's little-visited jewel; the Golfe de Valinco is home to the Mediterranean's great underwater wonder, red coral; and the Baie de Calvi contains one of the most highly rated sites in all Corsica in the wreck of a B-17 bomber (experienced divers only).

[ABOVE] ↗
Surfers, grab your
boards when the Silver
Dragon roars.

[TOP RIGHT] ↗
Only for those with true
grit – a Simpson Desert
cyclist forges a path
across the sand.

[BOTTOM RIGHT] ↗
You'll need wings on
your feet – and lots
of training – to run
in the footsteps of
Pheidippides.

DO: SURF THE QIÁNTÁNG BORE

COUNTRY China **TYPE OF ACTIVITY** Bore surfing
FITNESS/EXPERTISE LEVEL Surfing supremos only.
WHY NOW? To coincide with the year's largest wave.

DESCRIPTION A spectacular natural phenomenon occurs when the highest tides of the lunar cycle cause a wall of water to thunder up the narrow mouth of the Qiántáng River from Hángzhōu Bay in southeastern China. It is the largest such tidal 'bore' in the world, creating a wave so mythical that the Chinese call it the Silver Dragon.

Up to 3km wide and more than 7m high, the wave travels up to 40km/h, and the roar of it can be heard from about 20km away. The Qiántáng Bore occurs regularly through the year, when the highest tides occur at the beginning and middle of each lunar month, though the traditional time to witness it is as part of the Mid-Autumn Festival, around the 18th day of the 8th month of the lunar calendar. This date varies on Gregorian calendars but falls around the end of September a number of times before 2015. This is usually one of the highest bore tides of the year.

The Qiántáng Bore can be dangerous enough to watch – it was once said to have swept 10,000 people away – but it's also been attempted by surfers. In 2008 the Silver Dragon Surfing Championship was inaugurated, bringing in selected world-class surfers to ride the beast.

The Qiántáng River is one of up to 100 rivers around the world that experience these surge waves. Others include the Amazon, Dordogne and Severn Rivers. The latter, near Gloucester in England, is the heartland of bore surfing. Waves occur here over a four- or five-day period each month, and have been surfed for almost 10km.

↗ DO: SIMPSON DESERT CYCLE CHALLENGE

COUNTRY Australia **TYPE OF ACTIVITY** Mountain biking
FITNESS/EXPERTISE LEVEL High level of fitness and endurance required.
WHY NOW? To race a bunch of other nutters through the Australian desert.
DESCRIPTION Australia might be the land of sand and beaches but
after five days of pedalling through the interior sands of the Simpson
Desert you might think this less appealing than you once did. Billed as
the country's toughest mountain-bike race, the Simpson Desert Cycle
Challenge leaves the oasis of Purnie Bore in northern South Australia and
crosses around 590km (and 750 sand dunes) to another form of oasis –
the classic outback pub at Birdsville. Each day you'll pedal through around
120km of sand – get comfortable with having your bike slung over your
shoulder – and still you must average 12km/h to escape the ignominy of
being gathered up by the sweep van. www.desertchallenge.org

↗ DO: RUN IN THE SPARTATHLON

COUNTRY Greece **TYPE OF ACTIVITY** Ultramarathon
FITNESS/EXPERTISE LEVEL Train up if you're going to run this far.
WHY NOW? To feel like a Greek god or goddess.
DESCRIPTION Marathons the world over celebrate the run of the ancient
Greek Pheidippides from Marathon to Athens to announce a war victory
over the Persians. But how many honour his original run from Athens
to Sparta to rustle up help for the same fight against the Persians? Only
this one. Runners in this annual ultramarathon begin in Athens and
follow a 245km course believed to mirror Pheidippides' route as closely
as possible. At its highest point, the route rises to 1200m across Mt
Parthenio, where it is said that Pheidippides met up with Pan. In the
lingering summer heat, it's more likely now that runners will meet up with
fatigue. To keep runners in check, there are 75 race control points, each
with a cut-off time for any stragglers. The final cut-off is 36 hours, though
the 2009 winner came in a few minutes under 24 hours.
www.spartathlon.gr

↗ DO: SWIM THE CATALINA CHANNEL

COUNTRY USA **TYPE OF ACTIVITY** Marathon swimming
FITNESS/EXPERTISE LEVEL Superior fitness and endurance required.
WHY NOW? You'll probably be in the water for 12 hours, so let summer
warm it up first. **DESCRIPTION** Second only to the English Channel in the
minds of marathon swimmers, the Catalina Channel separates Catalina
Island from Los Angeles and was first crossed by swimmers in 1927 in a
race created as a response to the heavy publicity of English Channel swims.
At its shortest point, it's around 34km from the mainland to the island,
comparable to (if warmer than) its celebrity European equivalent. It has been
crossed in little more than seven hours, and by children as young as 12, but
attracts few people willing to challenge it – between 1927 and 2008 only
160 people swam the channel. www.swimcatalina.org

↗ **3 Peaks Cyclo-Cross**
www.3peakscyclocross.org.uk
A 61km cyclo-cross race, climbing 1500m
across three Yorkshire Dales' mountains.

↗ **Fish River Canoe Marathon**
www.fishmarathon.org.za
Two days (81.8km) of white-water paddling
through South Africa's semidesert Karoo.

↗ **MaXx Exposure**
www.trailbreak.co.uk/maxx_exp
Begin at sunset and try to mountain bike
120km of England's South Downs Way
walking track by sunrise.

↗ **Whitney Classic**
www.summitadventure.com
Cycle almost 220km through Death Valley to
Mt Whitney Portal, with climbs totalling more
than 4500m.

↗ PADDLE

More than 70% of the earth's surface is covered with water, so it's to be expected that a great number of the world's best adventure opportunities take place on or in H_2O. Divers have perhaps the best access to the treasury of marine sights, but it is kayakers and rafters who are often treated to the best of both worlds: ocean life and land views.

Kayaking finds some of its best moments in the climatic extremes, from weaving among the icebergs of Glacier Bay (p128) and Greenland's inner fjords (p106-7) – the spiritual home of kayaking – to the paradise-by-paddle of Fiji's Yasawa Islands (p161) and the islands sprinkled along Australia's Great Barrier Reef (p141).

While kayakers may cede much marine life to divers, they do not have to surrender it all. At some kayaking destinations, it's almost as though the marine wildlife is coming to you. In narrow Johnstone Strait (p124) off Vancouver

Island, kayaks have become the boat of choice for viewing pods of orcas as they hunt for salmon and rub skin from their bodies against pebbly beaches; while along Queensland's Hinchinbrook Island (p141), green sea turtles pop up with almost clockwork regularity and there's the rare chance of spotting a dugong.

Sea kayaking's wild sibling is white-water kayaking, which is akin to rodeo on water. Usually at home in the rapids of fast-charging rivers, it has also found a few ocean niches in places where the sea is stirred by rushing tides. Off Nova Scotia in Canada you can join the rafters at the mouth of the Shubenacadie River (p87) riding the world's highest tides, or discover why they call a certain tidal race off the Welsh coast the Bitches (p113) – getting bitch-slapped here has a whole new meaning.

If you like white-water, but not quite that much, you can always share the workload by experiencing river rapids from a raft. Some of the world's great rivers also make for some of the great rafting trips. The Colorado River (p144) can be rafted along its entire journey through the Grand Canyon (if you have two or three weeks); the upper Nile (p195) has four grade-5 rapids (grade 5 being considered the most powerful rapids a raft can run); and below Victoria Falls (p184-6), the so-called smoke that thunders the Zambesi River is considered to have the highest concentration of grade-5 rapids on earth. If you like it pure, Tasmania's Franklin River (p202) runs for more than 100km through a catchment that contains not a single human structure; while Turkey's Çoruh River (p91) rumbles between 1500m-high rock walls in the Yusefeli Gorge.

Inevitably, even rafting and kayaking have evolved into different, more adventurous pursuits. White-water sledging, or riverboarding, involves clinging to a modified boogie board and careering alone through the rapids. It's like rafting for one, and has its origins in the French Alps, but has been claimed almost as its own by New Zealand's all-conquering adventure industry (p13).

Kayaking's great leap forward has been extreme kayaking, which has taken white-water paddling to a whole new plane. In extreme kayaking, paddlers pitch themselves over waterfalls…and the bigger the better. Until just a few years ago it was believed a kayaker might only survive about a 20m drop. By early 2009, somebody had tested the theory by paddling over a 33m-high waterfall, then in March 2009 another kayaker barrelled over Brazil's 39m-high Salto Belo falls. A month later Tyler Bradt plummeted over 57m-high Palouse Falls in Washington state, smashing into the pool at the bottom about four seconds later at around 130km/h…and emerging entirely intact.

↗ **OCTOBER**

WEEK.01

GO:
BHUTAN

[ABOVE] ↗
A synthesis of the old
and the new, Bhutan is a
trekker's paradise high
in the Himalayas.

[RIGHT] ↗
Watch out for the
wild inhabitants
of the Selous.

WHY NOW? **THE SNOWMAN TREK CAN ONLY BE ATTEMPTED BETWEEN LATE SEPTEMBER AND MID-OCTOBER**

The Himalayan kingdom of Bhutan is not an ordinary place. It has one foot in the past and one in the future. Its farsighted leaders recognise the necessity of being part of the modern world, but they realise that once their forests and culture are destroyed, they can never be recovered. They have maintained their traditional culture, yet they have adapted what they need from modern technology. You'll find monks transcribing ancient Buddhist texts onto computers and traditionally dressed archers using the most high-tech bows and arrows.

Bhutan is a country of rolling hills and towering crags, with only small patches of cultivation and very little deforestation. It's often compared to Switzerland, not only because they're similar in size, but also because many parts of Bhutan look like the Swiss Alps, with green hills, chalet-like houses and snow peaks sticking out of nowhere.

↗ DO: **WALK SAFARI IN SELOUS GAME RESERVE**

COUNTRY Tanzania **TYPE OF ACTIVITY** Hiking/wildlife watching **FITNESS/EXPERTISE LEVEL** Moderate fitness required. **WHY NOW?** Walks operate through the dry season (June to October). **DESCRIPTION** Selous Game Reserve is one of the last great wild places: 55,000 sq km of untamed bushland, untouched forests, crocodile-filled lakes and emerald green floodplains. It's slightly larger than Switzerland, four times as big as the Serengeti, and the second-largest protected natural area in the world. Only the northern section of the park is open for tourism. Here you'll find hippos, elephants, wildebeests and zebras in abundance. The Selous is also one of the few wildlife areas in Tanzania that you're allowed to explore on foot. Walking safaris are conducted from all the reserve's hotels: a fantastic opportunity to see Africa up close without engine noise and diesel fumes. You can take three-hour hikes near the hotels or trek for days among dangerous animals, resting each night in catered camps. www.tanzania-web.com

Virtually the entire country is mountainous, and to see the best of Bhutan you should spend a week or more on foot, trekking through the great forested wilderness that covers most of the country. A trek provides the best opportunity to experience the real heart of Bhutan and to get an insight into the rural culture of the kingdom through contact with the local villagers and the staff accompanying you. Fewer than half the people who attempt the Snowman Trek actually finish it, either because of problems with altitude (you climb to passes above 5300m) or heavy snowfall on the high passes. Its season is short – late September to mid-October – and its commitment is long, covering around 25 days in country so remote that

if you find the passes blocked by snow, the only way out is by helicopter.

Bhutan's most popular route, walked by around 40% of trekkers to the country, is the nine-day Jhomolari Trek I, taking you to a high camp at Jangothang (4080m) for spectacular views of 7314m Jhomolhari. The trek is possible from April to early June and September to November, but the best chance of favourable conditions is in October or April.

Government rules dictate that all treks must be arranged as camping trips. www.tourism.gov.bt

[ABOVE] ↗
Get off the beaten track as you ease your way up to Kopra Ridge.

[TOP RIGHT] ↗
Hold on tight and let the river take its course.

[BOTTOM RIGHT] ↗
Cloud cover lies like wisps of fairy-floss across the mountain tops of the Karakoram Highway.

DO: **TREK TO KOPRA RIDGE**

COUNTRY Nepal **TYPE OF ACTIVITY** Hiking

FITNESS/EXPERTISE LEVEL Moderate level of fitness required.

WHY NOW? October and November are recognised as having the best trekking weather in Nepal.

DESCRIPTION It used to be that most trekkers came to Nepal to hike the Annapurna Circuit, but in recent years roads have begun to devour the track, dulling the experience for all but those who just want to tick off a famous name. In response, trekkers are being pushed out to the Everest region or in quest of new routes in the Annapurnas. In 2008 signs began appearing among the teahouses of Deurali, spruiking a new route up to Kopra Ridge, draping down from 7219m Annapurna South. It's clearly visible from the famous Poon Hill lookout, but rarely noticed.

The route branches off from the Annapurna Circuit at Deurali, just west of Tatapani, climbing to the alpine top of Kopra Ridge. Along a pilgrim's stop en route to the holy Lake Khaire, the ridge is now home to a trekkers' lodge, which peers deep down into the Kali Ghandaki, the world's deepest gorge, bottoming out almost 7000m below the summit of Dhaulagiri. Views also take in Annapurna South, Fang, Poon Hill and Dhaulagiri across the gorge.

The lodge is part of a community initiative throughout the area, with trekkers' funds from Kopra Ridge and four nearby community lodges going towards schools and other village projects. Even the ridge's air of untouched isolation comes with a twist, with the lodge serving as one of two solar-powered relay stations that transmit wireless internet signals to surrounding villages. A day's walk from any village, you can check your emails 3500m up Annapurna South.

Trekkers have been using the Kopra Ridge route for 30 years, but only in very small numbers, so the tracks are faint and guides are recommended.

↗ DO: RAFT THE GAULEY RIVER

COUNTRY USA **TYPE OF ACTIVITY** White-water rafting
FITNESS/EXPERTISE LEVEL Experience needed for independent trips.
WHY NOW? Get there as the water does. **DESCRIPTION** They call it the Gauley Season and it is quite simply one of the world's great white-water moments. Over six weekends each autumn, there are scheduled releases of water from the Summersville Dam in West Virginia to lower the Summersville Lake to its winter level. Up to 4 million litres a minute pours from the dam, and waiting for it are a host of rafters to ride its sudden, gut-churning rapids. As the Upper Gauley drops around 200m in 45km, it provides more than 100 rapids to negotiate, including several grade-five rapids, the highest grade a raft can run. Grab a paddle and brace for the deceptively named Sweet's Falls, a 5m plunge that helps make the Upper Gauley about the best white-water run in the United States.
www.nps.gov/gari

↗ DO: TRAVEL THE KARAKORAM HIGHWAY

COUNTRIES China and Pakistan **TYPE OF ACTIVITY** Adventure travel/cycling
FITNESS/EXPERTISE LEVEL High level of fitness if cycling.
WHY NOW? For clear skies and moderate temperatures, the best time to travel is September and October. **DESCRIPTION** The Karakoram Highway connects the Silk Road oasis of Kashgar, in China's Xīngjiāng province, with Islamabad, Pakistan's modern capital, via the 4730m Khunjerab Pass, the semi-mythical Hunza Valley and the trading post of Gilgit. It's been open to travellers only since 1986 and has assumed legendary status as one of the world's great adventure road trips. Within reach of the highway is some of the most awe-inspiring mountain scenery anywhere – the Karakoram boasts the highest concentration of lofty peaks and long glaciers in the world. A favourite way to make the 1300km crossing is by bicycle. It's a spectacular trip for cyclists who are super fit and have an appetite for the unexpected.

↗ DO: SAIL THE DALMATIAN COAST

COUNTRY Croatia **TYPE OF ACTIVITY** Sailing
FITNESS/EXPERTISE LEVEL Some sailing knowledge and experience handy.
WHY NOW? The sting of summer has gone but the Adriatic remains warm.
DESCRIPTION With almost 6000km of coastline and 1185 islands (of which only 66 are inhabited), it's little surprise that as much activity in Croatia takes place on the water as on the land. The long, rugged islands off the mountainous coast stretch all the way from Istria to Dubrovnik, making this a yachting paradise. Fine, deep channels with abundant anchorage and steady winds attract sailors from around the world, and throughout the region yachts can tie up right in the middle of all of the island action. A good place to charter a yacht is the city of Split, from where you can sail out past bucolic islands such as Hvar and Korčula before continuing south to nose into Dubrovnik beneath its magnificent town walls. Island circuits in and out from Split are also popular.

Jungle Marathon
www.junglemarathon.com
Run 100km or 200km through the Amazon region of northern Brazil.

Brompton World Championship
www.brompton.co.uk
Race for a world title on fold-up bikes.

Kalahari Augrabies Extreme Marathon
www.extrememarathons.com
Seven-day, 250km self-sufficient run through South Africa's Great Kalahari Desert.

Triple Crown
www.triplecrownbouldering.org
The first of three bouldering competitions in southeast USA; series two and three are held in November and December.

↗ OCTOBER
WEEK.02

GO:
VIETNAM

[ABOVE] ↗
Cast yourself adrift and explore the 3000 karst islands in Vietnam's Halong Bay.

[RIGHT] ↗
Paddling paradise awaits in the clear waters of the Yasawa Islands.

WHY NOW? OCTOBER OFFERS ONE OF THE BEST BALANCES BETWEEN HEAT AND COLD, DRY AND WET

Vietnam is a place of coast and mountains – there's 3451km of the former and 75% of the country is covered by the latter. Karst formations have been shaped into striking landscapes, with mountain tops sticking out of the sea like bony fingers. It sounds custom-made for exploration and adventure, though Vietnam is only just beginning to realise its potential.

Cyclists were among the first to add Vietnam to their wish-list. The Mekong Delta is cycling heaven, with barely a bump in its silted surface. The coastal route along Hwy 1 is an alluring and popular achievement, though the insane traffic makes it tough and dangerous. Better is the inland trunk road, Hwy 14, which offers stunning scenery and little traffic.

Halong Bay is undoubtedly Vietnam's natural wonder. Picture 3000 incredible islands rising from the emerald waters of the Gulf of Tonkin and you have a vision of greatness – it's been likened to Guilín and

↗ DO: KAYAK THE YASAWA ISLANDS

COUNTRY Fiji **TYPE OF ACTIVITY** Sea kayaking **FITNESS/EXPERTISE LEVEL** Basic kayaking experience required. **WHY NOW?** The Fijian winter is warming up, while the cyclone season is still a few weeks away. **DESCRIPTION** After the famous mutiny on the *Bounty* in 1789, Captain William Bligh paddled through Fiji's Yasawa Islands on his way to Timor. Given that he was being chased by Fijian canoes, he may not have enjoyed the experience as much as you will along this 90km-long chain of 20 ancient volcanic islands off the northwest corner of Viti Levu. Famed for lovely white-sand beaches, crystal-blue lagoons and rugged volcanic landscapes, the group forms a roughly straight line within the Great Sea Reef. Islands are no more than 10km apart, making for short paddles between landfalls. You'll find the best paddling along the western side of the islands, where you'll be sheltered from the prevailing southeast winds.

Krabi. Paddling among the karsts is an activity that has taken off in recent years and Halong Bay is now following hard behind Krabi as Southeast Asia's kayaking capital. Climbers are yet to really make their mark on the bay, though it's only a matter of time before the word gets out. Ninh Binh and Phong Nha could also offer some climbing competition.

The most popular diving area in Vietnam is Nha Trang, where there are around 25 dive sites, both shallow and deep. There are no wrecks, but some sites have good drop-offs and there are a few small underwater caves to explore. The waters support a good variety of soft and hard corals, and a reasonable number of small reef fish.

Surfing is also a new arrival on the Vietnamese scene – Mui Ne Beach is among the best spots, while experienced surfers head for China Beach in Danang.

Picking a best time to begin a Vietnamese adventure is a tough call, with monsoons hitting different parts of the country at different times. October offers one of the best balances between heat and cold, dry and wet.

[ABOVE] ↗
Compete in the legendary (lunatic?) Ironman World Championship if you dare.

[TOP RIGHT] ↗
Live life on the edge – the pencil-thin Yungas Hwy is the world's most dangerous road.

[BOTTOM RIGHT] ↗
For a holiday companion with a difference, make friends with a polar bear near Churchill.

DO: IRONMAN WORLD CHAMPIONSHIP

COUNTRY USA **TYPE OF ACTIVITY** Ironman triathlon
FITNESS/EXPERTISE LEVEL Superior fitness required.
WHY NOW? To swim, run and cycle among 1800 super-athletes.

DESCRIPTION It began as an argument in 1978 about who was fitter – cyclists, runners or swimmers – and morphed almost immediately into one of the world's great endurance events. Competitors must swim 3.8km, cycle 180km and then run a marathon-length 42km, all inside 17 hours. The best in the game complete the course in less than nine hours, with the record time of eight hours and four minutes set in 1996 by Belgian Luc van Lierde.

Harsh *kona* (leeward) conditions on the appropriately named Kona Coast on Hawaii's Big Island make the event the ultimate endurance test, even by triathlon standards. Heat reflected off the lava landscape commonly exceeds 38°C (100°F), making dehydration and heat exhaustion major challenges. Many contenders arrive weeks before the race just to acclimatise. On the day of the race, nearly 7000 volunteers line the course to hand out around 50,000L of water – more than 30L for each racer! Such are its challenges, the Hawaii Ironman was labelled 'lunatic' by *Sports Illustrated* as far back as 1979. In reward for all this punishment, the top male and female winners walk (or crawl) away with US$100,000 each.

To race at Kona you must first qualify, and each year around 80,000 triathletes attempt to snare one of the 1800 spots. There are 27 qualifying events held around the world, from Brazil to Australia to the Canary Islands, and each race is allocated a number of qualifying slots. Miss these and you can enter a lottery draw for US citizens (150 race positions available) or international competitors (50 positions).
www.ironmanlive.com

↗ DO: CYCLE THE WORLD'S MOST DANGEROUS ROAD

COUNTRY Bolivia **TYPE OF ACTIVITY** Mountain biking
FITNESS/EXPERTISE LEVEL Good bike control recommended.
WHY NOW? Come at the end of the dry season to avoid a muddy run.
DESCRIPTION The Yungas Hwy between the Bolivian capital La Paz and
the town of Coroico is officially the world's most dangerous road, at least
according to a 1995 Inter-American Development Bank report. Given that
an average of 26 vehicles disappear over its edge each year, the title is
well deserved. It's a gravel track only 3.2m wide – just enough for one
vehicle – with sheer 1000m drops, hulking rock overhangs, waterfalls
that spill across and erode the highway, and a growing reputation among
cyclists keen for an adrenaline rush. Bike hire is available in La Paz. Now all
you need do is watch those edges, drunk drivers and marauding trucks.

↗ DO: WATCH POLAR BEARS IN CHURCHILL

COUNTRY Canada **TYPE OF ACTIVITY** Wildlife watching
FITNESS/EXPERTISE LEVEL Not required.
WHY NOW? To share your holiday with big white bears.
DESCRIPTION There are no roads to Churchill, set on the shores of frigid
Hudson Bay, but that doesn't stop people getting here. What draws
almost every one of them is the town's status as the supposed polar-bear
capital of the world. Churchill is on the bears' migration route between
winters spent hunting on the frozen bay and summers spent on land,
and it's through October that they pass by the Manitoba town. You can
take day tours in purpose-built buggies, or you can stay (for a hefty fee) in
transportable 'tundra lodges'. Where you hope not to see a polar bear is
in town itself. Local authorities maintain a 24-hour vigil from September
to November, with gunshots fired at night to shoo away any town-bound
bears. You can reach Churchill by air or rail from Winnipeg.

↗ DO: MORNING GLORY CLOUDS

COUNTRY Australia **TYPE OF ACTIVITY** Natural phenomena/gliding
FITNESS/EXPERTISE LEVEL High level of expertise and experience
required if gliding.
WHY NOW? The Morning Glories usually occur from September to
late October. **DESCRIPTION** Arise at dawn for the chance to watch a
meteorological wonder roll into northern Australia's Gulf of Carpenteria.
The Morning Glory is a tubular cloud, or series of clouds, up to 1000km
in length, that rolls across the sky in the early morning, pushing great
updrafts ahead of it. It's these updrafts that have made it one of the great
gliding and hang-gliding adventures. First soared in 1989, Morning Glories
have carried gliders for more than 700km and up to six hours. The northern
Queensland town of Burketown makes a good base for both viewing and
soaring the Morning Glories.

↗ **Polar Circle Marathon**
www.polar-circle-marathon.com
Greenland marathon that includes 8km across
the ice cap.

↗ **Furnace Creek 508**
www.the508.com
Only 48 hours to cycle 817km, climbing
10,000m around a little place called Death
Valley.

↗ **Adventure Race Mexico**
www.adventureracemexico.com
Multiday, multidiscipline (including canyoning,
coasteering and rafting), 650km race through
Mexico.

↗ **Great Southern Adventure Race**
www.rapidascent.com.au
Two-day, 200km Australian stage race
featuring running, paddling, mountain biking
and rope work.

↗ OCTOBER

WEEK.03

GO:
NEW CALEDONIA

[ABOVE] ↗
*Vive la différence –
find French flair and
tranquil diving in New
Caledonia.*

[RIGHT] ↗
*If only someone could
invent a ski-lift for
sandboarding.*

**WHY NOW? THE BEST TIME TO VISIT NEW CALEDONIA IS
FROM SEPTEMBER TO DECEMBER, WHEN THE DAYS ARE
NOT TOO HOT AND STICKY, AND THERE'S LESS LIKELIHOOD
OF RAIN**

A *très* French island in the middle of the Pacific, New Caledonia is
surrounded by the world's largest coral lagoon, sections of which were
added to the Unesco World Heritage list in 2008, so it's little wonder that
diving here is king. In all there's around 1600km of reef, with the enclosed
turquoise lagoon around the main island of Grande Terre covering around
23,500 sq km. In addition to the barrier reef, near-shore fringing reefs
surround all the smaller outlying islands.

From the capital, Noumea, it's a short trip out to Amédée Islet, a marine
reserve with plenty of marine life, including sharks and rays and healthy
coral. On Île des Pins, a tranquil paradise of turquoise bays, white-sand
beaches and tropical vegetation, there are dives to caves and sites off

↗ DO: SANDBOARD AT SWAKOPMUND

COUNTRY Namibia **TYPE OF ACTIVITY** Sandboarding **FITNESS/EXPERTISE LEVEL** Good fitness for climbing the dunes. **WHY NOW?** It's one of the coolest times of the year in the Central Namib Desert. **DESCRIPTION** In the Central Namib Desert, Namibia's most popular holiday resort aspires to be an adventure centre (albeit dry) to rival Victoria Falls. Among such offerings as quadbiking and parachuting, sandboarding stands out as the town's signature activity. Hire a board and climb the high dunes around town, then – laying down or, if you're proficient at skiing or snowboarding, standing up – schuss down a 120m-high dune at speeds reaching 80km/h. Hire of a sandboard comes with gloves, goggles, transport to the dunes and enough sandboard polish to ensure a run as slippery as marbles. Now all you have to do is slog your way back to the top of the dunes.

the northern tip of the island, especially Vallée des Gorgones, to see soft and hard corals, eagle rays and leopard sharks. There's also good diving on the Loyalty Islands, a trio of sparsely populated islands with secluded beaches, hidden caves and deep holes. On the island of Ouvéa you can witness one of the ocean's great sights on foot, walking to natural shark nurseries near Unyee and in Lékiny Bay. Late each year, large sharks give birth in the warm shallow waters. Their hormones kick in, making them quiet (so they don't eat their offspring) and not dangerous to visitors.

The activity on New Caledonia is not all offshore. The Grande Randonnée 1 (GR1) is a 123km, five- to six-day walk that runs from Prony, at the southern end of Grande Terre, through Parc Provincial de la Rivière Bleue and north to Dumbéa. The trek goes from the sea through plains, forests, hills and streams, along mule tracks and into pond or marsh. The air might be moist, acrid or crisply alpine, and the views are always magnificent. Like French GRs, red-and-white markers guide trekkers. Along the route there are seven shelters and camping areas for trekkers. www.newcaledoniatourism-south.com; www.trekking-gr-sud-nc.com

[ABOVE] ↗
Tunnel into a
netherworld of caves,
including the World
Heritage–listed Škocjan
Caves.

[TOP RIGHT] ↗
Leap like a lemming
off the New River
Gorge Bridge.

[BOTTOM RIGHT] ↗
You can't beat a
paraglider's-eye view
over Turkey's
Ölüdeniz lagoon.

DO: CAVE IN THE KARST REGION

COUNTRY Slovenia **TYPE OF ACTIVITY** Caving

FITNESS/EXPERTISE LEVEL From clunkers to spelunkers.

WHY NOW? Slip into the caves between the summer crowds and the winter chill.

DESCRIPTION For cavers, there are few sexier words than 'karst' (limestone weathered into caves and fissures), which makes the eponymous Karst region in Slovenia a hot date for those who like the underworld. Thick layers of limestone deposits were laid down here millions of years ago. Earth movements then raised the limestone above sea level, where it was eroded by mildly acidic rainwater. Over hundreds of thousands of years, this slow, chemical erosion has produced limestone pavements, dry valleys, sinkholes, springs and, most notably, vast subterranean networks of caves and tunnels.

Foremost in the Karst region are the 5.8km long, 250m deep World Heritage–listed Škocjan Caves, carved out by the Reka River. The first section of the caves, called Paradise, is filled with beautiful stalactites, stalagmites and flow stones; the second part (called Calvary) was once the river bed. The Silent Cave ends at the Great Hall (Velika Dvorana), 120m wide and 30m high and a jungle of exotic dripstones and deposits.

The sound of the Reka River rushing through cascades and whirlpools below heralds your entry into the astonishing Müller Hall, with walls 100m high. To get over the Reka and into long, narrow Svetina Hall you must cross narrow Hanke Canal Bridge, 45m high and the highlight of the trip. Most visitors continue to Bowls Hall, remarkable for its rare bowl-like potholes; past Tominč Cave, where finds from a prehistoric settlement have been unearthed; and over a walkway near the Natural Bridge to a funicular, which carries you 90m up the rock face to near the reception area. Experienced spelunkers, however, can explore the 5km of caves and halls that extend to the northwest of Hanke Canal Bridge, ending at Dead Lake. www.park-skocjanske-jame.si

↗ DO: BASE JUMP AT BRIDGE DAY

COUNTRY USA **TYPE OF ACTIVITY** BASE jumping
FITNESS/EXPERTISE LEVEL Skydiving experience required.
WHY NOW? For the one day of the year you can throw yourself from New River Gorge Bridge.
DESCRIPTION Bridge Day might sound like a run-of-the-mill, small-town-America event in which the greatest danger is being trampled by baton-twirling marching girls, but wedged between the Eucharist service and the historic theatre production in Fayetteville's Bridge Day, there just happens to be a mighty BASE jumping event. Though BASE jumping is illegal here for 355 days of the year, on this one day, 450 BASE jumpers leap from the New River Gorge Bridge, opening their parachutes as they plummet 270m into the gorge – a drop of just eight seconds. BASE rookies can make their debut here, but only if you come packed with an extensive skydiving history (100 jumps minimum). If you prefer to maintain some contact with the bridge, you can also abseil from it. www.bridgeday.info

↗ DO: PARAGLIDE AT ÖLÜDENIZ

COUNTRY Turkey **TYPE OF ACTIVITY** Paragliding
FITNESS/EXPERTISE LEVEL Not required.
WHY NOW? To coincide with the International Air Games.
DESCRIPTION If you like the idea of plummeting off a cliff with another person strapped to your back, you won't find many better places than Turkey's resort town Ölüdeniz, set around a beautiful, sheltered lagoon. Many companies here offer tandem paragliding flights. The descent from Baba Dağ (Mt Baba), which is more than 1900m high, can take as long as 45 minutes, with amazing views over the lagoon, nearby Butterfly Valley and, on a clear day, out to the island of Rhodes. So popular is the sport in Ölüdeniz that it's now the venue for the paragliding International Air Games, held this week each October. www.babadag.com

↗ DO: VISIT AGDAM

REGION Nagorno-Karabakh **TYPE OF ACTIVITY** Adventure travel
FITNESS/EXPERTISE LEVEL Not required.
WHY NOW? A comfortable time to be travelling through the discomforts of the south Caucasus.
DESCRIPTION The self-declared republic of Nagorno-Karabakh was racked by war between 1989 and 1994 as Azerbaijan and Armenia fought for its control. In 1994 Agdam, a city of 100,000 people, was captured, sacked and looted. Tall, shattered tower blocks now stand deserted, past a sprawling city centre of one- and two-storey buildings. Shredded playgrounds sprout shrubs, streets are cracking open with trees, and ponds fill bomb craters. Beside a few soldiers and scrap-metal hunters, Agdam is as dead as Pompeii. The Ministry of Foreign Affairs of Nagorno-Karabakh doesn't permit a visit to Agdam, though some people go anyway. Don't venture beyond the mosque at the town centre. Determined travellers have managed to visit by hiring a taxi from Stepanakert; cameras are not welcome. Don't venture beyond the mosque at the town centre; climb one of the rickety minarets for a 360-degree, Hiroshima-like view of the city.

↗ **24 Hours of Moab**
www.grannygear.com
Mountain bike nonstop for 24 hours around the slickrock of Moab.

↗ **Becs-Pozsony-Budapest Supermarathon**
www.szupermarathon.hu
Five days to run, cycle or in-line skate 321km between Vienna and Budapest.

↗ **Fitzroy Falls Fire Trail Marathon**
www.fitzroyfallsmarathon.com
Marathon-length run around the sandstone escarpments south of Sydney; 5½-hour time limit.

↗ **Cape to Cape MTB**
www.capetocapemtb.com
Mountain bike 220km in four stages at Australia's southwestern edge.

GO: MOAB, UNITED STATES

[ABOVE] ↗
Slickrock Trail is a
mountain biker's Holy
Grail. If only you could
stick to the saddle the
way your knobblies stick
to the rock.

[RIGHT] ↗
Avoid crocodile-teeth
puncture marks in
your tyres as you
compete in the world's
longest and hottest
mountain-bike race.

WHY NOW? GO IN OCTOBER AND YOU CAN CATCH THE MOAB HO-DOWN BIKE FESTIVAL AS WELL

The Utah town of Moab would horrify its founding fathers and mothers. Established as a Mormon outpost, it has fallen to a cult of scabby, adrenaline-juiced mountain bikers who know only one kind of latter-day saint – those that can ride the Slickrock Trail without stacking.

Set at the heart of some of the United States' most striking desert, Moab's most famous feature is slickrock, the smooth sandstone named because horses found it so slippery. Beneath the knobbly tyres of a mountain bike it is, conversely, more like *stick*rock.

Foremost among the slickrock rides is the one that bears the name – the Slickrock Trail. A Holy Grail of mountain biking, Slickrock winds across the sandstone ridges directly above town, with glimpses of the Colorado River and Arches National Park as it circuits. Although around 100,000 cyclists follow its dashed lines every year, it's not a ride for the timid. It

COUNTRY Australia **TYPE OF ACTIVITY**
Mountain biking **FITNESS/EXPERTISE LEVEL**
Superior fitness required. **WHY NOW?** To pedal
madly through bulldust and croc country.
DESCRIPTION With even a name that's scary,
this 10-stage, 1260km event on Queensland's
Cape York Peninsula is billed as the longest
and hottest mountain-bike race in the world.
It begins in Cairns and loops inland through
Laura to Cooktown, returning through
rainforest along the Bloomfield Track to Cape
Tribulation. Roads are corrugated and deep
in bulldust, and stages are as long as 171km;
there's also the small matter of about 13,500m
of climbing. Even the shortest stage – 49km
into idyllic Cape Tribulation on the final day –
is no cruise, as it climbs through the Cowie
Range where road gradients are up to 33%.
And yes, there are crocodiles about in this
part of the world: you'll cross a few rivers and
creeks that are home to them.
www.crocodile-trophy.com

has climbs as steep as the pyramids and descents
that'll cramp your braking hand. If you come away
without 'bacon' (scabs) and you haven't pushed your
bike at some point, you've arrived as an authentic
mountain biker.

Cycling here, however, needn't be just about
belting around the Slickrock Trail. Rides can be
chosen as much for scenery as difficulties. Try
the swirling sandstone at Bartlett Wash, or hit
Canyonlands National Park for a few days of cross-
country pedalling on the White Rim Trail above the
Colorado and Green Rivers.

Get even closer to the rivers by indulging in
Moab's next best thing to slickrock – river runs
through water both flat and churning. A great number
of companies run an overwhelming variety of trips on
the Colorado and Green Rivers, and you can float like
an inland cruise or you can be buffeted silly by rapids.

To round out your week, you might try jet boating,
quadbiking or an extreme form of 4WDing in which
you remove your vehicle's doors, put on tyres like
doughnuts and head for tracks with names like Hell's
Revenge. You'll never think of Utah in the same way
again, especially if you come now when the Moab
Ho-Down Bike Festival is on. www.discovermoab
.com; http://moabhodown.chilebikes.com/

DO: MOUNTAIN RUN ON MT KINABALU

[ABOVE] ↗
What might first appear as a massive slab of chocolate cake is in fact a brutal way to burn off those extra calories.

[TOP RIGHT] ↗
A rising trend in low-impact travel – take only photos, leave only your shadow.

[BOTTOM RIGHT] ↗
Test your skills on the Violent Crumble or Cruel Britannia as you dangle precariously off Mt Araplies.

COUNTRY Malaysia **TYPE OF ACTIVITY** Mountain running

FITNESS/EXPERTISE LEVEL Superior fitness and good acclimatisation required.

WHY NOW? To compete in the Mt Kinabalu International Climbathon.

DESCRIPTION The British may cherish fell running, or mountain running, as something of a national pastime, but to find its most extreme challenge you must travel to Sabah for the annual Mt Kinabalu International Climbathon. Created in 1987 as a training exercise for park rangers to test their rescue skills, it began the following year as an international race, one that's now promoted as the 'world's toughest mountain race'.

In the Climbathon, competitors run up and down Mt Kinabalu (4095m), Southeast Asia's highest peak. From the race start at Timpohon Gate, runners ascend 2230m to Kinabalu's highest point, Low's Peak, before turning around and running back. The race covers a total distance of 21km, and the winner usually returns to Timpohon Gate in just under three hours; the cut-off time for stragglers is 4½ hours. Expect high temperatures and bath-like humidity at the base of the mountain and whatever the mountain gods throw at you on the top.

If this sort of high-altitude running sounds like just your thing, you needn't limit your experiences to Mt Kinabalu. The Climbathon is one of between six and eight races that make up the annual Sky Runner World Series. The season begins in May (and concludes on Kinabalu), and you can starve your running body of oxygen in places such as Switzerland, Spain, Andorra and the UK. Each race involves significant climbs and most are run above 2000m. One of the long-standing races is the International Skyrace Valmalenco-Valposchiavo, usually held in June and following former smugglers' tracks from Italy to Switzerland. http://climbathon.sabahtourism.com; www.buffskyrunner.com

↗ DO: BALLOON AT SERENGETI NATIONAL PARK

COUNTRY Tanzania **TYPE OF ACTIVITY** Hot-air ballooning
FITNESS/EXPERTISE LEVEL Not required.
WHY NOW? Witness the wildebeests from the air.
DESCRIPTION A memorable way to observe wildlife in the Serengeti
is from the air as you sail above the plains in a balloon. At the whim of
the airstream and accompanied by bursts of flame, you drift over the
park whose name translates as 'endless plains'. From the air you can
spot otherwise invisible hyena dens, tracks that crisscross the plains
like some gigantic web, and groups of zebras, wildebeests, hartebeests
and gazelles. The ride ends wherever the wind has blown you, and
your champagne breakfast (complete with linen tablecloths) may be
accompanied by whichever animals happen to be nearby. It's not a cheap
morning out but it's the only way you'll ever look down on a giraffe.
www.balloonsafaris.com

↗ DO: CLIMB AT MT ARAPILES

COUNTRY Australia **TYPE OF ACTIVITY** Rock climbing
FITNESS/EXPERTISE LEVEL Routes cover all grades.
WHY NOW? Spring offers the best conditions, with climbers settling into
the Pines for weeks. **DESCRIPTION** Mt Arapiles is an anomaly, a chunk
of quartzite seemingly dropped by mistake on the ironed-flat Wimmera
plain – something like Uluru (Ayres Rock) with a southern address. It's
also among the best climbing sites in the world, boasting more than 2000
routes, which range from basic to advanced, and have colourful names
such as Violent Crumble, Cruel Britannia and Checkmate. You can amble
up glorified scrambles or you can destroy your fingers on something like
Punks in the Gym (grade 31), which was once rated the most difficult
climb in the world. Another classic route is Kachoong (21) – if you've seen
just one photo of 'Araps' it's probably somebody hanging from the roof
on this route. To do Araps correctly, you should set up home in the Pines
camping ground – something akin to Yosemite's Camp 4 – at the base of
the mountain.

↗ DO: HIKE THE HOERIKWAGGO TRAIL

COUNTRY South Africa **TYPE OF ACTIVITY** Hiking
FITNESS/EXPERTISE LEVEL Moderate fitness required.
WHY NOW? For pleasant walking conditions amid wildflowers on
Table Mountain.
DESCRIPTION Discover one of the world's newest and most appealing
hiking experiences as you walk between Cape Town and the tip of the
Cape of Good Hope, crossing Table Mountain as you go. There are
several guided trail options available, offering two-day glimpses along the
Silvermine, Orange Kloof and Slangkop sections. The entire trail is slated
to be completed by the middle of 2010, offering a 97km, six-day walk
across one of the world's most recognisable mountains. There will be five
luxury tented camps along the trail in the finest African safari tradition.
www.sanparks.org/parks

↗ **Banff Mountain Film Festival**
www.banffmountainfestivals.ca
See the year's finest collection of adventure
films.

↗ **Grand Raid**
www.grandraid-reunion.com
Run 130km, with climbs totalling more than
7000m, to traverse the island of Réunion.

↗ **Wild Sau Dirt Race**
www.wild-sau.at (in German)
Austrian cross-country run through mud and
over obstacles, billed as the 'toughest 10km
of your life'.

↗ **Original Mountain Marathon**
www.theomm.com
One of the forerunners to adventure racing,
covering around 80km in two days; in the UK.

↗ NOVEMBER
WEEK.01

GO: SINAI PENINSULA, **EGYPT**

(ABOVE) ↗
Resonant with biblical history, the arid Sinai Peninsula contrasts with astounding marine diversity offshore.

(RIGHT) ↗
Reach stratospheric heights in the blink of an eye copiloting a MiG-25.

↘ **WHY NOW? SUMMER IS UNBEARABLE AND WINTER OFTEN SEES MT SINAI TOPPED WITH SNOW, SO VISIT IN BETWEEN THESE SEASONS**

Biblical and beautiful, Egypt's Sinai is a desert land conversely famous for its water activities. Sat like a cork in the neck of the Red Sea, the Sinai's southern coast between Tiran Island and Ras Mohammed National Park features some of the world's most brilliant and amazing underwater scenery. The crystal-clear water, the rare and lovely reefs and the incredible variety of fish have made this a diving and snorkelling paradise, attracting people from all over the globe to the sea Jacques Cousteau once said gave him the 'happiest hours of my diving experience'.

The resort of Sharm el-Sheikh, the epicentre of the diving industry, doesn't reflect the marine beauty, but it does have proximity to Ras Mohammed National Park, which covers the southern tip of Sinai and

COUNTRY Russia **TYPE OF ACTIVITY**
Adventure travel **FITNESS/EXPERTISE LEVEL**
Not required. **WHY NOW?** Most of your time
will be spent on the ground, and Russia
can be magical in autumn. **DESCRIPTION**
Plane spotters and thrill seekers unite, for
it's now possible to co-pilot a seriously quick
and impressive piece of aircraft. The MiG-25
'Foxbat' is a fighter jet that can fly at more
than twice the speed of sound (or around
3000km/h). One hour's drive southeast of
Moscow, tourist flights take to the high skies
from the formerly top-secret Zhukovsky Air
Base, rocketing away to an altitude of around
25,000m – the outer limit of the atmosphere,
from where you can see the curve of the
earth. For your money (starting at around
$US1500) you'll usually get your Russian visa,
several nights at one of Moscow's premier
hotels, transfers between airport, hotel and
Zhukovsky Air Base, an English-speaking
guide, flight instructions, training, a medical
check and, finally, the 30-minute flight.
www.flymig.com

offers arguably the Red Sea's finest diving. There are
20 dive sites within the park, including a selection
of wrecks, and Eel Garden and Shark Observatory
where you'll see – have a guess – eels and sharks.

Sinai's interior is as hard as its fringing corals.
Row upon serried row of barren, jagged, red-brown
mountains fill its southern end, surrounded by
relentlessly dry, yet colourful, desert plains. The
most famous of the mountains is 2285m Mt Sinai,
reputed to be the place where Moses received
the Ten Commandments, and now the peninsula's
favourite hiking destination. Begin at St Katherine's
Monastery and follow the camel trail or, if you're
feeling penitent, the 3750 Steps of Repentance to
the summit. It's customary to be here for sunrise,

and if you're planning to spend the night on top, as
many visitors do, come ready for a cold night.

Longer desert treks – up to a week or more – with
a Bedouin guide can be arranged in the village of
Al-Milga, 3.5km from St Katherine's. A guide is also
required if you fancy the five-hour climb to the top of
Gebel Katarina (2642m), Egypt's highest mountain.

[ABOVE] ↗
An ancient meteor strike on Mexico's Yucatán Peninsula has created a honeycomb world of caverns and sinkholes.

[TOP RIGHT] ↗
Reach out to a manatee (or is that a mermaid in disguise?) in Florida's Crystal River.

[BOTTOM RIGHT] ↗
Sleep under a blanket of desert stars on a camel trek in Tunisia.

DO: CENOTE DIVE IN YUCATÁN

COUNTRY Mexico **TYPE OF ACTIVITY** Cavern diving

FITNESS/EXPERTISE LEVEL Open-water dive certification required.

WHY NOW? The cenotes are clearest between about November and March.

DESCRIPTION In a cataclysmic collision 65 million years ago, a huge meteor struck the area that is now Mexico's Yucatán Peninsula, leaving a 284km-wide crater on the land's surface. Millions of years later cracks formed just below the crater's limestone surface and rainwater began filling the cavities these fissures created. Eventually the surface layer around the underground chambers began to erode and crumble, revealing the intricate vascular system of underground rivers and *cenotes* (pools, sinkholes) that lay beneath.

The Yucatán is now pitted with around 3000 *cenotes*, the most famous of which is the Sacred Cenote at the Mayan site of Chichén Itzá. This is an awesome natural well, around 60m in diameter and 35m deep, but it lacks the one feature that draws thousands of adventurers to the Yucatán each year – you cannot dive in the Sacred Cenote. Elsewhere on the peninsula, there are a number of *cenotes* that can be dived. Certified cave divers can delve to the caves' black depths but other divers will be limited to cavern diving, in which you're limited to staying within the area reached by sunlight. In most accessible caverns there are fixed lines to guide divers through the *cenote*. Popular *cenote* dives include Ponderosa (also great for snorkelling), near Puerto Aventuras, and Cenote Azul, a 90m-deep natural pool on the shore of Laguna Bacalar.

Cenote Dos Ojos is one of the most impressive caverns, with stalactites and stalagmites in an eerie wonderland. You can swim 500m through the *cenote* without leaving sunlight. This *cenote* also provides access to Nohoch Nah Chich, one of the largest underwater cave systems in the world. www.hiddenworlds.com

↗ DO: **SNORKEL WITH MANATEES**

COUNTRY USA **TYPE OF ACTIVITY** Snorkelling/wildlife watching
FITNESS/EXPERTISE LEVEL Basic swimming skills required.
WHY NOW? Good manatee numbers and you'll beat the winter snowbirds into town. **DESCRIPTION** With a walrus-like body that tapers to a beaver-like tail, the shy and elusive manatee is slow, nearly blind and known rather ingloriously as a sea cow, yet it's one of the state symbols of Florida. Around 3000 manatees are thought to live in Florida waters, and in the Crystal River in the state's north you can swim alongside them to ponder how on earth these huge grey aquatic mammals were ever mistaken for mermaids. Divers can pack away the tanks, as bubbles scare manatees, making this a snorkelling-only adventure. Try to choose a tour company that keeps the number of guests low – around six. Most also have a 'Manatee awareness program' but go with an outfit that incorporates this educational lecture into the tour itself and doesn't treat it as an optional, extra-cost feature.

↗ DO: **CAMEL SAFARI IN DOUZ**

COUNTRY Tunisia **TYPE OF ACTIVITY** Camel safari
FITNESS/EXPERTISE LEVEL Not required.
WHY NOW? November is one of the few times that conditions permit overnight treks. **DESCRIPTION** From the Tunisian town of Douz, camel trekking ranges from one-hour rides to days-long desert adventures. Overnight treks leave Douz in the afternoon, and involve about four hours riding before pitching camp at sunset. Guides prepare an evening meal of damper bread and stew, before you bed down beneath the stars then return the next morning. Longer expeditions – the only true way to cover enough ground to range into the Sahara – can range as far as the oasis town of Ksar Ghilane (seven to 10 days). If you trek in November, you'll not only have the best conditions, but the date harvest (which produces some of the best dates in the world) will also have just finished, and prices are generally cheaper.

↗ DO: **PARKOUR AT LISSES**

COUNTRY France **TYPE OF ACTIVITY** Parkour
FITNESS/EXPERTISE LEVEL Some free-running experience handy.
WHY NOW? You're going to run up a sweat, so come when Paris is cool.
DESCRIPTION Perhaps best known from the opening chase scenes in *Casino Royale*, parkour is an urban kind of gymnastics-cum-sprint-cum-hurdle race in which *traceurs* (parkour participants) dash between points, using city structures as part of the fun – climbing, leaping, hanging etc. Founded by David Belle, it had its origins in Lisses, at the southern edge of Paris, and this remains its heartland, with Lisses now home to an artificial climbing structure – the Dame du Lac, looking like a cross between a Mayan pyramid and an indoor climbing wall – that is considered the holy of parkour holies. Access issues have ruled the structure off-limits but Lisses doesn't disappoint *traceurs,* with many structures around town recognisable from various parkour documentaries.

↗ **Himalayan 100 Mile Stage Race**
www.himalayan.com
Run 160km over five days with views of four of the world's five highest mountains.

↗ **Mt Everest Bike Rally**
www.himalayan.com/b1.html
Five-day mountain-bike ride held in conjunction with the Himalayan 100 Mile Stage Race.

↗ **La Ruta de los Conquistadores**
www.adventurerace.com
Three-day, 320km mountain-bike race across harsh Costa Rican terrain; watch out for the 1000m climb.

↗ **Molesworth Muster**
www.bluedogevents.co.nz
An 80km mountain-bike ride along otherwise closed roads beneath New Zealand's Southern Alps.

GO: **HONG KONG, CHINA**

(ABOVE) ↗
Hong Kong is more than dim sum and downtown – get out and explore away from the tourist trail.

(RIGHT) ↗
Propel yourself to high-speed freedom with the Welsh wind in your sails.

↘ **WHY NOW? TRAILWALKER IS ON; NOVEMBER ALSO BREWS UP THE TERRITORY'S BEST WINDSURFING CONDITIONS**

Pack everything except your preconceptions and you might discover that über-urban Hong Kong is about more than downtown and dim sum. More than 7 million people call the territory home, but they're squeezed on to just 10% of the available land space, leaving around 1000 sq km of Hong Kong country open to exploration.

Walking trails in the territory are numerous, and include four long-distance paths. The 50km Hong Kong Trail cuts through five country parks on Hong Kong Island. The 70km Lantau Trail follows mountain tops from Mui Wo, doubling back at Tai O along the coast to where it started. The 78km Wilson Trail is unusual in that it begins on Hong Kong Island but crosses the eastern harbour to New Kowloon and carries on into the New Territories.

↗ DO: LAND YACHT AT PENDINE SANDS

COUNTRY Wales **TYPE OF ACTIVITY** Land yachting **FITNESS/EXPERTISE LEVEL** Beginners to wind warriors. **WHY NOW?** November is among the windiest months in southern Wales. **DESCRIPTION** With speeds of up to 120km/h, land yachting is exhilarating and also quite easy to pick up. The giant sandy beach at Cefn Sidan, in Pembrey Country Park, is an ideal spot to try out these wheeled demons, but it's nearby Pendine Sands that's considered *the* place to sail. Conditions are best with a southerly or southwesterly filling your sails (the typical wind in southern Wales at this time of year is a westerly). The hard, flat 12km beach at Pendine Sands was once a regular venue for land-speed records (most notably by Sir Malcolm Campbell). If you hear a loud bang as you're sailing, you probably haven't broken the speed of sound; unexploded munitions from a neighbouring testing ground are reputed to be found on the beach on occasions. To sail on Pendine you must join the Carmarthenshire Land Sailing Club (www.clscuk.com).

Hong Kong's longest path is the 100km MacLehose Trail across the Kowloon Peninsula. It's on this trail that you can also experience the phenomenon of Trailwalker, usually held this week in November. Created in Hong Kong in 1981 as an endurance training program for Gurkha soldiers (and subsequently spreading to the UK, Australia and New Zealand), participants must cover the MacLehose on foot in 48 hours (the Gurkhas had to do it in half that time).

The MacLehose Trail passes another Hong Kong outdoor icon: Lion Rock, a natural king of this urban jungle. Rising above Kowloon, it's also a cornerstone of Hong Kong's climbing scene, offering two- and three-pitch routes on its east and west faces. More than a dozen other Hong Kong crags also see climbing action, with the finest (and often busiest) routes found on Tung Lung Chau. Boulderers also have several playgrounds in which to perform their acrobatics.

Mountain-bike trails have opened in 10 country parks, birdwatchers can tick off 450 species (head to Mai Po Marsh for the best twitching), and the fact that Hong Kong's only Olympic gold medal came in windsurfing testifies to that sport's popularity – November brews up the territory's best windsurfing conditions. Hong Kong also has some surprisingly worthwhile diving spots, particularly in the far northeast. www.discoverhongkong.com; www.oxfamtrailwalker.org.hk/en; www.hongkongclimbing.com

[ABOVE] ↗
A maze you won't find your way out of. The Everglades offer 6070 sq km of labyrinthine waterways to paddle.

[TOP RIGHT] ↗
Bald is beautiful at the Alaska Bald Eagle Festival.

[BOTTOM RIGHT] ↗
A new take on *20,000 Leagues Under the Sea* – try snuba in Mauritius.

DO: TAKE THE WILDERNESS WATERWAY

COUNTRY USA **TYPE OF ACTIVITY** Canoeing/kayaking

FITNESS/EXPERTISE LEVEL Moderate fitness required.

WHY NOW? For pleasantly mild conditions (23°C average) and the least number of mosquitoes.

DESCRIPTION Covering the southern tip of peninsular Florida, the Everglades form the third largest national park in the USA, at around 6070 sq km, and the world's first national park created not for its scenery but for its biological diversity. It's the country's largest subtropical wilderness; it's World Heritage listed, an international biosphere and a wetland of international importance – quite simply, the Everglades are natural royalty.

Veined with waterways and estuaries, this watery maze is best explored by canoe or kayak. The chief paddling route is the Wilderness Waterway, a 159km journey through rivers and creeks (and, for a brief stint, in the Gulf of Mexico) along the Everglades' western edge, gliding by mangroves and sawgrass prairies.

The Wilderness Waterway begins in Everglades City in the park's north, winds through the Ten Thousand Islands (count them as you paddle past) and concludes at the Flamingo visitor centre at its very south. Allow about seven to nine days for the journey, and expect to see a few of the Glades' most famous inhabitants – alligators – possibly also more charming critters such as dolphins, manatees and roseate spoonbills.

Camp sites and camping platforms (known as chickees) are spread along the banks of the rivers and creeks, usually no more than 15km apart. Backcountry camping permits are required and can be obtained at the visitor centres in Everglades City or Flamingo. Canoes and kayaks can be rented in Everglades City. Be sure to travel with the necessary navigation charts – one turning can look very like another among the mangroves. The charts you'll need are numbers 11430, 11432 and 11433. www.nps.gov/ever

↗ DO: VISIT THE ALASKA CHILKAT BALD EAGLE PRESERVE

COUNTRY USA **TYPE OF ACTIVITY** Wildlife watching
FITNESS/EXPERTISE LEVEL Not required.
WHY NOW? To join the flocks at the Alaska Bald Eagle Festival.
DESCRIPTION Each year from October to February, more than 4000 bald eagles congregate along Alaska's Chilkat, Klehini and Tsirku Rivers to feed on spawning salmon. They come because an upwelling of warm water prevents the river from freezing, thus encouraging a late salmon run. It's a remarkable sight – hundreds of birds sitting in the bare trees lining the river, often six or more birds to a branch. The eagles can be seen from the Haines Hwy, where turnouts allow motorists to park and watch. The best view is between Mile 18 and Mile 22, where you'll find telescopes, interpretive displays and viewing platforms along the river. In the second week of November, nearby Haines is the venue for the Alaska Bald Eagle Festival, during which you can be accompanied to the preserve by noted naturalists. www.dnr.state.ak.us/parks/units/eagleprv.htm

↗ DO: UNDERSEA WALK IN MAURITIUS

COUNTRY Mauritius **TYPE OF ACTIVITY** Snuba
FITNESS/EXPERTISE LEVEL Not required.
WHY NOW? Get wet ahead of the approaching wet season.
DESCRIPTION The novel activity of undersea walking, or snuba, has caught on in a big way in Mauritius as it allows nondivers the chance to experience life below the waves. Participants don a weight belt and a diving helmet and stroll along the sea bed feeding the fish. Solar-powered pumps on the boat above feed oxygen to you during the 25-minute 'walk on the wet side', and divers are on hand in case there are any problems. In general, there's a minimum age requirement of seven years. The two prime spots for an underwater ramble are Grand Baie, in the north, and Belle Mare, on the east coast.

↗ DO: CLIMB PICO DE ORIZABA

COUNTRY Mexico **TYPE OF ACTIVITY** Mountaineering
FITNESS/EXPERTISE LEVEL Good fitness and climbing skills required.
WHY NOW? Climb on the fringe of the mountain's busiest season.
DESCRIPTION Mexico's highest mountain (5611m) is also the third-tallest in North America – only Denali (Mt McKinley) in Alaska and Mt Logan in Canada are taller. Orizaba is a dormant volcano with a small crater and a three-month snow-cap, and unless you have navigation skills and some experience of snow- and ice-climbing techniques you shouldn't attempt this climb without a guide. The most common route up Orizaba is from the north, using the small town of Tlachichuca as a base. From Tlachichuca, take a taxi to Villa Hidalgo at 3400m, then walk 10km to the mountain hut at 4200m. The climb from here is moderately steep over snow that's usually hard – it's not technically difficult, but crampons are essential, as are ropes and ice axes for safety. Most climbers leave the hut at about 2am to reach the peak for sunrise, before mist and cloud envelop the summit.

↗ Triple Challenge
www.triplechallenge.co.za
South African multisport event out of Pietermaritzburg; run, cycle and paddle more than 100km.

↗ 100km Pharaonic Race
www.egyptianmarathon.com.eg
Feel as old as the pyramids after running 100km through Egypt.

↗ Kendal Mountain Festival
www.mountainfest.co.uk
Visit the mountains from the comfort of a theatre chair in England's Lake District.

↗ Highland Fling
www.wildhorizons.com.au/highland-fling
Mountain bike 110km through the Southern Highlands of New South Wales, Australia.

↗ NOVEMBER

WEEK.03

GO: KWAZULU NATAL, SOUTH AFRICA

(ABOVE) ↗
The dramatic escarpment of the Drakensberg Mountains is the perfect setting for South Africa's most remote and rugged hiking.

(RIGHT) ↗
Although it's bright enough to read by, the electrifying Catatumbo Lightning display might distract you from your book.

WHY NOW? AT THIS TIME OF YEAR THE 'BIG FIVE' ARE DRAWN TO THE DWINDLING WATERHOLES IN THE PROVINCE'S PARKS

KwaZulu Natal is South Africa's most populous province, yet it's the kind of place where you can be surfing one day, swimming with sharks the next, viewing white rhinos the following day and then hiking across the jagged Drakensberg before your week is out.

Durban is the province's major city, and you can get busy without even leaving the city. Durban has surf and culture to match anywhere in the world. Given the right swell, the city has a range of quality breaks: South Break and Addington are normally the best beginner spots. The more experienced might want to range along the KwaZulu Natal coast to Westbrook, Ballito Bay and Zinkwazi Beach in the north, and Greenpoint, Scottburgh, Happy Wanderers, St Michaels and the Spot (all right-handers)

↗ DO: **WITNESS CATATUMBO LIGHTNING**

COUNTRY Venezuela **TYPE OF ACTIVITY** Natural phenomenon **FITNESS/EXPERTISE LEVEL** Not required. **WHY NOW?** Sightings are best from September through November. **DESCRIPTION** Centred on the mouth of the Río Catatumbo at Lago de Maracaibo, this strange phenomenon consists of frequent flashes of lightning with no accompanying thunder. The eerie, silent electrical storm, referred to as Catatumbo Lightning, can be so strong and constant that you will be able to read at night, and is said to be the world's largest single generator of ozone. Various hypotheses have been put forth to explain the lightning, but the theory that stands out is that cold winds descending from the Andes clash with hot, humid air evaporating from Lago de Maracaibo, producing the ionization of air particles responsible for the lightning. At this time of year there can be 150 to 200 flashes per minute.

in the south. Each produces rideable 1m to 2.5m-plus grinders over rock and sand bottom.

Deeper into the Indian Ocean, advanced divers who don't mind a shark or 200 will want to check out Protea Banks. At least 12 shark species frequent the banks. Look for grey reef, thresher, copper, sand, mako, tiger and even the occasional great white shark. For a more sedate and colourful diving experience, try the warm waters of Sodwana Bay.

One reason you'll want to come to KwaZulu Natal in November is to watch the wildlife at South Africa's oldest parks: Hluhuwe-Umfolozi and Greater St Lucia Wetlands. The former is the rhino capital of Africa, and also has KwaZulu Natal's only park with the full

complement of 'big five' creatures, all drawn at this time of year to the dwindling waterholes. Greater St Lucia is one of Southern Africa's most important coastal wetlands, famed for its crocodiles and, in November, humpback whales, whale sharks and nesting turtles.

Set on the border with Lesotho, the Drakensberg is South Africa's most enticing mountain range and will satisfy any mountain walker with its sheer, sharp peaks. Walk for a few hours or a few days; the southern end of the range offers some of the country's most remote and rugged hiking.

[ABOVE] ↗
Sample Rajasthan desert life on a camel safari.

[TOP RIGHT] ↗
Survey the seas surrounding the British Virgin Islands from the crow's nest of a crewed yacht.

[BOTTOM RIGHT] ↗
You need strong lungs and strong legs to run the Everest Marathon.

DO: **CAMEL SAFARI IN RAJASTHAN**

COUNTRY India **TYPE OF ACTIVITY** Camel riding

FITNESS/EXPERTISE LEVEL Not required.

WHY NOW? The most comfortable time for a camel safari is from October to February.

DESCRIPTION It's debatable whether the Rajasthan city of Jaisalmer is more famous for its sandcastle-like fort or for its camel safaris. No place better evokes ancient desert splendour and exotic trade routes, making it one of the most evocative places to begin a desert safari.

A camel journey into the Thar Desert offers a good way to sample desert life, but don't expect a sea of dunes. The Thar Desert is mostly barren scrub, sprinkled with villages and ruins. You'll come across tiny fields of millet, and children herding flocks of sheep or goats, whose tinkling neck bells offer a nice change from the sound of your farting camels.

The camel's reins are fastened to its nose peg, so the animal is easily steered. Stirrups make the journey a lot more comfortable. At resting points, the camels are unsaddled and hobbled. They limp off to graze on shrubs while the drivers brew chai or prepare food. The whole crew rests in the shade of thorn trees. At night you'll camp out, huddling around a tiny fire beneath a ceiling of stars and listening to the camel drivers' songs.

Most safaris last three to four days and the traditional circuit takes in Amar Sagar, where there's a garden, dried-up step-wells and a Jain temple; Mool Sagar, a run-down oasis with a Shiva Temple; Bada Bagh, a fertile oasis with a huge old dam and sandstone sculpted royal *chhatris* (centopaths) with beautifully carved ceilings; as well as various abandoned villages along the way.

More and more travellers are opting for remote safaris. You're driven in a 4WD for around 30km and then head off on your camel, avoiding the major sights and other safari groups. www.jaisalmertourism.com

↗ DO: SAIL THE BRITISH VIRGIN ISLANDS

COUNTRY British Virgin Islands **TYPE OF ACTIVITY** Sailing
FITNESS/EXPERTISE LEVEL Sailing experience required if bareboat
chartering. **WHY NOW?** It's the cusp of the high and dry season.
DESCRIPTION A felicitous combination of geography and geology
positions the BVI as sailing's magic kingdom. You've got a year-round
balmy climate, steady trade winds, little to worry about in the way of tides
or currents, a protected thoroughfare in the 56km-long Sir Francis Drake
Channel, and hundreds of anchorages, each within sight of one another.
These factors make the BVI one of the easiest places to sail, which
explains why more than a third of all visitors come to do just that. There
are three basic options: a sailing school; a bareboat charter (bare of crew
but fully equipped), with or without a skipper; or a more luxurious crewed
charter, complete with captain, cook and crew. A typical week-long
itinerary involves a sampling of the islands, while partially circumnavigating
Tortola. To hire a crewed yacht, contact the British Virgin Islands Charter
Yacht Society (www.bvicrewedyachts.com).

↗ DO: RUN THE EVEREST MARATHON

COUNTRY Nepal **TYPE OF ACTIVITY** Running
FITNESS/EXPERTISE LEVEL Good fitness and acclimatisation required.
WHY NOW? To race in the world's highest marathon. **DESCRIPTION**
Discover the painful feeling of running a marathon at heights usually
limited to mountaineers and hardy trekkers. With its starting line at Gorak
Shep (5160m), in the shadow of Mt Everest, it takes 10 days of trekking
just to get here. Then, with the temperature somewhere around -20°C, you
face the prospect of running 42km back to Namche Bazaar, dodging yak
trains and crossing rickety bridges only to clock a personal worst time –
most runners take twice as long to complete the Everest Marathon as
they do a normal marathon. To gain entry into this most difficult of races,
you must have experience of major cross-country, mountain running or
adventure events; road marathon experience is not sufficient.
www.everestmarathon.org.uk

↗ DO: HIKE IN THE SIMIEN MOUNTAINS

COUNTRY Ethiopia **TYPE OF ACTIVITY** Hiking
FITNESS/EXPERTISE LEVEL Moderate fitness required.
WHY NOW? Come early in the dry season (October to May) for green
landscapes and wildflowers. **DESCRIPTION** Far from Africa's beaten
mountain paths is a range unlike any other on the continent. The Simien
Mountains are made up of several plateaus, separated by broad river
valleys. A number of peaks rise above 4000m, including Ras Dashen
(4543m), the fourth-highest mountain in Africa. At the range's northern edge
is a 60km-long escarpment overlooking a land of rock pinnacles and mesas
for some of the finest views in Africa. All treks begin and end in Debark,
where the park headquarters are located. The most popular trekking routes
are along the western side of the massif, taking in the most impressive
sections of the escarpment. The most spectacular scenery is around the
Geech Abyss, while the classic Simien trek continues past Geech to the
summit of Ras Dashen; allow eight to 10 days for the return hike.

↗ **La Transtica**
www.latranstica.org
Seven days to run and raft from coast to coast
in Costa Rica.

↗ **Real Ale Wobble**
www.green-events.co.uk/events.php
Mountain bike up to 57km while quaffing
half-pints of ale at various checkpoints. Stick
around for the walkers' event a week later.

↗ **Ecomotion**
www.ecomotion.com.br
10-day, 430km team adventure race in Brazil;
disciplines include caving.

GO: VICTORIA FALLS, ZAMBIA/ZIMBABWE

[ABOVE] ↗
The thunderous roar and smoky spray of Victoria Falls is just the start of what the mighty Zambesi has to offer.

[RIGHT] ↗
There's nothing muddy about muck diving in PNG: it's a journey into history with an underwater garden thrown in.

WHY NOW? **THE ZAMBESI RIVER RAPIDS ARE RUNNING AT THEIR BEST**

Victoria Falls' thick, thundering curtain of water is so utterly overpowering it's regarded as one of the seven natural wonders of the world. Over this 1.7km-wide precipice, an average of 550,000 cu metres of water plummets 100m into the narrow Batoka Gorge every minute. In full flood, the spray – 'the smoke that thunders' – can be seen from 80km away.

Victoria Falls doubles as Africa's adventure capital, offering a staggering array of activities – some travellers have so much fun bungee jumping and/or rafting they forget to visit the falls! The headline act here are water activities, headed by some of the world's best white-water rafting. The Zambesi River below the falls is said to have the highest concentration of grade-five rapids of any watercourse on earth, and right now they are running at their best. Wild, low-water runs, taking in the winding 22km

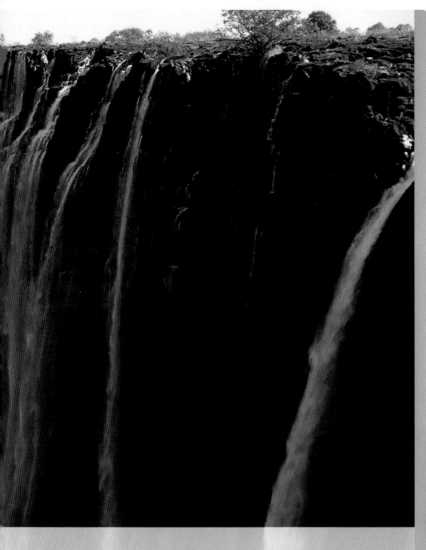

COUNTRY Papua New Guinea **TYPE OF ACTIVITY** Muck diving **FITNESS/EXPERTISE LEVEL** Not required. **WHY NOW?** Diving is best from October to March, when winds are lightest. **DESCRIPTION** Muck diving sounds like the ocean equivalent of bog snorkelling, but it's more akin to underwater macrophotography. Put simply, it's diving in silty water, enjoying the ocean's obscure smaller inhabitants, such as nudibranchs. PNG is the muck-diving world capital and Samarai Island is the epicentre. Anyone who can swim can witness the extravagant coral, fantastic tropical fish and the detritus of history side by side beneath the Samarai piers – Samarai was once the second-largest town in PNG but in 1942 Australian forces destroyed almost every building in anticipation of a Japanese invasion that never came. The easiest place to enter is just north of the Samarai Island wharf. To reach Samarai Island, jump aboard one of the public dinghies at Sanderson's Bay; the daily (except Saturday) crossing takes 1 ½ hours.

from rapids four to 18 (or 23) in Zimbabwe, or rapids one to 18 (or 23) in Zambia, operate from roughly 15 August to late December. All operators walk around grade-VI rapid nine, which is affectionately nicknamed Commercial Suicide.

If you want all the thrills of rafting without the raft, consider riverboarding, in which you surf the Zambezi with nothing between your body and the swirling maelstrom except a piece of foam.

Kayakers might be enticed here by images of kayaks tossed around in the Boiling Pot below the falls, but most canoeing and kayaking tours operate above the falls, paddling the wide river, exploring its mid-stream islands and shooting its mini-rapids.

Dry off with a quick leap from the Victoria Falls Bridge – at one time this 111m plunge was the world's highest bungee jump. If you have a few days left in your week, take your pick from horse, elephant and walking safaris, abseiling, high-wiring, microlighting, jet boating, a helicopter ride or drown your nerves with a spot of booze cruising. If it all sounds like an adventuring equivalent of a fast-food joint, you can even opt for an activity 'combo'...would you like a bungee jump with that?

[ABOVE] ↗
Take the slow boat to Timbuktu to encounter the people and landscapes of Mali.

[RIGHT] ↗
Skyjump is your chance to leap off a tall building in a single bound.

DO: **TIMBUKTU BY BOAT**

COUNTRY Mali **TYPE OF ACTIVITY** Adventure travel
FITNESS/EXPERTISE LEVEL Not required.
WHY NOW? The river's at its highest from August to mid-December.

DESCRIPTION The name Timbuktu has the very ring of adventure: remote, desert-licked and exotic. And it can still be an adventure to get here if you come on one of the large passenger boats that ply the Niger River between Koulikoro (60km northeast of Bamako) and Gao, via Korioumé.

Passenger boats run from August to mid-December, when the river is high, and you should expect a floating mass of jostling humanity for the five days of sailing between Koulikoro and Korioumé. Luxe and first class consist of two-berth cabins; second is a four-berth cabin; third is either an eight-berth or 12-berth cabin (although you can sleep and hang out on the upper deck); and fourth class is in the packed and basic lower deck (which even the most hardened travellers rate as the pits). Whatever class you're in, it'll be sweltering and the toilets will be flooded.

For a less gritty river experience, you can travel to Timbuktu by more traditional motorised canoes called *pinasse*. From the city of Mopti you can board a large, cargo laden *pinasse*, but this can be slow. A more serene, comfortable and quicker option is to get a group together and hire a tourist *pinasse*, journeying along the pale luminous swell of the Niger, banked by sand dunes, passing boats with rice-bag sails, makeshift villages, waving people and wading fishermen. You sleep on the river bank or in the boat. Nights are magical – silent and star-lit – but also cold, so pack a blanket or sleeping bag. It will take you about three days to reach Korioumé (18km from Timbuktu), from where you catch a shared taxi to Timbuktu.

↗ DO: SKYJUMP IN AUCKLAND

COUNTRY New Zealand **TYPE OF ACTIVITY** Cable-controlled BASE jumping
FITNESS/EXPERTISE LEVEL Not required.
WHY NOW? Spring...a wonderful time to spring from a tall building.
DESCRIPTION Think bungee jumping, but with a very urban, very Auckland twist. New Zealand's largest city also presents one of the country's largest adrenaline rushes: Skyjump, a 192m, cable-controlled BASE jump from the tallest building in New Zealand. Storeys above the gaming tables, restaurants and bars that fill the tower, you're fitted into a harness and a Superman-coloured suit and clipped to a cable. As you leap, a drum feeds out the cable, and you drop at a speed of around 85km/h by a fan descender. It's 20 seconds of superhero flight that almost impales jumpers on the city below. Instead, the descender – the sort used by Hollywood movie makers to film falling stunts (think *Entrapment* or *Titanic*) – slows the fall at the end, delivering you to earth on your feet. www.skyjump.co.nz

↗ DO: HILL-TRIBE TREK IN NORTHERN THAILAND

COUNTRY Thailand **TYPE OF ACTIVITY** Hiking
FITNESS/EXPERTISE LEVEL Good fitness required.
WHY NOW? The best time to trek is November to February, when the weather is refreshing, there's little or no rain and wildflowers are in bloom.
DESCRIPTION Thousands of visitors trek into the hills of northern Thailand each year, though many people feel awkward walking through hill-tribe villages and playing the role of voyeur. In general, the trekking business has become more conscious of the need to tread carefully in hill-tribe villages, and most companies limit the number of visits to a particular area and are careful not to overlap areas used by other companies. Chiang Mai and Chiang Rai are the main centres for hill-tribe trekking, while many people now also do short treks on their own, staying in villages along the way. It's not necessary to bring a lot of food or gear, just money for food that can be bought en route. The Tourism Authority of Thailand, however, discourages trekking on your own because of safety risks.

↗ DO: CRUISE THE SUNDERBANS TIGER RESERVE

COUNTRY India **TYPE OF ACTIVITY** Wildlife watching
FITNESS/EXPERTISE LEVEL Not required.
WHY NOW? Tiger sightings are most likely between October and March.
DESCRIPTION Home to one of the largest tiger populations on the planet, the lush 2585-sq-km Sunderbans Tiger Reserve seemingly floats atop the waters of the world's largest delta in West Bengal. The Royal Bengal tigers (estimated to number 274 in 2004) not only wander the impenetrable depths of the mangrove forests, but also swim the delta's innumerable channels. Although they're known to have an appetite for humans, tigers are typically shy and sightings are the exception, not the rule. Visiting independently is difficult, with seemingly never-ending permits, fees and tricky transportation connections. The West Bengal tourist department in Kolkata organises weekly boat cruises through the present high season. www.westbengaltourism.gov.in

↗ **Lake Taupo Cycle Challenge**
www.cyclechallenge.org.nz
Ride 160km around the New Zealand volcanic caldera, Lake Taupo.

↗ **Sani Stagger Endurance Race**
www.sanistagger.com
A knee-crunching marathon as you descend, then ascend, 1300m along the only road to cross South Africa's Drakensberg mountains.

↗ **Last Desert**
www.4deserts.com/thelastdesert
Run 250km across the Antarctic in six stages - just to get here you'll have to have run across two other deserts.

↗ **DECEMBER**

WEEK.01

GO: MÉRIDA,
VENEZUELA

[ABOVE] ↗
Ascend the Pico Espejo
by teleférico, the world's
highest and longest
cable-car system.

[RIGHT] ↗
Tysfjord treats visitors
to bright lights above
the surface, and gentle
giants below.

WHY NOW? IN DECEMBER, THE NORTHERN ANDES ARE
ENTERING THE DRY SEASON

Every continent should have a place that devotes itself to
bringing adventure and adrenaline to the masses. South America
has Mérida, set among the northern Andes, in the western corner of
Venezuela, and now entering its dry season. It's surrounded by beautiful
mountains, including the country's highest peak, 5007m Pico Bolívar, just
12km away. It's home to the famous teleférico, the world's highest and
longest cable-car system, running 12.5km from the bottom station of
Barinitas (1577m) in Mérida to the top at Pico Espejo (4765m), covering
the ascent in four stages. Even if you take the journey straight through
you'll be on the teleférico for around 1½ hours, though the cable car is
regularly shut down for repairs.

The list of adventure sports and outdoor activities on offer in Mérida
is longer than the menus in its restaurants – hiking, mountaineering,

↗ **DO: SWIM WITH ORCAS IN TYSFJORD**

↗ DO: SWIM WITH ORCAS IN TYSFJORD

COUNTRY Norway **TYPE OF ACTIVITY** Snorkelling/wildlife watching **FITNESS/ EXPERTISE LEVEL** Cold blood an asset. **WHY NOW?** Orcas generally arrive in late October and leave in January. **DESCRIPTION** Mid-autumn signals the arrival of migrating herring and, behind them, hundreds of orcas into Norway's Tysfjord, around 250km north of the Arctic Circle. For three months the killer whales stay, chasing herring while rugged-up wildlife watchers chase them. You can remain in the trawler or Zodiac for a surface view, or seize the rare (if chilly) opportunity to snorkel among these sleek giants. You'll be kitted out in dry suits and inner linings, and from the surface you can watch the orcas passing below. Sea eagles also have an appetite for Tysfjord herring, picking off the shoals as they're chased to the surface by the orcas. Lift your eyes from the fjord and you're also likely to be treated to the Northern Lights stellar spectacular. www.tysfjord-turistsenter.no/safari

birdwatching, paragliding, horse riding, rafting and mountain biking might just be the specials board. Mountains form the city's staple diet, and the most popular high-mountain trekking area is the Parque Nacional Sierra Nevada, east of Mérida, which has all of Venezuela's highest peaks, including Pico Bolívar, Pico Humboldt (4942m) and Pico Bonpland (4883m). Guided ascents are offered by most of Mérida's tour operators – Bolívar, particularly, is a mountaineering feat. The Parque Nacional Sierra La Culata, to Mérida's north, also offers some amazing hiking territory, and is particularly noted for its desert-like highland landscapes.

Paragliding is Mérida's most iconic adventure sport; there are even pictures of paragliders on the side of the city's garbage trucks. Tandem paraglides usually launch from Las González, an hour's drive from the city. From here you glide for 20 to 30 minutes down 850 vertical metres. Rafting is organised on several rivers on the southern slopes of the Andes, while canyoning is among the adventuring desserts.

If you'd rather look at animals than be one, Mérida is a centre for trips into Los Llanos, an immense plain savanna south of the Andes that is Venezuela's great repository of wildlife, particularly birds. It's also excellent ground to get close – not too close, mind – to piranhas, anacondas, caimans and capybaras.

[ABOVE] ↗
The jagged massif of the Torres del Paine rises above the waters of Lago Pehoé.

[TOP RIGHT] ↗
Make a splash in the subterranean wonderland of Waitomo.

[BOTTOM RIGHT] ↗
Mind the gap – test your nerves on a kloofing adventure.

DO: HIKE AT TORRES DEL PAINE

COUNTRY Chile **TYPE OF ACTIVITY** Hiking

FITNESS/EXPERTISE LEVEL Good fitness required.

WHY NOW? The shoulder summer season of December is one of the best trekking times.

DESCRIPTION Soaring more than 2000m above the Patagonian steppe, the Torres del Paine (Towers of Paine) are spectacular granite pillars that dominate the landscape of what is arguably South America's finest national park, Parque Nacional Torres del Paine. For hikers, this 181-sq-km park is an unequalled destination, with a well-developed trail network and *refugios* (mountain huts) and camping grounds at strategic spots.

For most trekkers the question is whether to circuit or to 'W'. Circuiting takes around eight days, while the popular W trek, named for the route's in-and-out shape, takes around five. Most hikers start both routes from Laguna Amarga – the W climbs to the spectacular Torres del Paine Lookout, immediately below the towers. With their mighty columns ringed by shelf glaciers and meltwater-streaked rocks, this is one of Patagonia's classic scenes. The W goes on via Los Cuernos and Lago Pehoé to Lago Grey, where the unstable, 200m-thick snout of Glaciar Grey continually sends blocks of ice – some as big as a house – plunging into the freezing waters. Patagonia's notoriously strong winds drive the icebergs across the lake to strand on the shore.

Walking the complete Torres del Paine circuit takes in the W plus the more remote back side of the massif. There are eight *refugios* for trekkers in the park, and the availability of hired camping equipment at all *refugios* and at Campamento Los Perros has made it theoretically possible to trek the circuit or the W without carrying a tent. For hikers on the circuit, however, this means covering the most difficult and remote stretch between Campamento Los Perros and Refugio Grey, including the crossing of the circuit's highest pass, in a long day. Some hikers find this is beyond them.

↗ DO: CAVE TUBE AT WAITOMO

COUNTRY New Zealand **TYPE OF ACTIVITY** Cave tubing
FITNESS/EXPERTISE LEVEL Rookies to full-blown spelunkers.
WHY NOW? Come early in summer to beat the high season.
DESCRIPTION The name Waitomo, which comes from *wai* (water) and *tomo* (hole or shaft), is appropriate: dotted throughout the countryside around this North Island town are numerous shafts dropping abruptly into at least 300 underground caves and streams. Tourism here began with sedate cave visits but in typical Kiwi fashion the list of things to do has become ever more daring. Cave tubing – floating through glow-worm-lit caves on inner tubes – has become Waitomo's signature activity, but even this simple activity now has more flavours than an ice-cream store. You can abseil up to 100m into caves; you can make belayed rock climbs out; and you can swim, leap and whoosh through the dark on flying foxes.
www.waitomocaves.com

↗ DO: KLOOFING IN SUICIDE GORGE

COUNTRY South Africa **TYPE OF ACTIVITY** Kloofing/canyoning
FITNESS/EXPERTISE LEVEL Swimming skills required.
WHY NOW? It's cold in the gorges so come when it's warm; the route is open November to April.
DESCRIPTION Kloofing is the South African term for the activity much of the rest of the world knows as canyoning. The object is to navigate your way through a narrow gorge or canyon, walking, scrambling, leaping into pools, swimming, abseiling, whatever it takes, until you emerge at the bottom, hopefully wetter and better for the experience. On the Western Cape – the heartland of kloofing – one of the most popular trips is through Suicide Gorge, where the leaps will at times make you feel that the gorge is very aptly named; some are almost 15m in height. The trail through the gorge is around 18km in length; access is through the Hottentots Holland Nature Reserve.

↗ DO: BUNGEE JUMP INTO A VOLCANO

COUNTRY Chile **TYPE OF ACTIVITY** Bungee jumping
FITNESS/EXPERTISE LEVEL Not required.
WHY NOW? Start the southern summer in the hottest of fashions.
DESCRIPTION Think of all the imaginable bungee jump scenarios and you probably still won't hit on this idea. In the Patagonian town of Pucón, you can leap from the skid of a hovering helicopter into the smoking, bubbling frenzy of a volcanic crater. This leap began as a TV stunt but struck the operators as a good commercial idea. The helicopter flies above the summit of 2847m Volcan Villarrica, and from here you dive into the sulphurous fog. The elastic cord stretches around 100m, leaving you dangling just 200m or so above the molten lava. And from here there's no easy way back into the helicopter. Instead you have a journey back to the airport hanging 100m below the speeding helicopter. This jump will cost you more than endorphins; it's priced at almost US$10,000.
www.bungee.com/bzapp/volcano

Kepler Challenge
www.keplerchallenge.co.nz
Run 60km through the Fiordland mountains along New Zealand's Kepler Track.

Goat Alpine Adventure Run
www.thegoat.co.nz
Get your horns around a 21km run to the ski fields of periodically eruptive Mt Ruapehu.

Grim Original
www.grimchallenge.co.uk
13km of muddy and wet running over an Aldershot (UK) army-vehicle testing ground.

Abu Dhabi Adventure Challenge
www.abudhabi-adventure.com
Six-day, 450km stage race that includes the uniquely local discipline of camel hiking.

↗ DECEMBER

WEEK.02

GO:
ANTARCTICA

[ABOVE] ↗
Worth the trip –
crabeater seals go with
the floe at Cape Renard.

[RIGHT] ↗
Get a grip on adventure
in France by rope-free
bouldering in the Forêt
de Fontainebleau.

WHY NOW? DECEMBER OFFERS UP TO 20 HOURS OF DAYLIGHT AND THE CHANCE TO SEE HATCHING PENGUINS
Antarctica, the earth's most isolated continent, must be earned, through either a long, often uncomfortable voyage or an expensive flight. Weather and ice – not clocks or calendars – set the schedule, and itineraries are subject to the continent's changing moods. What you'll find, however, is a spectacular wilderness of snow, ice and rock, teeming with wildlife.

Unless you're planning your own expedition, you'll visit Antarctica as part of a group tour, most likely on a ship. The most popular Antarctica trip involves an exploration of the Antarctic Peninsula, one of the continent's richest breeding grounds for seabirds, seals and penguins. Trips leave from Ushuaia, on South America's Tierra del Fuego, and you'll most likely make your first landing at one of the South Shetland Islands, a 540km chain of islands at the northern end of the Antarctic Peninsula with spectacular scenery and abundant wildlife.

↗ DO: BOULDER AT FONTAINEBLEAU

COUNTRY France **TYPE OF ACTIVITY**
Bouldering **FITNESS/EXPERTISE LEVEL**
Beginners to pros, but bring strong fingers.
WHY NOW? The sandstone is at its best in
the French winter. **DESCRIPTION** Look past
the elegance and splendour of Fontainebleau,
the former royal residence 67km southeast
of Paris, and you'll find its antithesis, the
gritty world of bouldering, at play in the Forêt
de Fontainebleau. To boulderers (who climb
near to the ground without ropes) this is the
enchanted forest, a place where they can't
see the trees for the rocks. 'Font' is prized for
its diverse routes and its collection of circuits,
in which problems are linked together into
a single route. The circuits might feature up
to 75 problems, and one stretches out for
around 10km. Each circuit at Font is colour-
coded according to its difficulty, with yellow
the easiest and black the most tendon-tearing.
http://bleau.info

On the Antarctic Peninsula your schedule will
depend on the expedition leader's judgment, though
most tours ultimately visit the same landing sites
because they offer easy access to wildlife, a station
or a museum. Likely landings include the former
British base-turned-museum at Port Lockroy; Neko
Harbor, where the glacier across from the landing
site often calves with a thunderous roar; and the US
Palmer research station.

You'll almost certainly call in at Paradise Harbor,
described in tour brochures as 'the most aptly
named place in the world'. That may be overstating it
a little but with its majestic icebergs and reflections
of the surrounding mountains, Paradise Harbor is
undeniably beautiful. It's a favorite place for 'Zodiac
cruising' around the ice that's calved from the glacier
at the head of the bay.

The Antarctic tour season is short – about four
months, with each month offering its own highlights.
Coming in December, at the height of the austral
summer, you'll find penguins hatching eggs and
feeding chicks, and you'll have up to 20 hours of
sunlight every day.

[ABOVE] ↗
Lower yourself 400m
into the abyss of the
Cave of Swallows.

[TOP RIGHT] ↗
Zorbing will turn your life
upside down and round
and round.

[BOTTOM RIGHT] ↗
Jump out of bed
early to spot
Madagascar's largest
lemur, the rare indri.

DO: ABSEIL INTO THE CAVE OF SWALLOWS

COUNTRY Mexico **TYPE OF ACTIVITY** Abseiling/rappelling
FITNESS/EXPERTISE LEVEL Abseiling experience crucial.
WHY NOW? For cool winter conditions to match the cool cave interior.

DESCRIPTION As its name might suggest, the Cave of Swallows, in the Mexican state of San Luis Potosí, has long been a favourite with twitchers, though curiously it is not home to swallows. Instead each morning thousands of white-collared swifts and green conures exit the cave (with its massive 60m wide entrance), flying in circles as they ascend gradually through the pit and then scattering into the skies. At night they return, freefalling into the cave to their nests.

For a while it was another sort of freefalling creature that put this cave on the adventuring map. One of the deepest caves in the world, and with a plunge of close to 400m from the cave entrance to the cave floor – you could stand the Eiffel Tower up inside the cave shaft – the Cave of Swallows became a favourite among BASE jumpers. Without a parachute it was about 12 seconds from the limestone cave lip to its floor, so the freefall was brief but exhilarating before chutes were deployed, spiralling BASE jumpers to the floor of the cave like a mirror image of the departing birds.

Environmental and safety concerns led to a ban on BASE jumping in the cave, so the way down now is by one of the world's longest abseiling descents – it's a few minutes down 400m of rope but about an hour of winching back out. Avoid abseiling at dawn or dusk so as to disturb the birds as little as possible.

The Cave of Swallows is about 300km from the state capital of San Luis Potosí city, near Ciudad Valles.

↗ DO: ZORB IN ROTORUA

COUNTRY New Zealand **TYPE OF ACTIVITY** Zorbing
FITNESS/EXPERTISE LEVEL Not required.
WHY NOW? Decent weather and Rotorua's holiday crowds are a week or two from arriving.
DESCRIPTION Zorbing is simple in theory: wriggle inside a large plastic ball and roll down a hill at speeds of up to 50 km/h. A cushion of air protects you from the hard bumps, while the centrifugal force pins your body to the ball in the manner of a gravity-defying show ride. It's dizzying and disorienting, but it wouldn't be a New Zealand adventure if there wasn't a way to spice up the activity even further. In this case, the evil sister is Zydro, where a bucket of water is poured into the Zorb, drenching you (and up to two other people inside the Zorb with you) as you scream your way downhill. Cold water or warm water, it's your choice.
www.zorb.co.nz

↗ DO: LEMUR TRACK IN PARC NATIONAL D'ANDASIBE-MANTADIA

COUNTRY Madagascar **TYPE OF ACTIVITY** Wildlife watching
FITNESS/EXPERTISE LEVEL Not required.
WHY NOW? The park fills up during Madagascar's high tourist season between July and September, though now is actually a better time to visit.
DESCRIPTION Parc National d'Andasibe-Mantadia consists of beautiful primary forest studded with lakes, and is the home of the rare indri, Madagascar's largest lemur. The wondrous indri has been described as looking like a four-year-old child in a panda suit, and is famous for its eerie wailing cry, which sounds like something between a fire siren and the song of an operatic tenor – it's an amazing creature to behold. There are about 60 family groups of two or five indris in the park; their cry, which can be heard up to 3km away, is used to define a particular group's territory. Indris are active on and off throughout the day, beginning about an hour after daybreak, which is usually the best time to try to see them.
www.parcs-madagascar.com

↗ DO: RAFT THE SOURCE OF THE NILE

COUNTRY Uganda **TYPE OF ACTIVITY** White-water rafting
FITNESS/EXPERTISE LEVEL Not required.
WHY NOW? Rafting is good year-round, with water levels constant, but December is one of the drier months in Jinja.
DESCRIPTION The source of the Nile out of Lake Victoria is one of the world's most spectacular white-water rafting destinations, and a place where you come to tackle the 'big four' – the source's four grade-five rapids (not the 'big five' usually sought in Africa). Rafting trips operate out of the town of Jinja (about 1½ hours by bus from the Ugandan capital, Kampala), and the growing list of white-water accoutrements is turning Jinja into one of Africa's burgeoning adventure destinations. The brave-hearted can try riverboarding, in which you take on the Nile armed only with a boogie board, or take instruction in white-water kayaking. Or you can just drop in from the 44m-high Nile High Bungee at the Jinja Nile Resort.

7 Cerros Medellin
www.7cerrosmedellin.com
Three-day urban adventure race through the streets and seven cerros (hills) of the Colombian city of Medellin.

Anaconda Lorne Surfcoast
www.rapidascent.com.au
Surf-oriented adventure race on Australia's surf coast: an ocean swim, beach run and ocean paddle take place beside standard stage events.

Action Asia Challenge Hong Kong
www.actionasiaevents.com
Single-day adventure race involving river-rock scrambling, ocean swimming and orienteering.

MICRONESIA

[ABOVE] ⬈
Make a dive for the 2000 islands of Micronesia scattered across the turquoise waters of the North Pacific.

[RIGHT] ⬈
Riding high on the back of a behemoth will give you a whole new perspective on Cambodia.

WHY NOW? DECEMBER TO FEBRUARY IS MANTA RAY SEASON IN MILL CHANNEL

In contrast to the vast North Pacific seas they span, the total land area of the 2000 Micronesian islands is so small that many world maps don't even bother to dot them in. But they are on every diver's map.

Micronesia's clear, 27°C waters teem with coral gardens and tropical fish. Around Palau, three ocean currents converge to bring in some of the most varied and dazzling marine life in the world. In Chuuk, the lagoon bed holds an entire Japanese fleet, frozen in time where it sank in February 1944. Complete with sake cups and skeletons, jeeps and tanks tied on board and fighter planes still waiting in the holds, the wrecks have been declared an underwater museum.

Thanks to Bikini Atoll's ominous nuclear history – the USA conducted 23 nuclear tests here in 1946 – the atoll has become one of Micronesia's premier dive sites, with divers massing to see the wrecks created by

COUNTRY Cambodia **TYPE OF ACTIVITY**
Elephant trekking **FITNESS/EXPERTISE LEVEL**
Not required. **WHY NOW?** The ideal time to
visit Cambodia is December and January,
when humidity levels are low, there's little
rainfall and a cooling breeze whips across
the land. **DESCRIPTION** Nestled against the
eastern border, Mondulkiri is Cambodia's most
sparsely populated province, with just two
people per square kilometre. This has helped
make it a great spot for elephant trekking.
The villages of Phulung and Putang, near the
provincial capital Sen Monorom, are the most
popular places to arrange a trek. Most of the
guesthouses around Sen Monorom, as well as
the tourist office, can arrange day treks, and it's
also possible to negotiate a longer trek with an
overnight stay in a Pnong village. For an original
elephant experience, spend a day at the
Elephant Valley Project, where you can learn
the art of the mahout, including an afternoon
ride to a waterfall where you can help wash
down the elephants.

the testing. One highlight is the USS *Saratoga*, the
world's only diveable aircraft carrier, which still holds
planes and racks of bombs. Another memorable dive
is the *Nagato*, the Japanese battleship from the deck
of which Admiral Yamamoto ordered his warplanes
to attack Pearl Harbor. Bikini is a great spot for diving
with sharks – grey reef sharks abound, and spotting a
silvertip on the wrecks is not uncommon.

Yap also has good diving, including virgin reefs
with excellent coral, vertical walls, sea caves, channel
drifts, schools of grey sharks and barracuda, sea
turtles and a couple of shipwrecks. Its most novel
attraction, however, is manta rays. From December
to February divers go to Manta Ridge in Mill Channel,
where a school of manta rays cruise about. These
gentle creatures, which can have a wingspan up to
3.6m, swim through the channel as divers cling to a
ledge about 9m below the surface. The manta rays
often come close enough to brush divers with their
wingtips.

The main air gateways into Micronesia are Honolulu
and Guam. www.visit-fsm.org

[ABOVE] ↗
The symmetrical cone of Ecuador's Volcán Cotopaxi lures mountaineers in search of a summit out of the ordinary.

[TOP RIGHT] ↗
The best way to avoid rush-hour traffic? Climbers scale the Sydney Harbour Bridge.

[BOTTOM RIGHT] ↗
Let fly on a zip-line through the canopy of the Costa Rican jungle.

DO: **CLIMB COTOPAXI**

COUNTRY Ecuador **TYPE OF ACTIVITY** Mountaineering
FITNESS/EXPERTISE LEVEL Mountaineering experience essential.
WHY NOW? December to February (and June to August) offer the best climbing conditions.
DESCRIPTION Volcán Cotopaxi (5897m), rising prominently 55km south of Quito, is Ecuador's second-highest peak, a symmetrical cone that forms the centrepiece of the country's oldest national park and its most popular outside of the Galápagos Islands. It's also the most popular high climb in Ecuador, no doubt due to a combination of its proximity, ease of access from Quito and its classic form.

The ascent is technically easy by mountaineering standards, but the route is crevassed, and climbers are killed almost every year. Glacier travel skills are essential and so is adequate acclimatisation. If you don't have such skills, hire a guide, preferably a member of Aseguim, the Ecuadorian professional guides association.

The ascent is generally commenced from a climbers' *refugio* (mountain hut) on the mountain's northern slopes soon after midnight, aiming to reach the summit in the early daylight hours, before cloud envelops the peak, and to descend before the snow softens. It normally takes five to seven hours to reach the summit and perhaps three hours to descend. Route details vary due to changes in the glacier. The view from the summit includes Chimborazo (6310m), Ecuador's highest peak and, owing to a bulge around the equator, the world's furthest point from the centre of the earth.

To get to the climbers *refugio* from Quito, take a bus south down the Panamericana and ask to be dropped off at the park entrance turn-off, just north of Lasso. There are usually vehicles waiting at the turn-off that will take you up to the *refugio* car park at 4500m. It's a 30-minute to one-hour walk from the car park up to the *refugio*, at 4800m.

↗ DO: CLIMB THE SYDNEY HARBOUR BRIDGE

COUNTRY Australia **TYPE OF ACTIVITY** Bridge climbing
FITNESS/EXPERTISE LEVEL Not required.
WHY NOW? Catch a summer dawn over Sydney Harbour.
DESCRIPTION Nominated by BBC viewers in 2003 as one of '50 things to do before you die', climbing to the top of the great metal coat-hanger that spans Sydney Harbour was once the domain of bridge painters. Now everyone can do it, with daily 3½-hour tours guiding visitors through the metalwork to the bridge's apex, 134m above the water of Sydney Harbour. You can climb during the day, at twilight, at night or, best of all, as the sun rises over the Tasman Sea and the harbour to break open a summer day. Such is the climb's popularity, bridge climbing has spread to the Auckland Harbour Bridge and Brisbane's Story Bridge.
www.bridgeclimb.com

↗ DO: CANOPY TOURS AT SANTA ELENA

COUNTRY Costa Rica **TYPE OF ACTIVITY** Zip line (flying fox) **FITNESS/EXPERTISE LEVEL** Not required. **WHY NOW?** Zip through the rainforest at about the driest time of year. **DESCRIPTION** In green and clean Costa Rica, the term 'canopy tour' might sound like a sedate peek into the foliage of a cloud forest but that would be a lie. Think instead of being strapped into a harness, hooked on to a cable-and-pulley system and sailing through the rainforest at high speeds á la *George of the Jungle*. Operators sell this as a great way to see nature, though the only way you're going to see a quetzal on one of these things is if you run smack dab into the poor bird. But what the heck; they really are a lot of fun. The zip-line craze began in the northwestern town of Santa Elena and there are now around 80 zip lines throughout Costa Rica. You'll still find many of them in Santa Elena and the neighbouring Quaker settlement of Monteverde.
www.monteverdeinfo.com; www.monteverdecostarica.info

↗ DO: PLYMOUTH–BANJUL RALLY

COUNTRIES England, France, Morocco, Mauritania, Senegal, Gambia
TYPE OF ACTIVITY Motoring rally
FITNESS/EXPERTISE LEVEL Not required.
WHY NOW? Cars leave from Plymouth through December.
DESCRIPTION Like the look of the Paris–Dakar Rally but haven't the necessary money or the speed? Perhaps the Plymouth–Banjul Rally is the event for you. To take part in this annual, noncompetitive rally, your vehicle must have cost less than £100 (Ladas are a favourite) and you must have spent no more than £15 on preparing the car. Then all you have to do is nurse the thing across six countries and 6000km into the Gambian capital of Banjul, where your car will be auctioned in aid of local charities. There's no fixed departure date and it'll probably take you around three weeks – you can take even longer if you want to look around a bit as you drive.
www.plymouth-dakar.co.uk

↗ **Morgan's Run**
www.ontrackclub.co.za
Bi-annual, 400km adventure race along the Eastern Cape coast in South Africa.

↗ **Sabie Experience**
www.sabieexperience.co.za
Four-day, 230km bike race around Sabie, South Africa's mountain-bike heartland.

↗ **Sheep Mountain 150**
www.sheepmountain.com
Very brisk 240km Alaskan dog-sled race; winner takes around 24 hours.

GO: LAPLAND, SCANDINAVIA

[ABOVE] ↗
Listen out for Santa's sleigh bells as you mush through Lapland's winter wonderland.

[RIGHT] ↗
Let slithering snakes massssage away the tension that has built up from having snakes slithering all over your face.

WHY NOW? VISIT NOW FOR FESTIVITIES AND FUN IN SANTA'S BACKYARD

Santa was here, though right now he's too busy to bother with visitors, so you'll need to find other Scandinavian distractions. Even with Lapland cloaked in the Polar Night, such distractions aren't difficult to find.

Begin in the Finnish city of Rovaniemi, the self-styled home of Santa Claus. Here, you'll find the Santa Claus Tourist Centre, the Santapark amusement park, Santa Claus Village straddling the Arctic Circle, an airport classified as Santa's official airport by the International Aviation Association, and a school for Santa assistants. When you've had your fill of the fat man in the red suit (is five minutes enough?), you'll discover that Rovaniemi is also a convenient base for dog- or reindeer-sledding, skiing, ice-fishing or snowmobile safaris.

Hop across the border to Sweden for a Nordic ski outing on Sweden's most famous hiking trail. Kungsleden (King's Trail) stretches 450km from

↗ DO: **RELAX WITH A SNAKE MASSAGE**

COUNTRY Israel **TYPE OF ACTIVITY** Massage
FITNESS/EXPERTISE LEVEL Not required.
WHY NOW? It's been a wild year, so wind
down in a wild way.
DESCRIPTION As the rest of the travelling
world relaxes over Christmas in spas that
pamper with mud wraps and hot rocks, head
to Talmei Elazar in northern Israel to discover
that adventure can be enjoyed laying down,
thanks to the soothing touch of snakes.
Here, one beauty spa – suitably attached to
a carnivorous plant farm – offers a treatment
that involves throwing onto your back half
a dozen nonvenomous corn snakes, milk
snakes and California and Florida king snakes
and letting their motion knead the tension
from your muscles…perhaps even as the
very presence of the snakes adds tension into
other parts of your body. It's a hell of a way to
slither out of one year and into the next.

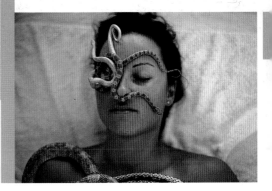

Abisko in the north to Hemavan in the south –
National Geographic once called this the 'last
remote wilderness in Western Europe'. If you want a
shorter outing on the trail, the most popular section
is the northernmost 100km between Abisko and
Nikkaluokta.

Eighteen kilometres from Sweden's northernmost
town, and 200km above the Arctic Circle, you'll also
find the Ice Hotel, reconstructed annually from tonnes
of ice taken from the local river. If you can wriggle out
from beneath your reindeer-skin blankets (the average
December temperature is around -13˚C), you'll find an
activity menu long enough to fill an entire week: take
a snowmobile for a night out at a wilderness camp;
venture to a moose wintering pasture; go mushing
on a dog-sled tour; go in search of the Northern
Lights on horseback or simply discover your inner
Scandinavian by hitting the hot tub.

If you'd like some adventure but can't resist
the Christmas moment, you're probably ripe for a
reindeer safari. Norway's Øvre Pasvik National Park
offers the most remote safari choice. Tucked hard
against the border with Finland and Russia, it's the
last corner of the country where wolves, wolverines,
lynx and brown bears still roam. Or you can return to
where you began, in Rovaniemi, for a reindeer sleigh
ride between Santapark and Santa Claus Village.
Ho, ho, ho. www.rovaniemi.fi

[ABOVE] ↗
The Franklin River wilderness is pure back-to-nature bliss, blending white-water adrenaline with majestic bush.

[TOP RIGHT] ↗
Mexico's Portrero Chico offers a dizzying array of climbing routes.

[BOTTOM RIGHT] ↗
A morning swim in the Med, an afternoon on the slopes.

DO: RAFT THE FRANKLIN RIVER

COUNTRY Australia **TYPE OF ACTIVITY** White-water rafting

FITNESS/EXPERTISE LEVEL Extensive white-water experience required if rafting independently.

WHY NOW? The rafting season is December to March – December offers reliable rainfall and good river levels. **DESCRIPTION** After an ardent and successful campaign to prevent it being dammed in the early 1980s, Tasmania's Franklin River is almost a byword for Australian environmentalism. Today, this wild river is also a rafting hotspot, offering a 100km-plus expedition-style adventure through Tasmania's pristine Southwest World Heritage region. Experienced rafters (or kayakers) can tackle it independently if they're fully equipped and prepared. For the inexperienced (about 90% of all Franklin rafters), tour companies offer rafting packages.

The trip down the Franklin starts below the Lyell Hwy, on the Collingwood River, and ends at Sir John Falls, on the Gordon River, taking around eight days. Rafters are usually met at Sir John Falls by a yacht, which takes them into the tourist town of Strahan. The greatest paddling rush – literally – comes in the Great Ravine, a 5km-long gorge bubbling with invitingly named rapids such as the Cauldron, Thunderush and the Churn. Expect to take at least a day to push, paddle and portage your way through the Great Ravine.

Water levels on the Franklin rise and fall like the stockmarket, and will have a major impact on the style of your trip. High-water will do much of your paddling work but can make the Great Ravine treacherous, while low-water can turn parts of your journey into a bushwalk, especially along the Collingwood River.

Visual highlights include the deep, still Irenabyss, and iconic Rock Island Bend (a photo of which fronted conservation campaigns in the 1980s) with its adjacent mossy waterfall, the unfortunately named Pigs Trough. www.parks.tas.gov.au.

↗ DO: CLIMB AT POTRERO CHICO

COUNTRY Mexico **TYPE OF ACTIVITY** Rock climbing
FITNESS/EXPERTISE LEVEL Low and high grades.
WHY NOW? Potrero Chico is a winter climbing wonderland.
DESCRIPTION With its limestone walls and sharp fins, the Potrero Chico canyon, around 1½ hours north of the city of Monterrey, has more than 600 marked climbing routes, both sport and traditional. It's considered among the best places in the world to learn the gymnastic artistry of rock climbing, but it's also a winter favourite for experienced climbers, offering everything from simple single-pitch sport routes to Mexico's most difficult climb, the 30m Sick Dimension (rated at 5.14b). It also contains one of the world's longest sport routes, the 24-pitch Time Wave Zero, a climb of around 700m. You can camp near the canyon at Rancho Cerro Gordo. Come for a few days and you may end up staying for the season.

↗ DO: SKI AT THE CEDARS

COUNTRY Lebanon **TYPE OF ACTIVITY** Skiing
FITNESS/EXPERTISE LEVEL Ski bunnies to Arctic hares.
WHY NOW? Feel festive by skiing on the nearest snow to Bethlehem.
DESCRIPTION Lebanon likes to boast that it's the only country in which you can ski in the morning and swim in the Mediterranean in the afternoon. It's an appealing mix in which to wind down from a busy year. Lebanon's highest and oldest ski field, the Cedars, is located less than 30km from the Mediterranean coast and people have been skiing here since the 1920s. It's less developed than other Lebanese ski resorts, but it's the second-most popular, particularly for those who actually ski (rather than pose). And with runs that begin around 3000m, the season usually starts in mid-December, ahead of other resorts in the country. There are also numerous off-piste opportunities at the Cedars if you're feeling more adventurous.

↗ DO: SEE ROBINSON CRUSOE ISLAND

COUNTRY Chile **TYPE OF ACTIVITY** Adventure travel
FITNESS/EXPERTISE LEVEL Not required.
WHY NOW? If you're feeling more Scrooge than Santa.
DESCRIPTION Wanting to spend this Christmas alone but with a tale to tell on your return? How about the island, 670km from the South American coast, named for its very solitude? In 1704 Alexander Selkirk was put ashore on the island (at his own request) after a dispute with his ship's captain. He lived here for four years, becoming the role model for Daniel Defoe's fictional *Robinson Crusoe*. Today, Robinson Crusoe Island is entirely national park (but for a small town of 500 people), receives less than 100 tourists a month, and is singularly serene. It's also developing a reputation as the best place to scuba dive in Chile. To reach the island, you can fly from Santiago de Chile or you can brave the seas for a couple of days by joining a naval supply ship or freighter out of Valparaíso.

↗ **Murray Marathon**
www.murraymarathon.ymca.org.au
Paddle 400km in five days along Australia's longest river.

↗ **Sydney to Hobart Yacht Race**
http://rolexsydneyhobart.com
Sail out of Sydney Harbour and through the Tasman Sea into Hobart's Derwent River.

↗ **Marathon des Dunes**
www.marathondunes.com
Three-day stage-race marathon (14km a day) through the Algerian Sahara, 650km south of Algiers.

WALK

Where there is land there can usually be walking, but in most walkers' minds not all lands are created equal. What elevates one walking trail or region above another is often subjective – is it scenery, remoteness, cultural interaction along the way, infrastructure such as huts and refuges? But still certain paths and walking areas have come to be accepted almost universally as the finest in the world.

If the best of the best share one common feature it is usually the presence of mountains; the world's most remarkable mountain chains have also inevitably created some of the most remarkable treks. At the high point of the Himalaya, with eight of the world's 10 highest peaks within its borders, Nepal has become synonymous with trekking. For many walkers this used to translate as the Annapurna Circuit, but in recent years the circuit has been all but devoured by roads, scattering trekkers to new destinations such as Kopra Ridge (p158).

The two top-10 peaks that don't belong to Nepal are in nearby Pakistan, and here you can trek along a glacier to the very foot of K2 (p118-19), the world's second-highest peak, for one of the planet's great mountain vistas. Other mountain treks that invariably appear in best-of lists include Torres del Paine (p190), Tour du Mont Blanc (p115), Milford Track (p44) and the Inca Trail (p86). Lesser-known mountain walking treats can be found in places far from the usual travel radar, such as Ethiopia's Simien Mountains (p183), the francophone Indian Ocean island of Réunion (p76-7), Bulgaria's Rila Mountains (p139) and among Venezuela's flat-topped *tepuis* (p12).

Mountains don't have a monopoly on good walking, however, with some coastlines just as inviting as an alpine view. Often, too, navigation at land's edge is as simple as keeping the sea to your left or right. Classic coastal trails include England's epic 1014km

South West Coast Path (p71), which has more up and down than some mountain trails; Vancouver Island's weather- and ocean-beaten West Coast Trail (p95); and Turkey's Lycian Way (p57), poised above the idyllic Aegean.

Forests may have enclosed views compared to a coastline or alpine ridge, but few things speak of idyllic walking quite like a green canopy. In California's Sequoia National Park, the Giant Forest is home to four of the earth's five tallest trees and is threaded by more than 60km of paths – the High Sierra Trail (www .nps.gov/seki/planyourvisit/high-sierra-trail .htm), the classic trans-sierra hiking route, begins through the Giant Forest on its 116km way across the Sierra Nevada. Western Australia's 964km Bibbulmun Track is another forest showcase, passing beneath a few more of the world's tallest trees around Walpole. Or you can settle for a floral forest in India's Valley of the Flowers (p125).

Even deserts invite footprints, and nowhere more so than in Australia's Red Centre where one of the world's newest and greatest treks, the Larapinta Trail (p75), rolls 223km along the mountain tops and gorges of the West MacDonnell Range. If you want more sand in your boots, you can follow the commandment to climb Egypt's Mt Sinai (p172-3) or commit to weeks of heat and deprivation along the 900km Israel National Trail (p53).

On most of these trails you'll probably see some wildlife, but if its animals – and big ones – you primarily want, there's always the prospect of an African walking safari: Tanzania's Selous Game Reserve (p157) and the continent's most famous national park, Kruger (p78), are the best destinations if you want to see your Big Five on foot.

↗ **INDEX**
ACTIVITIES

↗ **INDEX**

PLACES

↗ PHOTO CREDITS:
IN ORDER: CLOCKWISE ON SPREAD, FROM TOP LEFT

JANUARY WEEK 1
JTB Photo / Photolibrary
PCN Photography / Alamy
David Wall / Lonely Planet Images
Tim Hughes / Lonely Planet Images
Felix Hug / Lonely Planet Images

JANUARY WEEK 2
Austin Bush / Lonely Planet Images
imagebroker / Alamy
Mike King
Krzysztof Dydynski / Lonely Planet
Images
David Wall / Lonely Planet Images

JANUARY WEEK 3
David Else / Lonely Planet Images
Philip & Karen Smith / Lonely Planet
Images
Tim Rock / Lonely Planet Images
Douglas Steakley / Lonely Planet Images
Kevin Arnold / Getty Images

JANUARY WEEK 4
Gareth McCormack / Lonely Planet
Images
David Tipling / Lonely Planet Images
Joachim Löffel
Philip Game / Alamy
Mark A Johnson / Alamy

FEBRUARY WEEK 1
Jon Arnold Images Ltd / Alamy
Falk Kienas
Andrew Peacock / Lonely Planet Images
Eoin Clarke / Lonely Planet Images

FEBRUARY WEEK 2
Sara-Jane Cleland / Lonely Planet
Images
Mark Newman / Lonely Planet Images
Mark Harris / Fotolibra
Karl Lehmann / Lonely Planet Images
Christian Aslund / Lonely Planet Images

FEBRUARY WEEK 3
Martin Harvey / Photolibrary
David Else / Lonely Planet Images
Tim Rock / Lonely Planet Images
Andrew Bain / Lonely Planet Images
JTB Photo / Photolibrary

FEBRUARY WEEK 4
Paul Kennedy / Lonely Planet Images
ImageState / Alamy
WaterFrame / Alamy
Andrew Burke / Lonely Planet Images
Pierre Verdy / Getty Images

MARCH WEEK 1
Michael Eudenbach / Getty Images
Alaska Stock / Photolibrary
Barry Lewis / Corbis
Oliver Strewe / Lonely Planet Images
Stephen Alvarez / National Geographic
Stock

MARCH WEEK 2
Tim Rock / Lonely Planet Images
Mark Daffey / Lonely Planet Images
Andrew Bain / Lonely Planet Images
H Lansdown / Alamy
David Tipling / Lonely Planet Images

MARCH WEEK 3
Stefano Torrione / Photolibrary
Tom Cockrem / Lonely Planet Images
Sergei Remezov / Reuters / Corbis
Stu Smucker / Lonely Planet Images
Gareth McCormack / Lonely Planet
Images

MARCH WEEK 4
WoodyStock / Photolibrary
Frans Lanting / Corbis
Douglas Steakley / Lonely Planet Images
Sean Nel

CYCLE
Ray Laskowitz / Lonely Planet Images

APRIL WEEK 1
Zhan Tian / Dreamstime
Izzet Keribar / Lonely Planet Images
Patrice Coppee / Getty Images
Anders Blomqvist / Lonely Planet Images
David Epperson / Photolibrary

APRIL WEEK 2
Richard Wareham Fotografie / Photolibrary
Mike King
PatitucciPhoto / Getty Images
Greg Johnston / Lonely Planet Images
Joel Day / Alamy

APRIL WEEK 3
Holger Leue / Lonely Planet Images
Tom Boyden / Lonely Planet Images
Travelfile / Alamy
Darryl Torckler / Getty Images
Paul Greenway / Lonely Planet Images

APRIL WEEK 4
Theo Allofs / Corbis
Carol Polich / Lonely Planet Images
Klimberon / Dreamstime
LatinContent / Getty Images
Tom Brakefield / Corbis

MAY WEEK 1
Jane Sweeney / Lonely Planet Images
Felix Hug / Lonely Planet Images
Bruce Yuan-Yue Bi / Lonely Planet Images
Rodney Hyett / Lonely Planet Images
Andrew Bain / Lonely Planet Images

MAY WEEK 2
Jean-Bernard Carillet / Lonely Planet
Images
John Elk III / Lonely Planet Images
Emily Riddell / Lonely Planet Images
Jim Reed/Jim Reed Photography -
Severe & / Corbis
Christopher Herwig / Lonely Planet
Images

MAY WEEK 3
Norbert Eisele-Hein / Photolibrary
Christopher Pillitz / Getty Images
Philippe Body / Hemis / Corbis
Stephen Alvarez / Getty Images
Robert Harding Picture Library Ltd / Alamy

MAY WEEK 4
Andrew Peacock / Lonely Planet Images
Philip & Karen Smith / Lonely Planet
Images
Karl Lehmann / Lonely Planet Images
Michael Aw / Lonely Planet Images
Roger de la Harpe / Photolibrary

JUNE WEEK 1
Lewis Phillips / Photolibrary
mediacolor's / Alamy
Anders Blomqvist / Lonely Planet Images
Pixtal Images / Photolibrary
Anders Blomqvist / Lonely Planet Images

JUNE WEEK 2
Dennis Jones / Lonely Planet Images
David Epperson / Getty Images
Michael Gebicki / Lonely Planet Images
All Canada Photos / Alamy
Paul Kennedy / Lonely Planet Images

JUNE WEEK 3
Christer Fredriksson / Lonely Planet
Images
Stuart Westmorland / Corbis
Scott Darsney / Lonely Planet Images
Ali Kabas / Alamy
David Cheshire / Loop Images / Corbis

JUNE WEEK 4
Grand Tour / Corbis
Christophe Diesel Michot / Alamy
Dave Porter / Alamy
Bernard van Dierendonck / Photolibrary
Richard Wareham Fotografie / Alamy

JUMP
Tim Barker / Lonely Planet Images

JULY WEEK 1
Michael Gebicki / Lonely Planet
Images
Phil Rees / Alamy
Hermann Erber / Getty Images
Gavin Newman / Alamy
Peter Jordan_EU / Alamy

JULY WEEK 2
Rob Penn / Photolibrary
Robyn Beck / Getty Images
Rafa Rivas / Getty Images
Joel W Rogers / Corbis
Roland Weihrauch / epa / Corbis

JULY WEEK 3
Tim de Waele / Corbis
Ashley Cooper / Alamy
Hein van den Heuvel / Corbis
Steve Bentley / Alamy
Pep Roig / Alamy

JULY WEEK 4
Grant Dixon / Lonely Planet Images
Fotograferen.net / Alamy
Mark Newman / Lonely Planet
Images
Krzysztof Dydynski / Lonely Planet
Images

AUGUST WEEK 1
Frans Lemmens / Lonely Planet
Images
John Hay / Lonely Planet Images
Chris Cheadle / Alamy
Garry Weare / Lonely Planet Images
Mike Belozer / Getty Images

AUGUST WEEK 2
Barry Tessman / Getty Images
Chris Beall / Lonely Planet Images
Grant Dixon / Lonely Planet Images
Ethan Janson / Getty Images
Picture Contact / Alamy

AUGUST WEEK 3
Andrew Peacock / Lonely Planet
Images
Michael Patrick O'Neill / Alamy
Amos Nachoum / Corbis
Doug McKinlay / Lonely Planet
Images
Neil Robinson

AUGUST WEEK 4
Andrew Bain / Lonely Planet Images
Paul Kennedy / Lonely Planet Images
Gregg Bleakney
www.nordicventures.com
Lee Foster / Lonely Planet Images

SEPTEMBER WEEK 1
Witold Skrypczak / Lonely Planet
Images
Les Gibbon / Alamy
Luiz C Marigo / Photolibrary
Andrew Bain / Lonely Planet Images
Andrew Bain / Lonely Planet Images

SEPTEMBER WEEK 2
Liu Liqun / Corbis
Carl Yarbrough
Dawn Kish / Getty Images
Di Jones / Lonely Planet Images
Mark Daffey / Lonely Planet
Images

SEPTEMBER WEEK 3
Delphine Adburgham / Photolibrary
James Warwick / Getty Images
Seb Rogers / Alamy
Carlos Caetano / Dreamstime
Mark Daffey / Lonely Planet Images

SEPTEMBER WEEK 4
David Madison / Getty Images
Wendy Smith / www.everest-skydive.com
JS Callahan / tropicalpix / Alamy
Mike Hewitt / Getty Images

PADDLE
Ann Cecil / Lonely Planet Images

OCTOBER WEEK 1
Gavin Gough / Lonely Planet Images
Ariadne Van Zandbergen / Lonely Planet
Images
Andrew Bain / Lonely Planet Images
Lindsay Brown / Lonely Planet Images
Gareth McCormack Photography / Alamy

OCTOBER WEEK 2
Sean Caffrey / Lonely Planet Images
Mark Daffey / Lonely Planet Images
Jay Dickman / Corbis
Lee Foster / Lonely Planet Images
Craig Pershouse / Lonely Planet Images

OCTOBER WEEK 3
Peter Hendrie / Lonely Planet Images
Yvette Cardozo / Photolibrary
Jon Davison / Lonely Planet Images
Jason Bell / vertical-visions.com
AWPhoto / Alamy

OCTOBER WEEK 4
Whit Richardson / Aurora Open / Corbis
Oliver Strewe / Lonely Planet Images
Karl Lehmann / Lonely Planet Images
Tony Wheeler / Lonely Planet Images
Jonathan Chester / Lonely Planet Images

NOVEMBER WEEK 1
Mark Daffey / Lonely Planet Images
Sergei Chirikov / epa / Corbis
Greg Johnston / Lonely Planet Images
Michael Aw / Lonely Planet Images
Liquid Light / Alamy

NOVEMBER WEEK 2
Antonio D'Albore / Photolibrary
Nigel Hicks / Alamy
Snehitdesign / Dreamstime
John Hay / Lonely Planet Images
Steve Simonsen / Lonely Planet Images

NOVEMBER WEEK 3
Eric Nathan PCL / Photolibrary
Dennis Hallinan / Alamy
John Sones / Lonely Planet Images
Holger Leue / Lonely Planet Images
Reuters

NOVEMBER WEEK 4
Carol Polich / Lonely Planet Images
Robert Halstead / Lonely Planet Images
Patrick Ben Luke Syder / Lonely Planet
Images
David Wall / Lonely Planet Images

DECEMBER WEEK 1
Krzysztof Dydynski / Lonely Planet
Images
Jonathan Ball / Alamy
John Elk III / Lonely Planet Images
Andy Belcher / Alamy
Heinrich van den Berg / Getty Images

DECEMBER WEEK 2
Grant Dixon / Lonely Planet Images
Matthias Engelien / Alamy
Ken Smith / Alamy
Karl Lehmann / Lonely Planet Images
Micah Wright / Lonely Planet Images

DECEMBER WEEK 3
John Elk III / Lonely Planet Images
Aroon Thaewchatturat / OnAsia
Uros Ravbar / Lonely Planet Images
Holger Leue / Lonely Planet Images
Paul Kennedy / Lonely Planet Images

DECEMBER WEEK 4
Anders Ekholm / Photolibrary
Uriel Sinai / Getty Images
Grant Dixon / Lonely Planet Images
Christian Aslund / Lonely Planet Images
Corey Rich / Photolibrary

WALK
Gareth McCormack / Lonely Planet
Images

A YEAR OF ↗ ADVENTURES

A GUIDE TO THE WORLD'S MOST EXCITING EXPERIENCES

August 2010

PUBLISHED BY
Lonely Planet Pty Ltd
ABN 36 005 607 983
90 Maribyrnong St, Footscray,
Victoria, 3011, Australia

www.lonelyplanet.com

Printed through Colorcraft Ltd, Hong Kong. Printed in China
Cover image Philip & Karen Smith, Getty Images

Many of the images in this book are available for licensing
from Lonely Planet Images (LPI). www.lonelyplanetimages.com

ISBN 978 1 74179 976 7

LONELY PLANET OFFICES
AUSTRALIA Locked Bag 1, Footscray, Victoria, 3011
Phone 03 8379 8000 Fax 03 8379 8111
Email talk2us@lonelyplanet.com.au

USA 150 Linden St, Oakland, CA 94607
Phone 510 250 6400 Toll free 800 275 8555 Fax 510 893 8572
Email info@lonelyplanet.com

UK 2nd fl 186 City Rd London EC1V 2NT
Phone 020 7106 2100 Fax 020 7106 2101
Email go@lonelyplanet.co.uk

↗ VISIT WWW.LONELYPLANET.COM

**FOR MORE INFORMATION, LINKS TO EVENTS AND SPECIAL
OFFERS TO GET YOUR ADVENTURES UNDER WAY.**

↗ **COORDINATING AUTHOR** ANDREW BAIN
A reformed sportswriter, Andrew prefers adventure to avarice and can
usually be found walking or cycling when he should be working. He's
trekked, cycled and paddled in various parts of five continents, and is the
author of the book *Headwinds*, the story of his 20,000km cycle journey
around Australia, as well as Lonely Planet's *Walking in Australia*. He
confesses to naming his daughter after the Khmer word for 'mountain',
and once hallucinated that he was Reinhold Messner.

↗ **THANKS FROM THE AUTHOR**
Foremost thanks to all the Lonely Planet authors, without whose work
this project would have been as tricky as the Hillary Step. I'm grateful to
Chris Rennie for lending his surfing knowledge, and to a swag of expert
others for enduring my questioning about morning glories, land yachting,
maneless lions and the like. A big thanks to Bridget Blair and Janine
Eberle for their assistance in the summit team.

PUBLISHER Chris Rennie
ASSOCIATE PUBLISHER Ben Handicott
COMMISSIONING EDITORS Bridget Blair & Janine Eberle
IMAGE RESEARCHER Sabrina Dalbesio
DESIGNERS Mark Adams & Jennifer Mullins
LAYOUT Jim Hsu
EDITORS Trent Holden, Alison Ridgway, Dianne Schallmeiner
PRE-PRESS PRODUCTION Ryan Evans
PRINT PRODUCTION MANAGER Graham Imeson

↗ **WITH MANY THANKS TO**
Nigel Chin, Jessica Crouch, Liz Heynes, Charity Mackinnon, Kate Morgan,
Laura Stansfeld, John Taufa

FSC **Mixed Sources**
Product group from well-managed
forests and other controlled sources
www.fsc.org Cert no. SGS-COC-005002
© 1996 Forest Stewardship Council